Wondrous Events

Wondrous Events

Foundations of Religious Belief

James McClenon

University of Pennsylvania Press

Philadelphia

Cover art: *Ascent into the Empyrean* by Hieronymus Bosch
(Copyright CAMERAPHOTO-Arte, Venice).

Copyright © 1994 by James McClenon
All rights reserved
Printed in the United States of America

Library of Congress Cataloging-in-Publication Data
McClenon, James.
   Wondrous events: foundations of religious belief / James
McClenon.
      p.   cm.
   Includes bibliographical references and index.
   ISBN 0-8122-3074-4 (cloth). — ISBN 0-8122-1355-6 (pbk.)
      1. Parapsychology—Case studies.   2. Parapsychology—Religious
aspects.   3. Religion and sociology.   I. Title.
   BF1040.M328   1994
   133—dc20   94-20228
                                                                   CIP

Contents

Acknowledgments

The major theoretical orientation of this book is derived from the work of David Hufford (1982a). His comments have been very valuable. The Parapsychology Foundation provided me with grants in 1989, 1990, and 1991. These supported surveys of college students in North Carolina and Japan and funded production of a fifty-seven-minute video, *Wondrous Events: Foundations of Folk Belief*, produced by Emily Edwards of the University of North Carolina, Greensboro.

The National Endowment for the Humanities provided a grant allowing me to attend the summer seminar "Buddhism and Culture: China and Japan" at UCLA in 1989. I wish to thank the seminar directors, William R. LaFleur and Steven F. Teiser, whose comments and advice aided in writing Chapters 8 and 9.

Dr. Carl Becker and many American, Japanese, and Chinese students helped me collect survey data. The administrative staff of the University of Maryland, Asian Division, set up the program that facilitated my work in the People's Republic of China in 1986. Many students at Elizabeth City State University assisted me by gathering anomalous experience narratives between 1987 and 1993. I especially thank Thomas E. Chatman, Jr., Aretha Kelly, Ann Riddick, John Michael Tisdale, and Delois White. The 1990–91 Albermarle Writers Group read and commented on Chapters 4 and 6 and helped me recognize the aesthetic and dramatic qualities in wondrous event narratives.

I wish to thank many colleagues who made comments on portions of the manuscript: Henry H. Bauer, Carl Becker, Charles Emmons, George Hansen (whose efforts in catching errors are particularly appreciated), Erlendur Haraldsson, David Hufford, Joseph K. Long, Charles D. Orzack, Doug Richards, Peter M. Rojcewicz, Marilyn Schlitz, Donald H. Smith, Marcello Truzzi, Ron Westrum, and Michael Winkelman.

Patricia Smith, acquisitions editor at the University of Pennsylvania Press, provided encouragement for which I am grateful.

Referees and anonymous reviewers also made valuable comments on various sections of this work. Portions have been presented before professional groups or published in journals. Chapter 1 has appeared in print in two permutations:

"Social Science and Anomalous Experience: Paradigms for Investigating Sporadic Social Phenomena," *Journal of the American Society for Psychical Research* 85 (1991): 25–41.
"Social Scientific Paradigms for Investigating Anomalous Experience," *Journal of Scientific Exploration* 5 (1991): 191–203.

Chapter 2 has been published in alternate versions:

"Surveys of Anomalous Experience in Chinese, Japanese, and American Samples," *Sociology of Religion* 54 (1993): 295–302.
"Surveys of Anomalous Experience: A Cross-Cultural Analysis," *Journal of the American Society for Psychical Research* 88 (1994): 117–135.

Some of the narratives and discussion in Chapter 3 appeared in:

"The Experiential Foundations of Shamanic Healing," *Journal of Medicine and Philosophy* 18 (1993): 107–127.

Chapter 4 has been presented in alternate versions at two conferences:

"Hauntings and Poltergeists: Collective Behavior and Folk Religiosity," paper presented at the Southern Sociological Society meetings, Atlanta, GA, April 1991.
"Ghosts, Poltergeists, and Collective Behavior: Folk Religion and the Media," paper presented at the meetings of the Society for the Scientific Study of Religion, Pittsburgh, PA, November 1991.

Chapter 5 was first presented in a very different form:

"Thirty-three Asian Spiritual Healers: An Experience-Centered Approach," paper presented to the Southern Sociological Society, Norfolk, Virginia, April 1989.

A version of Chapter 8 was presented at a conference:

"Wondrous Events and Religious History in Medieval Asia and Europe," paper presented at the meetings of the Society for the Scientific Study of Religion, Washington, DC, November 1992.

Versions of Chapter 9 were presented at two conferences, then revised and published:

"Inscribing the Experience of Death: A Comparative Analysis of Medieval European, Japanese, and Chinese Narratives," paper presented at "Writing the Social Text, an Interdisciplinary Conference," University of Maryland, College Park, MD, November 1989.

"Near-Death Folklore in Medieval China and Japan: A Comparative Analysis," paper presented to the Southern Sociological Society, Louisville, KY, March 1990.

"Near-Death Folklore in Medieval China and Japan: A Comparative Analysis," *Asian Folklore Studies* 50 (1991): 319–342.

Chapter 11 was presented at two conferences:

"Wondrous Events in a Small Group: A Field Study," paper presented to the Southern Sociological Society, Chattanooga, TN, April 1993.

"Wondrous Events in a Small Group: A Field Study," paper presented to the Society for the Scientific Study of Religion, Raleigh, NC, November 1993.

Preface

This book is a sociological study of events labeled as wondrous. I make no claims regarding the physical causes of wondrous experiences. My theories and hypotheses pertain to the sociology of belief, medicine, religion, and folklore.

An experience-centered approach allows the researcher to use first-hand narratives as data (Hufford, 1982a). Rose (1989), Stoller (1989), and Narayan (1989) provide alternate pathways for this style of presentation. This approach permits more accurate portrayals of "what really happened" and "the way things really were" than a more traditional analysis would allow. Yet, paradoxically, I cannot claim to understand fully "what really happened" or to know "the way things really were," especially in situations where people may be seeking to deceive me. I argue, however, that this uncertainty is not problematic.

Sociologists and anthropologists are often unable to determine if their informants are lying or have reconstructed their memories of events. In my analyses here, however, I cannot be certain that my own observations are always valid since some of my respondents use deception. Although I have no method for evaluating sincerity quantitatively, this does not negate the value of an experience-centered approach. If observers *believe* that a particular event occurred, then that event is sociologically real. It affects those who believe in it. By the same token, if I have been misled, this deception suggests that others have been similarly misguided. Even in cases where I am virtually certain that informants have fabricated stories (see Chapter 6), their narratives are part of a folk tradition. The tales they tell are oral literature, accepted by believers as true.

Various readers have commented on aspects of this study. Skeptics have asked that I qualify descriptions of wondrous events with terms like "ostensible" or "alleged." They want me to state, for example, that an informant "believed she saw" a phenomenon rather than "she saw" the incident. They argue that the latter phrase suggests that the event was "real" rather than merely an experience leading to belief. Yet people accepting the authenticity of anomalous accounts regard these qualifiers as offensive. They feel such terms cast aspersions on the integrity of those reporting wondrous experiences.

My experience-centered approach uses informants' narratives as evidence. We need not make judgments regarding the authenticity of the respondents' accounts. Omission of qualifying terms does not imply support for their positions. On the contrary, it allows a clearer portrayal of what informants wish to convey, hence a more accurate presentation of the data.

The concept of "wondrous" includes an element of "not knowing." We can never know ultimate Truth on an intellectual level. Life is mysterious. As Emily Dickinson wrote, "Wonder is not precisely knowing and not precisely knowing not, a beautiful but bleak condition." Although I omit using qualifying terms, I acknowledge the bleak element of "not knowing" inherent within wondrous accounts.

Anthropologists have come to realize that a description of the way they gather information aids readers in interpreting ethnographic data. Since much of my material is qualitative, I offer the following chronology of my data collection activities.

In 1978, I began participant observation of the scientific parapsychological community. This research was conducted for my dissertation, sponsored by the University of Maryland. Between April and August 1979, I visited twelve major parapsychological research centers in the United States. The next summer I visited three European centers. As I pursued this research, I found that the scientific evaluation of psychical claims posed a question for sociologists of science: Why, after over a century of inquiry, have scientists been unable to resolve the issues regarding the existence of psychic phenomena?

In 1981, I polled a population of elite scientists within the American Association for the Advancement of Science (AAAS). I sent questionnaires to council members and selected section committee representatives. Respondents revealed more skepticism regarding paranormal claims than any group surveyed in recent decades. Their disbelief was far greater than that of either American college scientists or the general population (McClenon, 1982). This finding suggests that skepticism regarding paranormal claims varies directly with status in the scientific community.

Some sociologists argue that all groups must devise moral boundaries in order to maintain cohesion (Durkheim, 1938; Erikson, 1966). In the case of the paranormal, elite scientists apparently use latent ideological boundaries to label scientific deviance. They distinguish between science and "non-science" by rejecting psychical research.

Scientific boundaries are not created through philosophical argument but by scientific "gate-keeping" processes (McClenon, 1984).

During my participant observation of parapsychologists, I found that people sometimes contact parapsychological research centers in order to report haunting experiences. This led to more direct contact with those who claim such experiences. The Psychical Research Foundation suggested that I investigate a case in Baltimore where a family reported many anomalous events. The family heard unexplained voices, felt strange sensations, and saw unexplained movement of objects, as well as apparitional forms. I closely monitored this case for two years and have maintained contact with this family for more than a decade.

As I continued my investigation, I found that these types of episodes were not uncommon. I interviewed many people who believed they lived in haunted houses. Often they made special efforts to uncover "normal" explanations for their perceptions. For example, in one case, military police officers brought a police dog to their headquarters seeking signs of a recurrent apparitional intruder. I concluded that such phenomena were sociologically real since anomalous episodes had real effects on experiencers. I present the results of these field investigations in Chapter 4.

In 1981, I began an investigation of a group in Rolla, Missouri. The Society for Research on Rapport and Telekinesis (SORRAT) claimed that many anomalous events occurred during their meetings. They reported paranormal communications with deceased individuals through rapping sounds, paranormal movement of objects, and anomalous lights and sounds (Richards, 1982). The results of this investigation are presented in Chapter 11.

In 1982, I accepted a position as a lecturer with the Asian Division of the University of Maryland. During my Asian travels (1982–1986), I observed shamans and spiritual healers in Japan, Korea, the Philippines, Sri Lanka, Taiwan, Thailand, and the People's Republic of China. I report on these studies in Chapters 5, 6, and 7. I observed more than one thousand "psychic surgeries" in the Philippines (described in Chapter 6), participated in more than a dozen firewalks in Sri Lanka, Japan, and the United States (described in Chapter 6), and developed friendships with spiritual practitioners in Sri Lanka and Thailand (described in Chapters 5 and 7).

I also taught at the Northwestern Polytechnic University (NPU) in Xi'an, People's Republic of China, during the spring of 1986. I administered an "unusual experience" questionnaire to a random sample of NPU students (see Appendix). The same questionnaire was also administered at two other Chinese colleges. Because these students were raised during the Cultural Revolution (1966–1976) and had been selected for their orthodox adherence to traditional Marxist beliefs, they might, in theory, be considered devoid of religiosity, in the traditional sense. Surprisingly, they reported levels of anomalous experience equivalent to U.S. national samples.

After my return to the United States in 1986, I administered the same questionnaire to a random sample of University of Maryland dormitory residents. The narratives gathered from this population were similar to those from the Chinese respondents (McClenon, 1988a, 1990).

In 1987, I administered the same questionnaire to a random sample of students at Elizabeth City State University, a predominately black college in northeastern North Carolina. Later, in 1988, Dr. Carl Becker organized the administration of this questionnaire to Japanese students at Tsukuba University. An additional survey was administered to students at the University of North Carolina, Greensboro, in 1990. A quantitative analysis derived from these results is presented in Chapter 2.

Between 1987 and 1993, I collected more than one thousand anomalous experience narratives. Students in anthropology courses at Elizabeth City State University gathered many of these accounts. My collection allowed me to compare narratives from China, Japan, the University of Maryland, and the University of North Carolina at Greensboro. African-American, Caucasian-American, Chinese, and Japanese respondents reported similar forms of anomalous experience. These findings support the argument that some anomalous episodes occur independently of culture. I describe this research in Chapter 3.

I studied medieval Asian wondrous event stories while participating in a National Endowment for the Humanities seminar at UCLA during the summer of 1989. This allowed a cross-cultural perspective regarding the role of anomalous claims in the evolution of religious ideology. Chapter 8 includes a historical study of wondrous events in both medieval Asia and Europe. Chapter 9 compares medieval European and Asian accounts of near-death experiences.

The reader might note that the chronology of research differs markedly from the order of the chapters. Many of the events I observed over the years made little sense when I witnessed them. The final product, which you have before you, is an attempt to organize and systematize the body of findings.

This book is by no means the final word on wondrous events; many pathways remain unexplored. It does, however, illustrate the ways an experience-centered approach can be used to investigate anomalous episodes. Futures studies could test hypotheses derived from my analysis. Such studies might fall within the disciplines of anthropology, folklore, religion, and the sociology of medicine.

Chapter 1
Wondrous Events and Social Science

Throughout history, and all over the world, people have puzzled over reports of wondrous incidents. For the purposes of this study, wondrous events are defined as phenomena thought to exceed scientific explanation. Examples include extrasensory perception, apparitions, out-of-body and near-death experiences, spiritual possession, pain and heat immunity, psychokinesis (mind over matter), poltergeists (noisy spirits), miraculous healing, and contact with the dead. This study uses an experience-centered approach within a social scientific framework to test hypotheses regarding the incidence of, and social reaction to, anomalous claims.

This work has important implications for the sociology of religion and medicine. Many wondrous experiences support belief in spiritual powers or forces. They play a role in the development of religious ideologies. The universal elements that recur within these episodes contribute to uniformities within folk belief. However, the capacity for experiencing wondrous events is not evenly distributed. Some people report far more incidents than others. Those who possess the greatest ability to experience anomalous episodes tend to fulfill special roles within their societies. They develop and perform ceremonies that include wondrous exhibitions. Their performances initiate spiritual healings, support religious belief, and increase group cohesiveness. Group perceptions of wondrous effects have special impacts on both individuals and cultures.

Wondrous events are thought to be scientifically anomalous. This definition is limited to the scientific domain, a special subculture. Many traditional cultures have little concern for scientific explanations of wondrous events and some (Tibetan, for example) have no term for the *supernatural* since they regard all phenomena as part of the natural order. Yet all societies consider certain phenomena as beyond normal consciousness, outside the realm of ordinary experience.

Wonder is a relative term. For some observers, anomalous events inspire skepticism rather than wonder. When it comes to the miraculous, doubt springs eternal in many human hearts. Others apply religious reasoning to unusual phenomena. They reject the notion that wondrous events lack explanations since their convictions provide interpretations. Still, in most cases, belief, wonderment, and skepticism are rarely absolute.

The notion of wondrous events should be regarded as a category of convenience; it is a term referring to experiences having a variety of explanations. Determining which explanations are "valid" is beyond the scope of this study. Social scientific research makes conclusions pertinent only within the social domain.

Psychic phenomena, or *psi*, constitute an important category of such events. Because psychic phenomena have special impacts on religious belief, my central focus is on these types of claims. The glossary of the *Journal of Parapsychology* (Vol. 52: 375–378) defines *paranormal* as "any phenomenon that in one or more respects exceeds the limits of what is deemed physically possible on current scientific assumptions." *Extrasensory perception* (ESP) is defined as "paranormal cognition; the acquisition of information about an external event, object, or influence (mental or physical; past, present, or future) in some way other than through any of the known sensory channels." *Psychokinesis* (PK) is defined as "paranormal action: the influence of mind on a physical system that cannot be entirely accounted for by the mediation of any known physical energy." *Psi* is defined as "a general term used either as a noun or adjective to identify ESP or PK." Scientists who investigate psi are known as parapsychologists.

Psi has definition by elimination because only phenomena that cannot be explained scientifically are regarded as paranormal. This gives parapsychology a residual quality, since it focuses on topics that mainstream scientists spurn. Events found to have "normal" explanations—such as hypnosis, the homing behavior of pigeons, and Kirlian photography—are outside the realm of interest of parapsychologists because they now have scientific explanations (Blackmore, 1988; MacKenzie and MacKenzie, 1980).

Various anomalous phenomena, however, rejected in the past, have later been accepted as genuine. Reports of rocks that fell from the sky (meteorites) were once scorned by scientists, yet later were accepted (Westrum, 1977). Hypnosis, a phenomenon originally thought to be paranormal, has been accepted as a legitimate therapeutic procedure by many medical practitioners, though a complete explanation of the process eludes modern investigators. Through this process of legitimation, we would expect future scientists to devise accepted explanations for some of the "paranormal" phenomena discussed in this study.

Although parapsychologists feel they conduct valid research, they tend to be rejected as deviant. Their social treatment reflects the boundaries of a latent scientific ideology demarcating science from non-science. The "gate-keepers" of science, who edit journals and allocate funds, serve the scientific community by validating such borders. They treat highly peculiar claims with extreme skepticism. This process allows a more efficient allocation of scientific resources, which is a part of scientific rationality. Scientific institutions do not have sufficient time and money to investigate extremely far-fetched theories. The scientific rejection of parapsychological claims therefore creates an ideological demarcation for the scientific endeavor (McClenon, 1984).

I attempt to transcend the controversy regarding the ontological status of wondrous phenomena by working within established social scientific paradigms. I present theories, test hypotheses, and reach conclusions applicable within the sociology of religion, belief, and folklore. Therefore, in this study, I will not argue that psychic phenomena are real in a physical sense, nor attempt to prove that ESP, PK, psi, or paranormal events, as defined by parapsychologists, occur.

Psi, ESP, PK, and other wondrous events are *sociologically* real because they have real effects on those who experience them and their societies. Wondrous events are not a category of phenomena defined by physical parameters. The notion of *wondrous* is determined by ordinary people rather than by scientists doing experiments. When using the terms *psi*, *ESP*, and *PK*, I refer to socially labeled phenomena rather than to physical events, the status of which is uncertain.

Wondrous events include many incidents thought by most scientists to have normal, rather than paranormal, explanations. Firewalking and sleight-of-hand performances exemplify "normal" wondrous phenomena. Events involving fraud, misinterpretation, coincidence, and unusual physiological abilities can inspire wonder and have had impacts on religious ideology.

Many scholars regard ordinary events that have been interpreted religiously as the basic kind of religious experience. Peak experiences, such as seeing a beautiful sunset, hearing a moving musical performance, or being in love, have been labeled as wondrous. The present work defines *wondrous* in a narrower sense, focusing on the unexplained component within certain events. Scientifically anomalous events, as defined by common people, often stimulate religious explanations. It is in this context that I am using the term.

TABLE 1.1. The Differentiation of Anomalous Claims.

Variable (facts)	Relationship (processes)	
	ORDINARY	EXTRAORDINARY (ANOMALOUS)
Ordinary	A	C
Extraordinary (anomalous)	B	D

A = Ordinary science
B = Cryptoscientific claims
C = Parascientific claims
D = Crypto-parascientific claims

Source: Adapted from Marcello Truzzi, "Editorial: On Pseudo-sciences and Proto-sciences," *The Zetetic* 1 (Spring–Summer 1977): 7.

Marcello Truzzi (1977) classified anomalous claims on the basis of their relationship to other claims or observations (see Table 1.1). Ordinary science investigates the relationship between ordinary variables and relationships (A). Extrasensory phenomena are *parascientific* since their labeling involves the hypothesis that extraordinary relationships exist between ordinary facts (C). For example, a person dreams about witnessing an event and then later experiences the episode. Neither the dream nor the actual event is extraordinary, but the assumption of a paranormal relationship makes the phenomenon parascientific.

Large, unknown animals, lost continents, and unknown radiations constitute what Truzzi (1977) terms *cryptoscientific* claims (B). These phenomena, although associated with extraordinary facts, do not suggest extraordinary relationships between scientific variables. They are merely anomalous objects which, if fully documented under suitable conditions, would be accepted as authentic. Because these claims do not violate scientific canons to the degree that parascientific claims do, cryptoscientific assertions are less "wondrous." The present study places little emphasis on unidentified flying objects (UFOs) and large, unknown animals (such as Bigfoot, Sasquatch, or Yeti) since they have had less impact on religious beliefs.

Truzzi notes that some phenomena are *crypto-parascientific*, involving extraordinary facts coupled with extraordinary relationships (D). The classification of angels or devils falls within this category, since this presupposes spiritual realms and parascientific relationships. Religious observers tend to compound parascientific and cryptoscientific claims by using crypto-parascientific ideologies. For example, some religious observers feel that extrasensory perceptions (a parascientific claim) are produced by demons, thus positing a crypto-parascientific argument. They classify ESP events within a religious, crypto-parascientific framework.

When attributed to benevolent spiritual forces, wondrous events are regarded as miraculous. Kelsey (1987) notes four major attitudes toward this category. Miraculous accounts are perceived as (1) manifestations of God (Christian, Muslim), (2) results of illusion (rational materialism), (3) paranormal events (studied by scientific parapsychologists), or (4) the result of perceiving material reality as an illusion (Hinduism, Buddhism). Yet only a minority of people regard all wondrous events as illusion (option 2) or as scientific data (option 3). Humans, even across cultural borders, tend to evaluate anomalous phenomena within crypto-parascientific (religious) frameworks. The present study focuses on the means by which parascientific (and, in some cases, cryptoscientific) claims are reformulated into crypto-parascientific doctrines within folk religious contexts (transitions from categories B or C to D in Truzzi's scheme).

The demarcation between "ordinary" and "extraordinary" corresponds to the demarcation between the Western concepts of "normal" and "paranormal." This division evolved with advances in scientific knowledge. Newton's formulations allowed scientists to conceive of the universe as having immutable laws. Later, John Stuart Mill (1806–1873) sought to describe the methods of scientific investigation and the concept of causality. He set forth the Axiom of the Uniformity of the Course of Nature. He argued that every consequent has an invariable antecedent and that the cause of a phenomenon is the assemblage of its conditions (Mill, 1884/1973: 326, 327); because, as far as we know it, nature follows these laws, some claims are impossible (or labeled by believers as paranormal).

Jeremy Bentham (1748–1832) pondered the question of improbability and impossibility with regard to judicial evidence. Bentham noted that no criterion allows a listing of impossible events. Witnesses evaluate observations on the basis of disconformity to what they believe to be the established course of nature. They are sometimes motivated to accept perceptions and ideas that do not conform to natural laws. The principle instances associated with false notions are claims promising wealth, happiness, and the cure of diseases by inadequate means. According to Bentham, people's life experiences determine their concept of natural law and their motivations for accepting deviations from it (Mack, 1969).

Through empirical analysis, we can gain greater understanding of the factors that lead people to believe in violations of "natural" laws. An experience-centered approach indicates that perceptions of events labeled as paranormal provide support for crypto-parascientific doctrines. Although miracles are, to a degree, socially constructed using previously accepted crypto-parascientific standards, I will present evidence indicating that some wondrous events have features that transcend cultural boundaries.

Truzzi (1978) argues that three scales are important for evaluating anomalous claims: events are ordinary/extraordinary, witnesses are credible/non-credible, and narratives are plausible/implausible. Cultures differ in their use of these standards. Scientists are more skeptical when evaluating the paranormal than are nonscientists. Yet within all traditions, even scientific ones, people evaluate claims based on previously formed assumptions.

Variations exist even within a culture. About half of all Americans believe in extrasensory perception (Gallup, 1979; Gallup and Newport, 1991). About one in three accept the reality of Bigfoot or Sasquatch (Gallup, 1979). The percentage believing in ghosts has increased from 11 percent in 1978 to 25 percent in 1990 (Gallup and Newport, 1991). Nine percent have "seen or been in the presence of a ghost," and 14 percent had been in a house they felt was haunted (Gallup and Newport, 1991). Survey data indicate that evaluations of anomalous events are determined, in part, by the observer's cultural, ideological, and geographic point of reference. The Loch Ness Monster, for example, stimulates greater belief in Scotland than it does in the United States. Western Americans harbor more faith in Bigfoot than do Easterners.

Even with variations in evaluation, some elements within wondrous experience appear to be universal. This book develops a set of arguments, based on observation, which assert that:

1. Wondrous events are sociologically real. Some types have universal features that shape folk belief.
2. Wondrous events provide a foundation for belief in spirits, souls, life after death, and anomalous powers. They also have qualities that stimulate skepticism.
3. Those with the greatest capacity for experiencing wondrous events often engage in ceremonial performances. They produce wondrous events for audiences, often triggering belief and psychosomatic healing.
4. Many of the processes surrounding wondrous performances can be explained within sociological paradigms.

These arguments are associated with three types of wondrous events, categorized according to their settings. *Primary* wondrous events are spontaneous anomalous experiences. Examples include involuntary extrasensory perceptions, out-of-body experiences, precognitive dreams, and apparitions. *Secondary* wondrous events are performed. Examples include mediumship, firewalking, shamanic sleight-of-hand exhibitions, and staged demonstrations of extrasensory perception. *Tertiary* wondrous events are perceived after an individual witnesses a wondrous performance or believes in a particular ideology. Miraculous healings and culturally specific religious experiences, such as seeing the Virgin Mary, exemplify this type of phenomenon.

Individual forms of wondrous experience occur within more than one context. Extrasensory perceptions, for example, ensue spontaneously (a primary event), as part of a psychic's performance (a secondary event), or as a result of a psychic's instructions (a tertiary event). These categories focus attention on the social context surrounding anomalous experiences and further illustrate the basic arguments of this book.

1. Wondrous events are sociologically real.

Wondrous events need not be experimentally validated to be studied by social scientists. A large percentage of many different populations accept these phenomena as real (Haraldsson, 1985; Greeley, 1975, 1987). Like racial prejudice, sexual discrimination, and social hierarchy, wondrous events are socially defined variables having special qualities and measurable effects. Wondrous events, as defined within this study, need not be preceded by such terms as "ostensible" or "alleged," since these episodes are *perceived* by observers as real. Some informants may be lying or engaging in fraud, but this problem does not negate the experience-centered approach. Wondrous accounts are a form of oral literature, accepted by believers as valid. As W. I. Thomas (1928: 572) explained, "If men define situations as real, they are real in their consequences." Because many people consider psychic phenomena to be real, their beliefs have real effects.

Some forms of wondrous experience have universal features, contributing to equivalent beliefs across cultures. Hufford (1982a) developed his "experiential source" theory based on this finding within his study of sleep paralysis experiences. In Newfoundland, he collected supernatural assault narratives (by an entity termed the "Old Hag" by his respondents) and found a surprisingly high incidence within his sample (23 percent). His American respondents, unfamiliar with Newfoundland's folk beliefs regarding the Old Hag, described similar events with equivalent imagery and frequency. He noted primary elements (impression of wakefulness, paralysis, real settings accurately perceived, and fear) in *all* cases and secondary features (for example, sensation of presence, difficulty breathing, apparitional perceptions) in *many* cases. Hufford's definitions of primary and secondary features (referring to elements within supernatural assault experiences) differ from my concept of primary and secondary wondrous events (primary incidents are spontaneous; secondary events are part of a performance).

Hufford refuted a *cultural source* hypothesis that suggests the Old Hag experiences are derived entirely from cultural conditioning. His data supported an *experiential source* hypothesis that suggests that primary and secondary elements within these episodes transcend culture and that the Old Hag may be a source, rather than a consequence, of belief.

Hufford noted that many scholars have attempted to fit descriptions of the Old Hag into previously conceived psychological or psychoanalytical theories. This has resulted in distorted notions that do not correspond to the empirical data. Although unable to establish the causal source of Old Hag episodes, his approach demonstrates that these events constitute genuine anomalies within the folklore paradigm.

Hufford's experience-centered approach provides a methodological foundation for my work. The basic unit of data is the *memorate*, a story told as a personal experience and believed by the respondent to be true. The objective is to delineate the degree to which memorates are cultural products and to determine which elements within a collection of memorates are universal.

This methodology can be extended to other forms of anomalous experience (Hufford, 1982a; 1985a, b; 1987a, b, 1992; Rojcewicz, 1987). Episodes such as extrasensory perception, out-of-body, near-death, apparitional, and contact-with-the-dead experiences can be analyzed within this paradigm. The cultural and experiential source theories lead to clearly testable hypotheses. If the cultural source theory is valid, experiences will occur only within cultures that support them. The experiential source theory predicts that certain phenomena, such as déjà vu, sleep paralysis, ESP, clairvoyance, psychic contact with the dead, and out-of-body (OBE) and near-death experiences, contain universal elements that occur in all cultures. Such experiences are instrumental in *causing* changes in belief, rather than merely being *caused by* belief. If the anomalous experiences of many respondents show details contrary to their expectations but similar to the experiences of others with whom they do not share psycho-social factors that could account for those similarities, then the experiential source theory is supported. We could then argue that primary elements cause cross-cultural convergences of folk belief. Verification of the hypothesis that socially real psi has the power to modify belief in a specific direction would transform presently accepted theories regarding the evolution of occult beliefs and establish a new paradigm within folklore and religious studies.

Psychical researchers, engaging in cross-cultural studies, have already gathered evidence supporting the experiential source theory. For example, Haraldsson (1985) compared data from national samples of citizens polled regarding frequency of paranormal experience. Although the percentage claiming ESP, clairvoyance, and contact with the dead varied from country to country, these experiences were reported in all countries. Sheils (1978) noted that OBE beliefs appear in about 95 percent of the world's cultures and are striking in their uniformity. He tested conventional explanations for these beliefs and found them inadequate. Irwin (1985a) also reviewed surveys of OBEs and attempted to identify universal features. Osis and Haraldsson (1977) presented cross-cultural data regarding near-death experience that support belief in primary elements (for example, feeling separate from one's body, sense of movement, encountering spiritual beings, and communicating with a powerful entity). Emmons (1982) surveyed a random sample of Hong Kong residents and found evidence that apparitional experiences manifest some universal elements (images in these experiences had anomalous qualities similar to those of other cultures). Stevenson's (1970) cross-cultural study of children's reincarnation memories indicated cultural influences within these memorates, as well as the probability that common features also exist.

Survey techniques and analysis of cases can also reveal replicable patterns, even when data are gathered from a single culture. Gurney, Myers, and Podmore (1918/1886) conducted the first large-scale survey of apparitional experiences, verifying a statistically improbable relationship between crisis apparitions and death. West (1948) found an equivalent high rate of apparitional experience. L. Rhine's (1981) studies of psychic experiences supply the largest body of evidence, suggesting that patterns exist within paranormal reports. Palmer's (1979) survey of a random sample of Charlottesville, Virginia, residents offers a more recent study. Other research data also reveal patterns in reports of anomalous experience and guidelines for a continuation of this avenue of research (Bennett, 1987; Gallup, 1982; Gauld and Cornell, 1979; Greyson and Flynn, 1985; Haraldsson, 1988–89; Lundahl, 1982; Mitchell, 1981; Ring, 1980; Rogo, 1982a). Case material can be found in Evans (1984, 1987, 1989) and Gooch (1984).

Chapters 2 and 3 present data that support the claim that primary features exist in déjà vu, night paralysis, extrasensory perception, out-of-body, and contact-with-the-dead experiences within Chinese, Japanese, Caucasian-American, and African-American samples. Chapter 4 notes commonalities within field investigations of haunting and poltergeist cases.

2. Wondrous events provide a foundation for folk religious beliefs.

More than one thousand experience narratives from the United States, China, and Japan were gathered as part of this study. In these narratives informants often describe universal features, supporting folk belief in spirits, souls, life after death, and anomalous capacities. Features within these narratives coincide with listings in Thompson's *Motif-Index of Folk-Literature* (1966).

Although wondrous events do not compel belief in religious doctrines, faith relieves the cognitive dissonance that anomalous episodes often create. Chapter 8 presents historical evidence that wondrous events contributed to a convergence of medieval Buddhist and Christian beliefs in spirits, souls, prayers, special mediators, and life after death. Chapter 9 focuses on medieval Asian and European near-death experience accounts. These narratives show commonalities that contributed to similarities in Buddhist and Christian concepts of the afterlife.

Psychic phenomena, or *psi*, have qualities that elicit skepticism as well as faith. Parapsychologists have often been unable to convince their critics of the existence of paranormal faculties. Although many researchers believe that they have confirmed the existence of psychic phenomena (Wolman, 1977), skeptics question the validity of these claims (Kurtz, 1985). Some parapsychologists suggest that psi has an elusive "hiding" quality, a characteristic that hinders its verification (Braud, 1985). This belief is based on both laboratory and field experiences. When referring to psi's hiding quality, I do not mean to personalize the term but rather to refer to a folk belief supported by research observations. Chapters 10 and 11 provide examples of the types of experience contributing to skepticism regarding psi and belief in psi's hiding quality.

3. Those with the greatest capacity for experiencing wondrous events often engage in ceremonial performances.

Persons who report frequent spontaneous wondrous events find they must adjust to these phenomena (Chapter 5). This often entails playing a special role. Many societies have standard methods for becoming a spiritual healer. Those reporting frequent spontaneous wondrous incidents (primary events) sometimes gain the skills required to perform regular demonstrations (secondary events). Shamanic performances may entail extrasensory feats, sleight-of-hand ability, dissociative trance, and heat immunity (Chapter 6 reports on some participant observation studies).

Long (1977) cites more than one hundred cases of wondrous phenomena in the anthropological literature, most of which entail performances. Some researchers have sought to prove the authenticity of secondary anomalous claims within an anthropological context (Giesler, 1984, 1985a, b, 1986; Winkelman, 1981). Winkelman (1982) proposes that magical performances originated with innate psychic abilities. Psychic phenomena in the laboratory are forms of performance that constitute secondary wondrous events.

Wondrous performances often function as a stimulus for tertiary experiences, particularly psychosomatic healings. Although the possibility exists that some cures truly defy scientific explanation, most successful psychic treatments result from shifts in attitude and belief and can be classified as psychosomatic.

4. Many of the processes surrounding wondrous performance can be explained within sociological paradigms.

Wondrous events are often affiliated with collective behavior. The study of collective behavior entails examination of relatively unorganized patterns of group interaction. It includes the analysis of crowds, riots, panics, fads, fashions, rumors, mass hysteria, and social movements. Collective behavior is typically viewed as an adaptive response to new or ambiguous situations. It is often associated with emotional arousal and social strain (Le Bon, 1969/1895; Park and Burgess, 1921; Perry and Pugh, 1978; Turner and Killian, 1957). Many forms of psychic phenomena, such as hauntings, poltergeists, and miracles, are sporadic, spontaneous, affiliated with emotional arousal, and related to group processes. As a result, these events may be evaluated as forms of collective behavior.

UFO phenomena have already been recognized as an appropriate topic within the field. Miller (1985) devotes a chapter to UFOs, reviewing the data regarding witnesses, organizations, and public awareness. Bennett (1987), Greeley (1975, 1987), Lyons and Truzzi (1991), McCready and Greeley (1976), and Truzzi (1972) offer a similar body of evidence regarding psychic experiences.

Theories predicting the patterns, form, and dissemination of rumors aid in understanding the transformation of anomalous memorates into supernatural folklore. Within Shibutani's (1966) framework, rumor is a recurrent form of communication through which people attempt to construct a working interpretation of ambiguous situations by pooling their intellectual resources. Sociologists have long recognized that rumors are not always incorrect. People without adequate information regarding a topic generally attempt to gather information from as many sources as are readily available. The collective result is not necessarily inaccurate or implausible but is rather a substitute for news obtained through institutional channels. Rumor is "improvised news": "If the demand for news . . . exceeds the supply made available through institutional channels, rumor construction is likely to occur" (Shibutani, 1966: 57). The traditional scientific network's failure to address issues regarding the paranormal has apparently created conditions in which informally gathered information is transmitted through uninstitutionalized channels, evolving into folk beliefs.

Social scientists can trace the means by which people use reports of the paranormal to formulate social knowledge regarding wondrous events. For example, narrators often describe their experiences to others. Their reports are shaped by memory, story-telling ability, and perception of audience needs. A rumorlike process of oral transmission molds these narratives, shaping, leveling, and sharpening them to fit cultural requirements. Yet the existence of universal features within some types of wondrous experience produces ideological convergences of religious belief. Folk beliefs in spirits, souls, life after death, and anomalous capacities are almost universal.

Collective behavior orientations can also provide a framework for analysis of group processes. For example, Smelser's (1962) *value-added* theory proposes that seemingly spontaneous collective behaviors are the result of a combination of necessary, causal factors. Smelser's theory is presented as a chain in which the predicted behavior occurs only if all elements are present in a specific order. Smelser's approach, borrowed from the economics of manufacturing, hypothesizes that stages exist within collective behavior processes: (1) *structural conduciveness*, the basic parameters imposed on behavior by culture, (2) *structural strain*, derived from deprivations or from inconsistencies between values and norms, (3) *generalized belief*, which provides a focus for collective action, (4) *precipitating factors*, events triggering activity, (5) *mobilization of participants for action*, and (6) *the operation of social control activities*. This orientation has proven useful for the analysis of panics, riots, crazes, and other forms of collective behavior.

Value-added theories can also be applied to haunting incidents. Many cases involve a progression of events, occurring within cultural parameters, seemingly related to group tensions. Precipitating events trigger mobilization for action. Although hauntings differ from other forms of collective behavior, researchers can note the degree to which events fit previously conceived value-added theories. The theories often can be reformulated when empirical evidence exposes their deficiencies. Chapter 4 presents findings from haunting and poltergeist investigations that support a modified value-added approach.

Analysis of social data regarding wondrous events may sometimes have direct bearing on present parapsychological hypotheses. For example, if poltergeist activity occurs more frequently around prepubescent adolescents, as psychical researchers suggest, we might then predict that the mean age of such agents would be less in societies whose youth reach maturity at an earlier age.

At the same time, social scientific investigators may find patterns within group processes unique to paranormal experiences. During an ethnographic study of spiritual healers in the Philippines, I noted that extremely anomalous events were most frequently reported during the original phase of folk healers' careers (seemingly primary events). These reports attracted crowds that required management. Psychic practitioners then orchestrated ritualized performances, attempting to meet the needs of mass audiences (secondary events). Many healings resulted (tertiary events). Practitioners who lacked competent advisors, business acumen, charismatic personalities, or suitable ideologies did not maintain the public interest required to establish an ongoing enterprise.

Although social scientists in the past have tended to attribute reports of unusual experiences to collective delusion (for examples, see Johnson, 1945; Medalia and Larsen, 1958; Miller, 1985), more recent researchers have used alternate approaches to study anomalous events. Miller (1985: 111), for example, concludes that "[g]enerally . . . the data from these studies show only minimal support for the mass hysteria image and explanation of collective behavior." Miller's interactionist perspective and Smelser's (1962) value-added theory do not reject the possibility that *authentic* psychic phenomena may contribute to unusual experiences.

Although the research conclusions regarding the correlates to belief in ESP are unclear (Zusne and Jones, 1982), the data generally indicate that belief is not related to pathology. Frequency of mystical experience, operationally defined by Greeley (1975) as a feeling of being lifted out of one's body by a powerful spiritual force, correlated positively with psychological well-being. Emmons and Sobal (1981b) found within an American national sample that those accepting paranormal claims suffered from fewer deprivations than those rejecting them. Believers tended to be better educated and more wealthy than skeptics.

Social scientific analysis of wondrous events could increase understanding of religious movements. The study of recruitment into religious cults, sects, and movements is an area ripe for innovation since, in general, sociologists have paid little attention to wondrous events. The deprivation/ideological appeal orientation places emphasis on the tendency for potential recruits to have needs that fit the movement's ideology (Glock and Stark, 1965). Social networks theory, an alternate but not exclusive perspective, emphasizes the importance of human relationships in religious recruitment and retention (Stark and Bainbridge, 1980). People often are attracted to a religious group because their friends or relatives are members. The potential convert's "structural availability," that is, freedom from previous temporal and ideological commitments, is also important (Snow et al., 1980).

Wondrous events play a role in these processes. Those feeling the need to explain psychic experiences may join innovative religious movements that place emphasis on anomalous events. Ellwood (1977) presents a history of innovative religious movements in America, from Swedenborg's doctrines to Zen Buddhism. In all probability, participants in these groups were influenced by wondrous experiences as well as by deprivations, social networks, and structural availability. Chapters 8, 9, and 11 present cases exemplifying groups' use of wondrous events to attract new members.

The decline in the explanatory power of religious institutions may coincide with an increased acceptance of wondrous events. This argument corresponds with Stark and Bainbridge's (1985) theory that secularization contributes to the growth of cults and sects. Cerullo (1982) argues that the 1882 founding of the British Society for Psychical Research was motivated by the desire to believe in a nonmaterial, eternal, yet scientifically verifiable component of the human personality, "a secular soul." Likewise, Emmons and Sobal (1981a) hypothesize that modern belief in the paranormal constitutes a functional equivalent to religious faith. In national survey data, they found that those with "no religion" or who state that religion is "not at all important," were more likely to believe in ESP than religious respondents. According to Greeley's (1975) national survey data, those scoring high on an index based on self-reports of déjà vu, extrasensory perception, and clairvoyance were slightly *less* likely to go to church than average Americans but more likely to believe in human survival after death, to have certainty about fundamental religious beliefs, to be religious optimists, and to consider themselves religious agnostics (Greeley, 1975: 15; McCready and Greeley, 1976).

Various theorists have attempted to explain the origin of religiosity as a product of individual experience. Lang (1968/1898) suggested that wondrous events played an important role. Assorted scholars suggest that perceptions of psychokinesis and extrasensory events are possible origins of magical traditions (de Vesme, 1931; Long, 1977; Winkelman, 1982). Lowie (1924) and Tylor (1920) hypothesize that the misinterpretation of physiological or physical phenomena may be responsible for religious sentiment. Otto (1953) attributes the religious impulse to a sacred universal force, the numinous. Although these theorists have been criticized for placing insufficient emphasis on social factors, the experiential elements they discuss probably did play a role in stimulating religious sentiment among early humans.

The capacity to perceive anomalous phenomena may have a genetic component. If so, wondrous events could have had important impacts on human prehistory. Richard Broughton (1988: 187), a former president of the Parapsychological Association, argues, "If you want to know how [psi] works, first find out what it's for." He hypothesizes that psi contributes to individual human survival, but that perception of its incidence is obscured because too much psi ability is dysfunctional. Those exhibiting excessive psi capacities are often persecuted.

My collection of anomalous narratives provides very few examples of wondrous events contributing to a person's survival or reproductive success. Wondrous episodes more often support religious beliefs, such as faith in an afterlife or in occult connections crossing space and time. Psi seemingly has little impact on people's success in transmitting their genes.

A social scientific orientation can view wondrous events as functional for entire societies, rather than for individuals. Wondrous events support unifying religious beliefs. Because of the relationship between psychic phenomena and spiritual healing, evolutionary processes may have shaped the capacity to experience wondrous events. Those more responsive to therapeutic suggestions, often embedded within ceremonies involving altered states of consciousness and wondrous performance, may have had higher survival rates.

It is dysfunctional for groups to acquire *absolute* belief in occult interpretations of wondrous phenomena since such faith can be irrational. Mundane explanations exist for many wondrous perceptions and skepticism assures a connection to reality. If everyone felt certain of a pleasant afterlife, for example, suicide would seem a logical choice to many. The restricted development of the capacity to perceive wondrous events may be related to evolutionary factors. Human groups are most adaptive when they contain both believers and skeptics. The ability to experience psi seemingly has an obscured quality since reports of psychic phenomena stimulate both belief and skepticism.[1]

Wondrous phenomena have had important impacts on modern religious ideologies. Miraculous events were instrumental in the origin and development of Christianity (Smith, 1978; Ward, 1982). Zurcher (1959) notes the use of miraculous performances by monks spreading Buddhism in China (reviewed in Chapter 8). The eighth-century monk Kyokai was the first of various Japanese writers to propagate Buddhism in Japan by collecting, transcribing, and disseminating miracle stories (Nakamura, 1973; reviewed in Chapters 8 and 9). Although beyond the scope of my analysis, wondrous events have affected other religions as well (Kelsey, 1987).

The results of my study can be interpreted within the context of Stark and Bainbridge's (1985) theories. They provide a model that predicts the future of religion. They argue that *compensators* are the basic stimuli for religious belief (p. 6). Compensators are defined as the belief that rewards will be obtained in the distant future or in some other context that cannot be immediately verified. Religions are "human organizations primarily engaged in providing general compensators based on supernatural assumptions" (p. 8). "[S]upernatural assumptions are the only plausible source for many rewards that humans seem to desire intensely" (p. 431).

Stark and Bainbridge argue that secularization creates fertile grounds for sect and cult development. "Sect formation is, in part, a response to early stages of weakness in the general compensators provided by the conventional churches. Cult formation tends to erupt in later stages of church weakness, when large sectors of the population have drifted away from all organizational ties to the prevailing faiths" (p. 445). Much data support their argument. Localities with lower rates of traditional church attendance have higher rates of cult activity.

Stark and Bainbridge depict the market features I observed in my investigations of spiritual healers. Cults often demonstrate skillful free enterprise, both in competition with each other and with more traditional groups (p. 183). Cults have the potential to become cult movements, which can, in turn, evolve into churches. Stark and Bainbridge review the literature regarding group processes occurring during the transition from cult to church. They argue that basic mechanisms related to upward mobility and regression toward the mean can be applied to sect and cult movements. Their formulations provide testable hypotheses that specify factors related to the development of client cults to cult movements.

Wondrous experiences are one factor influencing this process. Although I present alternate arguments regarding the future of magic, Stark and Bainbridge's (1985) framework explains my findings within the context of a sociology of religion. Cults have been extremely important within religious history and wondrous experiences and performances are critical within many of these groups. Recurring patterns surrounding wondrous events allow predictions concerning the future of religion.

Summary

Hufford's (1982a) cultural source and experiential source theories lead to testable hypotheses regarding wondrous events. If the experiential source orientation is valid, we would predict that primary features exist in some forms of wondrous experience, features that contribute to commonalities in folk belief. This hypothesis is supported by survey data (see Chapters 2 and 3). Narratives from individuals reporting hauntings and poltergeists also contain primary features (see Chapter 4).

Wondrous events can also be analyzed using theories of collective behavior and the sociology of religion; haunting and poltergeist experiences occur within collective behavior processes (see Chapter 4). At the same time, psychic practitioners reveal common patterns within their socialization and performance, and in their effects on audiences (see Chapters 5, 6, and 7). An analysis of medieval Buddhist and Christian history reveals the impacts of wondrous events on religious traditions (see Chapters 8 and 9). The traits unique to wondrous experience are also apparent within the history of scientific investigation of psychic phenomena (see Chapter 10) and in a study of a modern group making psychic claims (see Chapter 11). Further, the capacity for wondrous experience may have genetic components. These findings allow predictions regarding future religious beliefs (see Chapter 12).

My analysis is open to verification, reformulation, or refutation. It is far from complete. My social scientific orientation points toward further theoretical development as well as testable hypotheses.

Chapter 2
Surveys of Anomalous Experience: A Cross-Cultural Analysis

Scholars often assume that wondrous perceptions are cultural products originating simply from religious need and scientific ignorance (Schumaker, 1990; Singer and Benassi, 1981; Hufford, 1982b, 1987a, 1990). Such suppositions are derived from what Hufford (1982a) labels the cultural source theory. This theory, associated with disbelief in the paranormal, assumes that scientific education reduces, and religious belief increases, the incidence of wondrous experience. In this study, these hypotheses were tested by analyzing survey data from Caucasian-American, African-American, Chinese, and Japanese college populations regarding déjà vu, sleep paralysis, extrasensory perception (ESP), contact with the dead, and out-of-body experience (OBE).

The findings provide little support for the cultural source theory. This evaluation coincides with that of Fox (1992). Using U.S. General Social Survey data from 1984, 1988, and 1989, Fox found that reports of paranormal experiences were higher among women but were otherwise unaffected by age, race, education, income, marital status, or religious preference. An alternative to the cultural source model suggests that dissociative and related capacities regulate the incidence of anomalous experience. Dissociation refers to the ability to maintain simultaneously two or more relatively autonomous cognitive or emotional activities, some being outside the conscious domain. This dissociative model links primary wondrous events with naturally occurring states of consciousness.

The Cultural Source Theory

The cultural source theory is based on an implicit set of assumptions regarding the power of culture to shape experience. According to this theory, respondents' cultures are thought to determine the frequency and forms of their anomalous reports. The theory has been shaped by the evolution of scientific paradigms and the role of anomalous experience within religious history.

Within the context of the cultural source theory, many types of anomalous experiences are thought to result from existential anxiety or deprivation (Schumaker, 1990; Zusne and Jones, 1982). Anomalous reports are assumed to originate from lies, hoaxes, misinterpretations of ordinary events, failure to recognize coincidence, psychological needs, and mental malfunctions. Occult beliefs affiliated with such accounts are self-validating because they alleviate feelings of helplessness and anxiety (Snow and Machalek, 1982). The proliferation and longevity of supernatural doctrines are therefore thought to reflect social disorders, tension, and flaws in the scientific education system (Kaagan, 1984; Singer and Benassi, 1981).

Although the cultural source theory rarely has been articulated clearly, studies by several researchers are representative. Brunvand (1981) portrays modern folklore as a collection of narratives heard from a "friend of a friend," rather than traditions evolving from memorates. Finucane (1984) likewise reveals correlations between apparitional accounts and social needs, placing little emphasis on similarities within firsthand reports. Such scholarship assumes that correspondences between specific cultures and their folklore accounts demonstrate that anomalous episodes are cultural products. Cultural source theorists tend to ignore the distinction between firsthand and secondary accounts.

The high incidence of miraculous reports within religious histories seemingly supports the cultural source theory. Faith apparently increases frequency of anomalous experience. The Christian Gospels contain well over two hundred items about Jesus' miracles or claims to wondrous powers (Smith, 1978: 109). Of the 2,532 biographical descriptions within *Butler's Lives of the Saints* (Thurston and Attwater, 1956), 29 percent include miraculous accounts (White, 1982). Medieval Chinese and Japanese documents also connect anomalous experiences with religious belief (Ch'en, 1964; McClenon, 1991; Nakamura, 1973; Zurcher, 1959). The cultural source theory, in its most common form, specifies that those claiming greater religiosity should therefore report more anomalous episodes and that anomalous experience should be more prevalent within certain denominations.

According to the cultural source theory, scientific education should reduce the frequency of paranormal reports and belief in wondrous claims. Scientists tend to be more antagonistic toward religious arguments, placing greater emphasis on empirical findings. Prominent social theorists including Emile Durkheim, Sigmund Freud, and Karl Marx advocated forms of agnosticism, typically coupled with skepticism toward the supernatural. Their doctrines provide paradigms for modern sociological and psychological formulations regarding religion. Most academic discourse on the supernatural, rather than being "culture-free," advocates a "culture of disbelief" since paranormal experience is regarded as being entirely a product of culture (Hufford, 1982b, 1983a, 1985a, 1987a).

Previous Surveys

Greeley (1975) presented the first major analysis of randomly sampled national data regarding anomalous experience. He found that almost one-fifth of the U.S. population reported frequent paranormal experiences and that these episodes were unrelated to any obvious forms of pathology. Respondents answered questions about déjà vu, ESP, contact with the dead, clairvoyance, and mystical experiences. His ESP question asked, "Have you thought you were in touch with someone when you knew that it was impossible?" Contact with the dead was measured by asking, "Have you thought you were really in touch with someone who had died?"

During recent years, other representative national surveys of psychic experience and paranormal beliefs were conducted using the same questions (Davis and Smith, 1990; Fox, 1992; Greeley, 1987; Haraldsson, 1985; Haraldsson and Houtkooper, 1991). Table 2.1 compares percentages of respondents reporting déjà vu, ESP, and contact with the dead within European and American national samples. Variations in frequency of reports among groups would seem to reflect cultural traits specific to each country (Haraldsson, 1985; McClenon, 1988a). For example, a relatively low percentage of citizens in Denmark claimed ESP and contact-with-the-dead experiences, while a high percentage of Icelanders and Americans reported such episodes.

Various studies have found relationships between religious variables and reporting of anomalous events. Those scoring high on Greeley's (1975: 15) Psi Scale of anomalous experience were more likely to consider themselves religious agnostics. Yet these respondents were likely to have greater certainty about fundamental religious beliefs. Within a San Francisco sample, Wuthnow (1978) found that religiosity correlated positively with paranormal experience.

Some studies support the argument that paranormal beliefs constitute a functional equivalent for organized religion (Bainbridge and Stark, 1980a, b; Emmons and Sobal, 1981b). According to these sources, belief in the occult may counteract the existential anxiety

TABLE 2.1. Percent of Respondents Reporting One or More Anomalous
Experiences.

	Déjà vu	ESP	Contact with dead
American National Samples:			
United States (1973)	59	58	27
United States (1984)	67	67	42
United States (1988)	67	65	40
United States (1989)	64	58	36
European National Samples:			
Great Britain		36	26
Northern Ireland		24	12
Republic of Ireland		19	16
West Germany		35	26
Holland		27	11
Belgium		18	16
France		34	23
Italy		38	33
Spain		20	16
Malta		28	19
Denmark		14	9
Sweden		23	14
Finland		35	15
Norway		18	9
Iceland		33	41
Total for Western Europe		32	23

Sources: Greeley (1975, 1987), Fox (1992), Haraldsson (1985).

associated with the prospect of death in the same manner as religious
faith. Respondents reporting no religious preference, or for whom
religious beliefs were unimportant, were more likely to believe in
nonreligious paranormal phenomena (Emmons and Sobal, 1981b).
Similarly, areas of the United States where interest in the paranormal is
highest show the lowest level of traditional church attendance (Bainbridge and Stark, 1980b). Yet other studies found significant positive
relationships between paranormal beliefs and religiosity (Emmons,
1982; Haraldsson, 1981; Irwin, 1985b; Thalbourne, 1984; Tobacyk
and Milford, 1983), and some found no significant correlations (Gallup
and Newport, 1991; Murphy and Lester, 1976; Sheils and Berg, 1977;
Thalbourne, 1981).

The relationship between religion and occult belief may be mediated
by scientific education. As argued above, various studies support the
argument that those with scientific training are less susceptible to

occult experience and belief. Wagner and Monnet (1979) polled a random sample of American college professors and found that professors of the humanities, arts, and education were more likely to believe in ESP than were natural and social scientists. Padgett, Benassi, Singer (1981) and Otis and Alcock (1982) reached similar conclusions: study of the sciences was related to less belief in psychic phenomena. Council members and selected section committee representatives of the American Association for the Advancement of Science were far less likely to have had anomalous experiences or to believe in ESP than were average American citizens (McClenon, 1982, 1984). Elite scientists and physicians—those listed in *Who's Who in America*—showed far greater doubt regarding the possibility of contact with the dead and the validity of near-death experiences than did ordinary Americans (Gallup, 1982).

Yet the hypothesized negative correlation between scientific training and belief in psychic claims may be culturally specific. Jahoda (1968) found no significant relationship between scientific training and the persistence of traditional (paranormal) beliefs among students at the University of Ghana. The present study sheds light on this issue through analysis of data from a variety of ethnic and cultural sources, including Caucasian-American, African-American, Chinese, and Japanese student samples.

Hypotheses

The following hypotheses were developed from the cultural source theory:

1. Anomalous experiences will occur more frequently among those claiming no religious belief or preference than among Catholics, Protestants, Jews, or Buddhists.
2. Those reporting greater religiosity will claim more frequent anomalous experiences.
3. Students majoring in scientific or technical curriculums will report fewer anomalous experiences and less belief in ESP than those studying other fields. These relationships should be especially pronounced among third- and fourth-year students. Third- and fourth-year science students will demonstrate greater skepticism regarding ESP than lower-level science students because they have been more fully exposed to scientific training.

Due to the range of findings in the research literature, two-tailed tests of significance are appropriate for hypotheses 1 and 2 because significant results in either direction support the cultural source theory. (Statisticians refer to the ends of the normal curve as "tails" and statistical tests taking both ends into account are termed "two-tailed" tests.) The three hypotheses in category 3 require one-tailed tests of significance since no cultural source proponent suggests that scientific education *increases* the experience of, or belief in, anomalous events.

Methodology

Student samples are particularly appropriate for investigating hypotheses dealing with scientific education. Within these groups we can determine direct influences from recent exposure to scientific training. Data were gathered through questionnaires administered to randomly selected student samples at (1) three colleges in Xi'an, People's Republic of China in 1986, (2) the University of Maryland, College Park, in 1987, (3) Elizabeth City State University, Elizabeth City, North Carolina in 1988, (4) Tsukuba University, Tsukuba, Japan in 1989, and (5) the University of North Carolina, Greensboro, in 1990. Questionnaires had previously been sent to council members and selected section committee members of the American Association for the Advancement of Science in 1981 (McClenon, 1982, 1984).

The survey populations exemplify radically different cultural groups. The elite American scientists were mainly older male Caucasians (mean age: 55 years; 80 percent male). More than three-quarters of the University of Maryland and University of North Carolina at Greensboro (UNCG) students were Caucasian. UNCG, formerly a women's college, furnished a sample of which 67 percent were female. Elizabeth City State University (ECSU) is a predominately black college in northeastern North Carolina. The three Chinese colleges in Xi'an (Northwestern Polytechnic University, Xi'an University of Medical Science, and the Shaanxi Finance and Economic Institute) educate China's academically gifted students. Tsukuba University is an elite Japanese college within commuting distance of Tokyo.

The three colleges in the People's Republic of China were surveyed by questionnaires (accompanied by pre-addressed return envelopes) given to students in randomly selected dormitory rooms (McClenon, 1988a, 1990); 40 percent of the sample responded. The same method was used to poll students at Tsukuba University, using a questionnaire translated into Japanese under the supervision of Dr. Carl Becker; 33 percent responded. University of Maryland dormitory residents were randomly selected by computer and mailed the same questionnaire; 42 percent responded. Random samples of classrooms were selected at Elizabeth City State University and at the University of North Carolina,

Greensboro. Students filled out and returned the questionnaire while they were in class, assuring high response rates.

The questionnaire used Greeley's (1975) déjà vu, ESP, and contact-with-the-dead questions. It also asked respondents to supply their sex, age, academic class and major, and answers to questions regarding frequency of sleep paralysis, OBE, belief in ESP, religious preference, and self-perceived religiosity (see Appendix for exact format).

Chinese students were asked about "sixth sense," rather than extra-sensory perception, since they have no equivalent word for ESP. Chinese respondents were not polled regarding religiosity or religious preference because Xi'an students, at the time of the survey, did not confess to religious proclivities. Such questions would be labeled politically incorrect (McClenon, 1990).

Methodological obstacles exist in all cross-cultural analyses. Groups from different cultures may react differently to questionnaire instruments. Respondents may inflate or conceal the extent of their unusual experiences. Nonresponse may bias results. Methodological variations also complicate comparison between groups. These problems do not negate the value of cross-cultural questionnaire research.

Sociologists also must deal with contradictory demands when devising survey instruments (Neuman, 1991). Lengthy questionnaires, with multiple questions regarding each variable, are capable of establishing internal reliability. Yet brief questionnaires achieve higher response rates and are less subject to nonresponse bias. Although I do not recommend it wholeheartedly, my unusual experience questionnaire has the value of brevity and also permits comparison with previous American and European surveys.

Various checks indicate that the data probably reflect self-perceived experience. Some of the findings have reduced my concern regarding nonresponse bias. For example, data gained from elite scientists and University of Maryland respondents—requiring the stimulation of reminder postcards—did not differ significantly from those returning mailed questionnaires within a week (McClenon, 1984, 1990a). I gave the questionnaire to thirty-three Chinese academics who attended my lecture at Lanzhou University in 1986 (the contact-with-the-dead question was omitted for political reasons). Their responses revealed a level of anomalous experience equivalent to other Chinese samples (20 of 33, or 61 percent, reported ESP episodes, and 14 of 33, or 43 percent, claimed out-of-body experiences). Their discussion of the survey instrument indicated that their responses reflected personal experiences. The instrument was also appraised by students in a sociology of religion class at the University of Maryland in 1987. They revealed frequencies of experience equivalent to those within the random sample of the college dormitory population. Furthermore, they described their interpretation of questionnaire items and indicated that their responses were associated with specific experiences. Finally, anomalous narratives provided by the Lanzhou academics, the sociology of religion students, and respondents to the random sample surveys were equivalent to those described in the psychical research literature.

Japanese and American respondents were asked if they would agree to be interviewed. The percentage providing names and telephone numbers varied from 9 percent (UNCG) to 17 percent (ECSU). These individuals were questioned to determine the degree to which quantitative response reflected personal experience. Some respondents were interviewed on more than one occasion to observe alterations. Virtually all respondents had clear experiences in mind corresponding to each claim. Repeated narratives showed only slight variation.

Between 1987 and 1993, a thousand anomalous accounts were collected for this study in northeastern North Carolina, many by students in anthropology classes at Elizabeth City State University. The narrative forms of these accounts coincide with data obtained through the questionnaires.

By interviewing respondents, I found weaknesses in the survey instrument used in this study. People's answers to forced-choice questions did not always closely reflect their personal experience. For example, many individuals claiming "contacts with the dead" described subjective impressions without sensory verification. Other "contacts" involved apparitions, ESP, or PK. The "contact" question failed to differentiate these experiences. Other items presented similar ambiguities. A few respondents reported déjà vu episodes that contained extrasensory elements, for example.

Response to experiential questions in the study often reflect the human construction of social realities. For example, those who believed in survival after death were more prone to claim contacts with the dead. People believing in ESP were more likely to label unusual correspondences as paranormal. Although the items in the questionnaire are subject to multiple interpretation, this problem does not invalidate their use. They are justified by their brevity and comparability, rather than by their value for determining the authenticity of specific forms of psychic experience. Episodes *perceived* by respondents as valid have real effects on their beliefs.

Greeley's questions have been useful to previous sociologists of religion. Fox's (1992) analysis, for example, reduces faith in the cultural source theory since he found little correlation between anomalous experience and social variables. MacDonald (1992) found that the frequency of contact-with-the-dead reports was most affected by gender and an interaction effect between race and religious imagery. Although Greeley's questionnaire items have limitations, my use of them allows comparison with previous studies.

Results

Table 2.2 compares the percentages of those reporting one or more anomalous experiences. Chinese students generally demonstrated the highest percentages of such experiences and belief in ESP. The elite scientists tended to report the lowest levels of psychic episodes and beliefs. The Japanese claimed lower rates of contact with the dead, OBE, and belief in ESP than did the other student groups.

Religious Preference

American religious preferences were categorized as Protestant, fundamentalist-type Protestant, Catholic, Jewish, other, or none. Japanese responses were classified as Buddhist, Catholic, other, or none. No chi square tests regarding religious preference and anomalous experience achieved statistical significance at the .05 level within American or Japanese groups.

Religiosity

The percentage of students who regarded themselves as religious varied among samples. Seventy-eight percent of the ECSU students, 74 percent at UNCG, 47 percent of the Maryland students, and 15 percent of the Tsukuba Japanese claimed to be "extremely" or "somewhat" religious.

Self-reported religiosity was significantly associated with forms of anomalous experience in two samples. A significantly higher percentage of UNCG students claiming to be "slightly" or "not at all" religious reported OBEs than those claiming to be "extremely" or "somewhat" religious (25 percent vs. 15 percent, $p < .01$, two-tailed difference of proportions test). A significantly higher percentage of the more religious Japanese students also reported sleep paralysis episodes (70 percent vs. 45 percent, $p < .05$, two-tailed test). These cases were encountered within the context of twenty tests of significance (p values were not corrected for multiple analysis). The UNCG OBE/religiosity analysis was as follows: chi square $= 7.25, df = 1, p < .01; r = 0.09, N = 511, p = .06$, two-tailed test. The Japanese sleep paralysis/religiosity data produced the following: chi square $= 4.95, df = 1, p < .05; r = 0.24, N = 130; p = .011$, two-tailed test.

TABLE 2.2. Comparison of Sample Surveys.

Percent reporting one or more experiences

	N	PERCENT RESPONDING	DÉJÀ VU	SLEEP PARALYSIS	ESP	CONTACT WITH DEAD	OBE	BELIEF IN ESP*
Elite American Scientists	339	71	59	**	26	10	20	20
University of Maryland students	214	42	89	37	44	25	27	66
University of NC, Greensboro students	532	98	86	32	42	20	18	60
ECSU (African-American students)	391	99	80	50	35	25	18	68
Chinese student random samples (three colleges)	314	40	64	58	71	40	55	76
Tsukuba University Japanese students	132	33	88	50	35	10	13	61

*Percent considering ESP "a fact" or "a likely possibility."
**Elite scientists were not polled about sleep paralysis experiences. The OBE question for elite scientists was that used by Greeley (1975), which differed from that used on the other surveys.

Scientific Training

Data from the University of Maryland, UNCG, ECSU, and Tsukuba University demonstrated no significant differences between those majoring in fields associated with science (social science, natural science, computer sciences, math, engineering, and architecture) and those majoring in fields less related to scientific studies (liberal arts, education, business, and others) with regard to sleep paralysis, ESP, OBE, and contact with the dead. The only significant relationship occurred with regard to déjà vu among ECSU students, an unremarkable finding since twenty-four tests of significance were conducted and p values were not corrected for multiple analysis. In this case, chi square = 4.25, $df = 1$, $p < .05$. Eighty-four percent of ECSU nonscience majors versus 75 percent of the science-related majors reported déjà vu.

Analysis of Japanese and U.S. data comparing junior and senior science-related majors to equivalent nonscience majors with regard to the experience variables and belief in ESP revealed no significant differences. Significant variations existed among the Chinese colleges with regard to reporting of anomalous experiences (McClenon, 1990). These findings have little bearing on the hypothesized relationship since all the Chinese students attended colleges specializing in physical, medical, or social scientific training. Students from the technical college (NPU) tended to report anomalous experiences less frequently— although they claimed higher levels of belief in a sixth sense—than did those at the medical or economic colleges (McClenon, 1990).

Upper-level (third- and fourth-year) science majors, according to the hypotheses, would be expected to report less belief in ESP than lower-level science majors, since the advanced students had been exposed to more scientific training. No significant differences were found in the predicted direction. Among University of Maryland and UNCG samples, belief in ESP was *greater* among upper-level science students than at the lower level. At the University of Maryland, 51 percent of young science majors were believers, compared to 69 percent of the older ones ($p > .95$, one-tailed difference of proportions test). At UNCG, 48 percent of the younger UNCG science majors believed in ESP while 66 percent of the more advanced students were believers ($p > .95$, one-tailed difference of proportions test). These relationships were opposite to that predicted by the cultural source hypothesis.

Further Analysis

As was found by Greeley (1975), the anomalous experience variables were highly correlated with each other. ESP, contact with the dead, and

OBE were significantly intercorrelated in all samples ($p < .05$). Déjà vu and sleep paralysis correlated significantly with other experience variables in most samples.

A "psi index" was created by summing up the values for ESP experience, contact with the dead, and OBE, on the basis that these reports (1) were significantly correlated with each other in all samples, (2) some respondents attributed religious significance to these experiences, though claiming no religious preference, (3) these accounts were equivalent to those reported within religious literature, and (4) parapsychologists regard these reports as sometimes violating established scientific principles. Experience variables were scored "1" if the respondent reported no experiences, "2" for reporting an experience "once or twice," "3" for "several times," and "4" for "often"; the psi index thus varied from 3 to 12.

Table 2.3 reveals significant variations in the distribution of the psi index across samples (chi square $= 392$, $p < .001$). All samples contained individuals who had no experiences and were skeptical of paranormal claims. Yet even among the elite scientists, of whom 64 percent reported no experience, 5 percent reported frequent episodes. Two cells pertaining to nonexperiencing and highly experiencing Chinese students contributed 69 percent of the chi square value. Nonexperiencing and highly experiencing elite scientists contributed another 9 percent to the chi square value. If elite scientist and Chinese data were omitted, the other samples continue to demonstrate significant differences (chi square $= 27.9$, $df = 12$, $p < .01$). This analysis replicates Haraldsson's (1985) findings. Diverse cultural groups report different levels of anomalous experience.

Belief in ESP and frequency of sleep paralysis correlated significantly with the psi index within all samples (see table 2.4). Only within the Japanese sample did frequency of déjà vu experience not correlate significantly with the psi index.

Within Caucasian-American samples, age was significantly correlated with belief in ESP (University of Maryland: $r = .22$, $N = 209$, $p < .01$; UNCG: $r = .115$, $N = 525$, $p < .01$). Within both groups, younger science majors tended to be more skeptical; older ones revealed percentages of belief in ESP equivalent to college-educated Americans. Outlying ages affected these correlations (13 UNCG students and 1 Maryland resident were over 30 years old). Chi square tests were conducted to check for these effects. Within the Maryland data, chi square $= 7.02$, $df = 3$, $p = .07$. The UNCG data produced the following: chi square $= 8.19$, $df = 3$, $p < .05$. In general, older Caucasian-American students showed greater belief. Although we might suppose that belief increases with age due to greater exposure to experience, ESP experi-

TABLE 2.3. Distribution of Frequency of Anomalous Experience.

Sample vs. Percentage in Category of Psi Index

PSI INDEX = ESP + CONTACT WITH DEAD + OBE	UNIVERSITY OF MD	UNCG	ECSU	CHINESE	JAPANESE	ELITE SCIENTISTS*
3 = no experience	44%	46%	50%	14%	60%	64%
4 = once or twice of one type of experience	18%	26%	23%	15%	15%	16%
5 = once or twice of two types or several times of one type	16%	14%	14%	16%	9%	9%
6 = once or twice of all three types, several times of two types, or many times of one type	12%	7%	6%	13%	8%	6%
7 or higher = many times *and* several times of at least two types	10%	6%	7%	41%	8%	5%
coefficient alpha:	.62	.52	.63	.46	.66	.57

*The OBE question on the elite scientist poll was that used by Greeley (1975), differing from that used on the other surveys.

Chi Square = 392
df = 20
p < 0.001

TABLE 2.4. Pearson Product Correlations Between Psi Index and Other Major
Variables.

	Belief in ESP	Déjà vu	Sleep paralysis	Age	Religiosity
University of MD	.31[c]	.38[c]	.27[c]	.03	.02
University of North Carolina Greensboro	.34[c]	.25[c]	.12[b]	.12[b]	−.07
ECSU (African-American)	.15[b]	.32[c]	.15[b]	.09	−.02
Three Chinese colleges	.12[a]	.26[c]	.16[b]	.09	*
Tsukuba University (Japanese)	.26[b]	.14	.27[b]	.12	.13

*Chinese students were not polled regarding religiosity.

a: $p < .05$ two-tailed test
b: $p < .01$ two-tailed test
c: $p < .001$ two-tailed test

ence among Maryland students showed very little correlation with age ($r = -.07$, $N = 209$, not significant). Among the Greensboro students, ESP experience increased significantly with age ($r = .11$, $N = 524$, $p < .05$).

A multiple regression analysis of the psi index on self-reported religiosity, academic major, age, and sex of respondent revealed that these variables offer little predictive capacity regarding the incidence of psi episodes (see Table 2.5). Age had slightly greater predictive capacity than did class standing and was used in place of class standing in the model. Of all variables, only age, within the University of Greensboro sample, created a significant t ($p = 0.011$). The significance test for each variable only reflects how much that variable contributes to predicting the psi index *in addition* to the other variables in the model. When two variable are correlated, it is less likely that they will appear to make significant individual contributions. Within the Greensboro data, for example, SEX correlated with HOWREL, the variable related to religiosity ($r = 0.193$), and AGE correlated with MAJOR ($r = 0.134$). Because AGE was most correlated with PSI ($r = 0.12$, $p < .01$, two-tailed test), the predictive contributions of the other variables were reduced. Variables other than AGE did not reveal statistically significant individual correlations with psi. Subsequent analyses indicated that area of academic study does not affect incidence of psi experiences to any appreciable degree, even if religious preference, religiosity, age, or class standing are controlled.

Discussion

Although frequencies of anomalous experience varied cross-culturally, hypotheses regarding a relationship between religious preference or

TABLE 2.5. Regression of Psi Variable on Self-Reported Religiosity, Academic
Major, Age, and Sex of Respondent.

	Univ. of Maryland	Univ. of NC, Greensboro	Eliz. City St. Univ., NC	Tsukuba Univ., Japan
HOWREL				
Coefficient	0.040	−0.101	−0.067	0.305
T	0.306	−1.356	−0.559	1.546
MAJOR				
Coefficient	0.130	0.056	0.143	0.174
T	0.527	0.376	0.916	0.512
AGE				
Coefficient	−0.020	0.039	0.030	0.052
T	−0.305	2.549[a]	1.612	0.617
SEX				
Coefficient	−0.370	−0.002	0.008	−0.205
T	−1.530	−0.016	0.053	−0.710
Constant	4.711	3.501	3.520	2.458
Multiple correlation coefficient	0.136	0.137	0.105	0.181
Squared multiple R	0.019	0.019	0.011	0.033
N	206	502	376	123

a: probability = .011.
Variable Names and Descriptions:
HOWREL   How religious do you consider yourself?
       4 = extremely, 3 = somewhat, 2 = slightly, 1 = not at all.
MAJOR   Dummy coded 1 if non-science academic major.
AGE   Age of respondent.
SEX   Dummy coded 1 if male.

scientific training and frequency of anomalous experience were not
supported in the study. The effects of self-perceived religiosity were
highly sporadic. In the context of the study, knowledge of a respondent's religious preference, religiosity, or scientific training did not
contribute greatly to the ability to predict frequency of anomalous
experience. Although socialization seemingly affects the incidence of
anomalous reports, as indicated by variations in frequency of reports
among samples, the data provide little support for the traditional
cultural source orientation.

These findings generally replicate those of Fox (1992), who, using
U.S. national survey sample data from 1984, 1988, and 1989, found
that paranormal experiences were higher among women but unaffected by age, race, education, income, marital status, and religious
preference. Cultural source and deprivation theories fail to explain the
incidence of reported paranormal experience.

An Alternative Model

An alternative model better explains the scattered and meager relationships between religiosity and anomalous reports. The incidence of anomalous experience is associated with various psychological variables, all of which are in turn correlated with dissociation. Frequency of psychic experience has been found to be correlated with hypnotic suggestibility (Nadon and Kihlstrom, 1987; Richards, 1990a; Wagner and Ratzeburg, 1987; Wickramasekera, 1989; Wilson and Barber, 1983), the Tellegen absorption scale (Irwin, 1985b; Nadon and Kihlstrom, 1987; Palmer and Van der Velden, 1983), and fantasy-proneness (Wilson and Barber, 1983). Although this body of research reveals consistent results, correlations tend to be less than 0.3.

Dissociation, a capacity related to hypnotic suggestibility, may be most closely related to anomalous experience. Richards (1991) reported that, within a population of frequent psychic experiencers, the Dissociative Experiences Scale correlated moderately with most forms of psychic report (Pearson's r varied from .3 to .4). Richards (1990b: 56) defines dissociation as "a variety of states that take place out of the conscious awareness of the personality that normally has executive control of the body." The Dissociative Experiences Scale asks respondents to mark a line showing what percentage of the time a specific statement applies. Sample statements include, "Some people have the experience of driving a car and suddenly realizing that they don't remember what has happened during all or part of the trip," and, "Some people find that they sometimes are able to ignore pain."

Capacities for dissociation, hypnosis, absorption, and fantasy-proneness are fostered through a variety of pathways. These include child abuse, positive encouragement by adults during childhood, and fervent engagement in absorbing activities such as meditation, dancing, acting, reading, or viewing movies. Ross and Joshi (1992) reported that their psychic experience index correlated significantly with secondary features of multiple personality disorder ($r = .23, p < .004$); the number of DSM-III-R dissociative disorders positive ($r = .21, p < .009$); childhood sexual abuse ($r = .20, p < .02$); and the number of sexual abuse perpetrators ($r = .22, p < .006$). Irwin (1985b, 1992) also found that child abuse is correlated with psychic experience and belief.

Although a growing number of findings link childhood trauma and dissociative experiences with psychic experiences, most researchers argue that psychic experience should not be considered as indicative of pathology. A high percentage of psychic experiencers have not been severely traumatized and reveal no indications of mental disorder. Dissociation and psychic experience should be regarded as normal human capacities that have not been thoroughly studied in nonclinical populations (Heber et al., 1989; Hufford, 1992; Richards, 1991; Ross and Joshi, 1992).

These studies support an alternate model linking cultural features to the incidence of wondrous experiences. The alternate theory hypothesizes that activities contributing to the development of the dissociative, hypnotic, and absorptive faculties enhance the capacity for anomalous experience. Furthermore, societies exhibiting high rates of dissociative-type and other unusual experiences may be expected to report more anomalous episodes. The data do not support the argument that dissociative-type traits *cause* anomalous experiences since psychic episodes occur among some individuals revealing low levels of these attributes.

This alternate theory coincides with experimental findings. Parapsychologists such as Honorton (1977, 1985) report that ESP occurs more regularly during altered states of consciousness (Honorton et al., 1990). Certain spontaneous anomalous experiences may involve retrieval of information during the onset of particular types of dissociative states.

Some religious practices, such as fervent prayer, chanting, or meditation, encourage dissociative states and are hypothesized to increase the incidence of anomalous experience. Yet the model predicts that highly religious people who report few dissociative experiences should experience few wondrous events. These formulations coincide with the present study's finding of few correlations between religiosity and anomalous experience. The alternative model is not sophisticated enough to explain why specific forms of anomalous experience vary in incidence across cultures; it merely suggests that factors contributing to dissociative experience also contribute to increased reports of anomalous events.

Childhood trauma is hypothesized to stimulate dissociative capacities leading to anomalous experience (Irwin, 1992). This relationship may also help explain variations within my data. During the Chinese Cultural Revolution (1966–1976), many Chinese children viewed public beatings, executions, and unusual social turmoil. Such social unrest may have contributed to higher rates of Chinese anomalous experiences. Shamanic beliefs, repressed but still prevalent in Chinese culture, probably also created an environment supportive of dissociation.

Several studies indicate that hypnotic suggestibility, a trait related to dissociation, is relatively stable during the course of a life (Hilgard, 1965) and that it has a genetic component (Morgan, 1973). The capacity for anomalous experience probably has similar characteristics. Folklore and anecdotal accounts from many societies describe paranormal capacities as spontaneous for many, cultivated by others, and inherited by some.

The alternate model, suggesting a relationship between anomalous experience and dissociation, differs from the original cultural source orientation derived from a "culture of disbelief" (Hufford, 1982a, 1985a, 1990). The "disbelief" theory attributes anomalous experience to pathologies, ignorance, and misperceptions. But according to the alternative model I have described, the capacity for anomalous experience is a trait influenced by both genetic and cultural variables, affiliated with naturally occurring psychological capacities.

Dissociation and related altered states should not be conceived as pathological. These naturally occurring mental states were (and still are) valuable in shamanic healing. Shamanism constituted the major health care system in early societies. Groups lacking members with dissociative abilities, and the capacity to experience anomalous events, were at a disadvantage. Mental faculties encouraging wondrous experience appear to be a product of human evolution.

Conclusion

The findings do not sustain the hypotheses that religious needs increase the frequency of anomalous experiences, while scientific training reduces them. Self-reported religiosity was sporadically associated with some types of anomalous experience. Scientific training, particularly within Caucasian-American groups, did not reduce the frequency of anomalous reports or belief in extrasensory perception. The survey data suggest that the culture of disbelief, prevalent among academics and elite American scientists, is not widespread among undergraduates.

Although the survey samples revealed great variety in frequency of claims of unusual experiences, the finding that moderate levels of anomalous experience exist within all surveyed groups implies that the capacity to perceive these episodes is culturally universal.

Chapter 3
A Cross-Cultural Comparison of Wondrous Event Narratives

Cultural source and experiential source hypotheses can be effectively evaluated through examination of firsthand anomalous accounts. The analysis in this chapter is based on a collection of more than a thousand narratives from northeastern North Carolina and about 150 accounts from the University of Maryland, Tsukuba University (Japan), three colleges in Xi'an in the People's Republic of China, and from elite scientists of the American Association for the Advancement of Science.

Hufford's (1982a) cultural source and experiential source theories allow for clearly differentiated hypotheses regarding the characteristics of anomalous stories. If all anomalous experiences are produced entirely by the respondent's culture (the cultural source theory), we would expect each cultural group to present unique story forms, reflecting cultural variation. If certain types of anomalous experiences contain elements transcending culture (the experiential source theory), we should find that these narratives can be categorized on the basis of these features, no matter which cultural group furnished the report.

Analyses of the narrative collections in the present study support the experiential source hypothesis. Although the percentage of people reporting episodes varies cross-culturally, some forms of anomalous narrative reveal universal features. These categories include apparitions, precognitive dreams, waking extrasensory perceptions, night (or sleep) paralysis, out-of-body experiences, synchronistic events, déjà vu, and certain occult practices (consulting psychic practitioners, for example). By gathering, categorizing, and analyzing narratives from a variety of cultural groups, we can delineate universal features.

Methodology

Each questionnaire administered in my study contained the item, "If you have had a very unusual experience, would you describe it briefly?" American and Japanese respondents were asked if they would grant an interview and, if so, to give their name and telephone number. About 8 percent of those replying furnished narratives. Approximately 150 narratives were obtained through this process. Respondents permitting further inquiry were contacted and asked to elaborate on their experiences.

More than a thousand narratives were collected by anthropology students at Elizabeth City State University between 1988 and 1993. They interviewed friends, relatives, and neighbors in and around Elizabeth City in northeastern North Carolina. A video of some of these presentations portrays the informants' sincerity (Edwards and McClenon, 1993).

The data gathered support the experiential source hypothesis. Few accounts contain features that identify them as specific to a particular culture. The narratives fall within natural clusters (for example, apparitions, precognitive dreams, and out-of-body experiences). To demonstrate the cross-cultural relevance of these groupings, I provide sample cases for each category from Chinese, Japanese, Caucasian-American, and African-American students, as well as from elite American scientists. Many of the features apparent within these narratives are listed in Thompson's (1966) *Motif-Index of Folk-Literature*, suggesting that individual experiences engender certain motifs.

Previous researchers have devised categorization systems for psychic reports. Rhine's (1981) groupings reflect definitions used in laboratory investigations of ESP and psychokinesis. Virtanen (1990) and Bennett (1987) developed frameworks appropriate for folklorists. My surveys, discussed in the previous chapter, used Greeley's (1975) questionnaire items. Unfortunately, Greeley's questions have contributed to the conceptual confusion surrounding the phenomena, because they do not coincide with the other researchers' groupings or with naturally occurring patterns.

My list of unusual experiences is not exhaustive. I provide examples of frequently occurring forms merely to illustrate their primary features. Some accounts could be classified in more than one category. For example, some déjà vu episodes include extrasensory perceptions and could be classified in either category. Apparitional events may also involve ESP. Space restrictions do not allow for a complete discussion of the many variations in each category. Although precognition is a form of ESP, I discuss waking ESP episodes separately from precognitive dreams, since precognitions occur more frequently and have a different quality when experienced during sleep.

1. *Apparitions* are visual perceptions of a seemingly paranormal nature. Because some apparitions are regarded as "contacts with the dead," these accounts often contribute to belief in life after death. Thompson's *Motif-Index* includes categories E200–E599, "Ghosts and other revenants."

2. *Precognitive dreams* are dreams of future events or situations that are later found to be valid. These episodes support belief in predestination and prophesy. The *Motif-Index* cites D1812.3.3, "Future revealed in dream."

3. *Waking extrasensory perceptions* (ESP) are impressions, while awake, of external events or objects gained in some way other than through the known sensory channels. These events are thought to occur as a result of paranormal communicative capacities. The *Motif-Index* cites D1812, "Magic power of prophecy"; D1819.1, "Magic knowledge of another's thought"; D1820, "Magic sight and hearing"; D1825, "Kinds of magic sight."

4. *Night paralysis* entails subjective impressions of wakefulness, feeling unable to move, and realistic awareness of actual environment. Night paralysis is equivalent to the medical concept of sleep paralysis, but refers to informants' perceptions rather than to their physiological condition. These episodes are often associated with intense fear as well as sensations of supernatural phenomena. They can contribute to belief in spiritual entities, particularly demons. The *Motif-Index* lists F471.1, "Nightmare. Presses person in dream," and D2072, "Magic paralysis." Related to night paralysis are F471.2, "Incubus comes in sleep has sex," and F471.2.1, "Succubus: female incubus."

5. *Out-of-body and near-death experiences* comprise perceptions of feeling outside of one's body. These events support belief in the existence of a soul and life after death. The *Motif-Index* lists E720, "Soul leaves or enters the body"; E721, "Soul journeys from the body"; E177, "Resuscitated man relates visions of beyond"; and E374, "Dead returns to life and tells of journey to land of dead."

6. *Synchronistic events* are anomalous, or unlikely, correspondences, often thought to reflect cosmic warning or control. Some forms of synchronistic events are believed to indicate life after death because an unusual phenomenon coincides with someone's death. The *Motif-Index* includes B733.2, "Dogs howling indicates death"; D1812.5, "Future learned through omens"; F960.2, "Extraordinary nature phenomena at death of holy person"; N101, "Inexorable fate"; and Q147, "Supernatural manifestations at death of pious person."

7. *Déjà vu* is the feeling of previously having had an experience when this was not the case. These sensations sometimes support belief in predestination, cosmic connections, or reincarnation.

8. *Psychokinesis* (PK) is paranormal action or physical effect without muscular cause. Although I did not collect sufficient Japanese and Chinese firsthand reports to compare narratives, I hypothesize that universal features exist in PK accounts, as reflected by several *Motif-Index* listings (e.g., E402.1.5, "Invisible ghost makes rapping or knocking noise"; F1083, "Object rises into the air"; F1083.0.1, "Object floats in air"; F473, "Poltergeist. Invisible spirit").

9. *Occult experiences and practices* include a variety of perceptions and behaviors related to performance and belief (consulting psychics, use of a Ouija board, folk healing, etc.). Many elements within these experiences are culturally specific. Yet some occult activities result in anomalous experiences that contain universal features. The *Motif-Index* devotes a chapter to magic and many other citations, such as V221, "Miraculous healing by saints."

The narratives in my collection are strikingly parallel to those gathered by previous researchers in the United States (Hufford, 1982a; Rhine, 1977, 1981), Canada (Hufford, 1982a), Finland (Virtanen, 1990), Great Britain (Bennett, 1987; Gurney et al., 1918; Sidgwick and Committee, 1894; West, 1948), and Hong Kong (Emmons, 1982). I have yet to conduct statistical analyses equivalent to those of Rhine (1981) and Virtanen (1990). I do, however, provide a few descriptive statistics in my discussion of cases, derived from analysis of a preliminary sample (approximately half) of my North Carolina narratives.

Apparitions

Apparitions are perceptions, involving the known senses, of a seemingly paranormal nature. The objects of these experiences are often labeled as ghosts, phantoms, specters, shades, or spirits. In northeastern North Carolina, older people refer to such perceptions as "haints." An image, sound, odor, or sensation may occur or disappear without explanation, leaving the reality of the event in question. Apparitional accounts were the largest category in my collection (approximately 30 percent).

Most respondents felt their perceptions were caused by an external entity, particularly the spirit of a deceased person. Sample narratives portray the cross-cultural consistency of apparitional experiences:

One night as I lay restlessly sleeping, I had a visitor. My grandmother, dead for three years, was standing by my bed, stroking my head . . . assuring me that everything was going to be alright. [African-American student]

Two years ago on the anniversary of [my father's] death . . . I prayed at his grave for a few brief moments and I turned towards my car. I saw him sitting in my car, but the closer I got the less I saw, and when I was close enough the vision disappeared. [Caucasian-American student]

My whole family [lived by a cemetery. One night] the other people were fast asleep . . . I saw a female standing in the door. I looked at her for a long time . . . [she vanished, but later reappeared]. It wasn't an unreal image. It is a real fact. [Chinese student]

I once saw the ghost of a dog we had owned, sitting on top of a grave. . . . My mother and younger sister also said that they had seen its ghost, too. [Japanese student]

When I was moving out of my apartment after graduate school, I thought I saw an apparition in the living room as I lay in my bed. I had rented the apartment furnished and the lady who rented it to me recently died. It appeared to me that the apparition might have been of this deceased lady checking to see that I did not take any of her possessions when I left for a new residence. However, I would not swear I saw a ghost, as other explanations are possible. [Elite American scientist]

These narratives coincide with motifs in Thompson's list: E320, "Dead relative's friendly return"; E334.2, "Ghost haunts burial spot"; E521.2, "Ghost of dog"; E419.10, "Concern of ghost about belongings of its lifetime." The stories illustrate a variety of reactions to apparitional experiences. Some people identify the apparition as a deceased friend, neighbor, or relative, and they view the event as an indication of life after death. Even within groups rejecting occult belief, many experiencers are certain that their perceptions were not illusions. For example, the atheist Chinese student states, "It wasn't an unreal image. It is a real fact."

Respondents often acknowledge that their accounts could stimulate skepticism, and they supply corroborating evidence to support their claims. For example, the Japanese student reports that family members had seen the same image (E421.5, "Ghost seen by two or more persons; they corroborate the appearance"). Some skeptical experiencers are immune to the argument that apparitions have supernatural origins. For example, the elite scientist can think of "other explanations" for his experience, allowing him to maintain an agnostic attitude.

Some apparitions generate evidence that has a bearing on the issue of life after death. Apparitions have demonstrated willful temperaments, seemingly indicating the survival of a deceased person's personality. Psychical researchers have collected cases where apparitions have supplied previously unknown information that was later found to be true (Gauld, 1977). For example, ghosts have correctly prophesied and revealed locations of concealed wills, hidden money, or bodies requiring reburial (E545.17, "The dead foretell the future"). Yet such cases are rare. Only a few of my informants ascribed paranormal abilities to apparitions.

A more common form of evidential account is the "crisis apparition." Experiencers perceive images or sounds coinciding in time with someone else's bodily death or exposure to danger. For example, an apparition of a husband, thought to be in good health, might appear to his wife at the time of his death in a distant location (E364, "Dead returns to say farewell"; D1827.1.4 "Sounds heard from distance at time of death"). Sometimes respondents inform others of their experiences prior to the verification of the corresponding death. During the 1880s, Gurney, Myers, and Podmore (1918/1886) collected 702 evidential cases and concluded that these episodes demonstrated a paranormal factor. Later, the British Society for Psychical Research conducted a "Census of Hallucinations." Statistical analysis indicated a correlation between the incidence of crisis apparitions and the associated deaths. The committee argued that the correspondence could not be explained as coincidence (Sidgwick and Committee, 1894).

More recent studies have uncovered similar cases. West (1948) conducted an equivalent but smaller survey of British hallucinations. He found no evidence that the frequency of hallucinations was declining in comparison with the previous British studies. In about 11 percent of the reported cases, experiencers felt their perceptions were "veridical" since they corresponded with some external event. My collection includes many reports of apparitional images and psychokinetic phenomena coinciding with the death or emergency of a relative, friend, or neighbor. Soji Otani has collected veridical accounts from Japanese World War II widows who perceived apparitions of their husbands at the time of the spouses' deaths.

Virtanen's (1990) Finnish accounts are in accord with those in my collection. Over 75 percent of my cases and 95 percent of Virtanen's accounts involve apparitional sightings by a single person. Some people report apparitions that remain invisible to their companions (E421.1.1, "Ghost visible to one person alone").

Finucane (1984) noted that apparitional accounts tend to reflect the interests and needs of the society within which they occur. Catholics have a greater probability of perceiving ghosts who claim residence in purgatory, for example. This evidence suggests that apparitions reflect subconscious processes rather than spiritual forces. Only a few of my cases show direct correspondences between informants' beliefs and their accounts. For example, some stories include demonic images, culturally specific to Christian societies. The following story fits *Motif-Index* G303.3.1.1, "The devil as a large, strong man":

I had a soft light in my room. I was wide awake. I do not smoke, drink, or partake of drugs. There appeared a man before me. . . . He was very tall, possibly 7 feet tall. His hair was black, coarse, and pressed back firmly. His skin was smooth but very red. His eyes were dark and filled with hate. He was clean-shaven. His teeth were perfect. He smiled, but his lips were tight. He had horns that were white and partially covered with black hair. . . . He wore a robe (black) with a high neck. The robe extended to the floor and covered his feet. His hands were long and bony. I cannot tell you that I saw Satan. I can only describe what I saw. He held a red tarantula in his hand. He threw it at me. He said, "Go get her!" He missed. I said, "Oh, no you don't!" I ran out into the hall. When I looked back, the figure and the spider were gone. I searched everywhere for the spider. It must have returned with its owner (I'm not joking about what I saw.) [Caucasian-American adult]

Yet such indications of cultural influence on anomalous experience are rare. My narrative collection contains only a handful of reports regarding demons, religious figures, or other themes reflecting a particular culture. I was surprised that so few respondents furnished the forms of mystical and religious experiences that other researchers have found prevalent (for example, Hay and Morisy, 1978). Evidently, the connection between culture and anomalous experience is more complex than most cultural source theorists suppose. Although people's responses were probably shaped by cues within survey and interview questions, the narratives indicated no clear correlation between content of apparitional narrative and religious needs.

Some respondents reported events that they claimed violated their expectations yet which coincided with folkloric conceptions. For example, a Chinese student who denied belief in ghosts or religion furnished an account that coincided with the Chinese folk belief that ghosts can cause illness. His narrative includes motifs E265.1, "Meeting ghost causes sickness," and E533, "Ghostly bell."

When I was small, grandfather passed away. My grandmother was alone, so I stayed with her every day. One night, I woke up and looked at the oil lamp on the table. . . . I saw a big black hand take up the lamp and then put it down. . . . Simultaneously, I felt as if I heard a bell ringing at the front gate. The next day I was ill. . . . There was no bell at our front gate.

Apparitions are like dreams in that their content is related to subconscious processes. They differ in that: (1) Respondents often claim a normal state of consciousness during their incidence; (2) apparitions are perceived as having exterior origins while dreams occur internally; (3) apparitions are more often perceived simultaneously by groups than are dreams; (4) apparitions more frequently stimulate belief in spiritual forces than do dreams; (5) apparitions generally provide less narrative content than do dreams.

Apparitions are easily classified by the type of object seen. More than 20 percent of apparitional accounts in my analyzed subsample and 7 percent within Haraldsson's (1988–89) collection were of unidentified humans. Most apparitional narratives contained few dramatic features. The existence of many uneventful episodes does not coincide with the common, skeptical argument that all apparitional episodes are produced by the fear of death. Yet anomalous perceptions of mundane objects can also stimulate wonderment:

One summer night, when I was sitting outside to enjoy the cool, I saw a bag of lime dropping down from a building. However, nothing dropped down in fact. [Chinese student] [E530, "Ghosts of objects"]

More typically, people see human figures. I include two similar stories from very different cultures, both of which fall under *Motif-Index* E425.1.1, "Revenant as lady in white":

I saw a white woman dressed in all white walking in the field. She had on a white dress, white shoes, and a big white hat. . . . I looked more closely and she seemed transparent. I could see right through her. The more that I looked at the woman the more afraid I became. . . . No one would believe me, [but] I know that I saw that woman. My family still tries to give me excuses about what I saw. [African-American adult]

I looked outside the window and saw an old woman in white clothes standing in the middle of our courtyard, facing our window. . . . I told my mother to look at her but my mother said she'd seen nothing and blamed me for talking nonsense. I was very much frightened to look at this old woman. Some time later she disappeared. I have been wondering about this thing but can't get an answer. I didn't see her coming in, nor going out. I dare say that she came down from the sky and disappeared like a ghost. . . . I wish this mysterious thing would not remain a mystery during all my life! [Chinese student]

Apparitional lights are classified by the environment within which they are observed. When moving in the sky, they are often labeled as unidentified flying objects (UFOs). Those observed in cemeteries are assumed to be spirits (E530.1, "Ghost-like lights"). In the swamp areas of northeastern North Carolina, such lights are often labeled "jack-o-lanterns" or "jack-ma-lanterns" and thought to be malevolent spirits (F491.1, "Will-o'-the-Wisp leads people astray"). Various folklore stories, as well as firsthand accounts, describe the negative consequences of investigating such lights.

The impact of an apparitional narrative on an audience is affected by its aesthetic or dramatic qualities. *Aesthetics*, in this context, can be defined as those qualities which resonate with an audience's needs, producing a sense of truth, completeness, balance, drama, or beauty.

Aesthetic qualities determine the value placed on an account by its listeners. Many firsthand reports have few aesthetic features:

I saw a blurred figure walking through my house [which] disappeared immediately. [African-American student]

My grandmother said that one night while walking to church through the swamp, she saw a man with no head and he walked from the right side of the road and went over to the left side. [Student respondent interviewed African-American adult]

One night when I went to bed, I woke up and a figure was floating above my bed. I didn't recognize the figure and it vanished. [Caucasian-American student]

But narratives with sufficient aesthetic qualities will be retold periodically, becoming part of local folklore. Aesthetics involve more than just textural features; narrators also use facial expressions and body movements to enhance their tales. Videotaped presentations reveal a variety of performance skills (Edwards and McClenon, 1993).

Aesthetic qualities determine which stories are disseminated. Only a small percentage of accounts are found suitable for retelling. The following account illustrates story-telling ability in textural form. An African-American adult reports her experience to an anthropology student:

I was only 13 years old at the time [Aunt Sue died] but I remember as if it were only yesterday. . . . [One evening] I heard a knock on the door. It was a peculiar knock like nothing I ain't never heard before. I went on over to the door (and Lord knows I ain't lying to you child) and there was Aunt Sue standing there as if she wasn't dead or nothing! Child, I was so a-scared that I almost toppled over backwards from the shock! . . . Aunt Sue just stood there and looked at me and I gawked back at her and not once did my nappy-headed pappy come out of his room. . . . She walked towards me and I let out one powerful scream. I thought the entire neighborhood would come to see what was the matter but nothing happened and my pappy was still asleep. Aunt Sue laid something on the end table and then she vanished right in front of my face! I couldn't believe my eyes. I was afraid to walk over to the table. . . . I went straight away to bed and tried to forget the whole thing. I passed it off as a bad dream caused by those two-day-old collards I had eaten. When I got up the next morning, I did my usual chores and I finally made my way over to that end table. Lo and behold, there was a gold locket that Aunt Sue was buried with. I was so a-scared that I called Pa in to take a look at it. We both just stared at each other and didn't say a mumbling word. [E544.1, "Ghost leaves object after appearance"]

Some respondents report frequent and regular apparitional experiences. They develop especially robust belief systems regarding life after death. For them, the paranormal becomes normal and their certainty provides a foundation for occult performance and spiritual healing (see Chapter 5). Students gathered the following sample cases from African-Americans reporting frequent experiences:

[Alice] told me that for every night for exactly five years, at the beginning of each month her grandfather would appear to her and talk to her. She said she wasn't frightened about this because her and her grandfather were so close and she knew he wouldn't do anything to harm or hurt her. . . . [Alice] said that whatever her grandfather said would happen did indeed occur. . . . Alice said that people always wondered how she would always have good luck. She knew this was because of grandfather's teachings and advice. [E320, Dead relative's friendly return; E545.17, The dead foretell the future; E585, Dead person visits earth periodically]

[R.] says she has contacts with her dead uncle. When something bad is happening or someone is sick, he'll sit down on her bed and let her know if things will be okay. [E320, Dead relative's friendly return]

The existence of universal features in these accounts supports the experiential source hypothesis. Most stories do not support the argument that they originated from religious needs or from the fear of death. Many episodes are uneventful, many are entirely secular, and many have nothing to do with death. As a result, the cultural source theory does not correspond very well with the data.

Precognitive Dreams

Precognition, a type of ESP, refers to the gaining of information about the future through nonsensory means. Twelve percent of my North Carolina narratives were *precognitive dreams*, the gaining of information about the future while sleeping (D1812.3.3, "Future revealed in dream"). *Contemporaneous ESP* refers to the paranormal perception of events while they occurred. Although contemporaneous ESP and precognition can occur in both the sleeping and waking states, precognitions occur more frequently during dreams. Rhine (1981) found that 75 percent of the precognitions in her collection of 3,290 narratives occurred during dreams. Only 40 percent of contemporaneous ESP events among her cases transpired in the dream state.

My data replicate the patterns noted by Rhine (1981) and Virtanen (1990). The precognitive dreams in my collection differ in narrative structure from waking precognitive events (D1812.4, "Future revealed by presentment: 'knowledge within'" and D1825.1, "Second sight. Power to see future happenings"). Non-dream precognitions generally convey less information and have less imagery.

Some examples illustrate the primary features within precognitive dreams:

Once I dreamed I was going to a funeral and the very next day my great-grandmother died. The funeral was just like in my dream. . . . I just kind of sat there and thought to myself that I had already been [here] once before. [African-American student]

I dreamed my grandmother died and [I] knew when, where, and how. I was also aware of the last time I was to see her and knew I would not be at the funeral. [Caucasian-American student]

Once I had a terrible nightmare at night [that I would be hit by a car]. I was hit by a running car the next morning. [Chinese student]

I often saw dreams which I took to be precognitive. . . . For example, I saw an erupting volcano (about a year before Mt. Mihara erupted); an airplane crashing (which I later took to be the JAL crash). . . . I sometimes saw test problems in my dreams (which actually turned out to be problems on the real test when I took it). [Japanese student]

On three occasions in my life (early, not recently), I dreamed of events that occurred in advance of their actually happening. Two of the events involved the deaths of individuals—one expected, but not imminent; the other, unexpected. [Elite American scientist]

Precognitive dreams, like apparitional experiences, can pertain to extremely important life events, particularly death or accidents (as in the American and Chinese examples), or to mundane perceptions (the Japanese report of seeing examination problems). In both precognitive dreams and in non-dream precognition, death is a common theme.

As in Virtanen's data, most of the precognitive dreams in my collection focus on death or tragedy. Other topics included everyday events—births, travel, finding lost items, lottery numbers, and special events within personal relationships.

Most narratives seem not to reflect religious needs. For example, one respondent who had an unusual name reported dreaming that he had robbed a bank and was fleeing from the police. The next day, as he approached the bank, police cars converged on it. Later he read in the newspaper that a bank robber, whose name was exactly the same as his, was apprehended while fleeing in the same direction as in his dream.

Respondents who experience frequent precognitive experiences come to believe that the universe has a structure that allows for the viability of prophesy. These episodes support folk belief in fortune-tellers (D1311, "Magic object used for divination"; D1812, "Magic power of prophecy"; M302, "Means of prophesying"). My data coincide with Virtanen's (1990) in that precognitions rarely pertain to national events or major individual decisions. Ironically, the types of information most often requested of psychics (health, wealth, love) are not very much in evidence among my spontaneous precognition cases.

Waking Extrasensory Perceptions (ESP)

Extrasensory perception entails gaining information through nonsensory means, a category that includes *precognition*. The most typical forms of ESP narratives within my data were *precognitive dreams*, discussed previously, and *waking ESP*. Examples of waking ESP illustrate its primary features:

One day I received a phone call at 5 A.M. informing me of my grandfather's death. I knew that the call would inform me of his death prior to the call. I could feel something was wrong. [African-American student]

Sometimes, I can tell when things are wrong back home without coming in direct contact with them. I call home when I have a "feeling" and Mom tells me something bad has happened—such as the time my grandfather died, my sister broke up with her serious boyfriend, and Dad was very sick. [Caucasian-American student]

During my study in the university, I am far away from my family and have no relatives here. But quite a few times I have had the premonition that something wrong had taken place in my family. I felt very upset and eager to go home. When I was actually at home, I found either my parents had been ill or [that] there had been something wrong with them. [Chinese student]

When I was at home, some thirty seconds before the telephone would ring, I would know that the telephone was going to ring and whom [the call] was from. [Japanese student]

Recently, at dinner (7:30 P.M.), I "knew" that an ill friend of friends (whom I knew only casually) had died. Two days later, we learned that he died that evening, when I had the "feeling." [Elite American scientist]

As with the precognitive dreams, waking ESP narratives frequently involve deaths, illness, or accident; yet they can also be about mundane events, such as the identity of a telephone caller. Episodes often reflect special emotional bonds between people.

Some incidents reflect knowledge of inanimate objects, events that parapsychologists label clairvoyance:

Sometimes when I'm playing cards with my grandmother, I don't know how she does it, but she will seem to know what card will turn up next, even before it's been turned over. [Caucasian-American student]

Like precognitions, these episodes are rarely associated with clearly articulated religious ideologies. Most respondents express wonderment rather than religious awe. They do not feel the need to reformulate their religious beliefs. Experiencers who depend purely on scientific schemata are sometimes disturbed by ESP episodes since these events seemingly defy mechanistic concepts. Those who report frequent ESP episodes come to feel that they have unique capacities.

The features that are predominant in my collection of ESP narratives correspond with those of other researchers. Most ESP reports have a personal focus, involving known individuals. A sizable percentage of these accounts focus on mundane events. Only a few refer to events of national import.

Night Paralysis

Night paralysis has primary features that include subjective impressions of wakefulness, paralysis, and realistic perception of actual environment. I use the term night paralysis, rather than sleep paralysis, to refer to the content within informants' narratives rather than to their physiological states. Night paralysis has secondary features that are sometimes reported by experiencers: feelings of intense fear, spiritual presences, pressure on the chest, hearing footsteps, seeing ghostly figures, and other anomalous perceptions, all within the context of the actual environment (Hufford, 1982a). Although the elite scientists were not asked about this type of experience, and did not supply night paralysis narratives, other groups did:

I felt I couldn't move for some reason. . . . The feeling was so strange because it almost felt like I was confined by another force other than my own. [African-American student]

The most unusual experience I have had was waking up one night and being terrified and unable to move. I felt there was someone in the room with me. It seemed to last a long time. [Caucasian-American student]

I dreamed of an old friend who had died several years ago. . . . I was woken up. I felt I couldn't move, though my mind was awake. I tried to take up my hand but it was futile. [Chinese student]

I suddenly became aware of an orange-colored light covering the whole side of the room beyond the foot of my bed. . . . I tried to get up, but my body wouldn't move. (I think I was barely able to move my fingers.) . . . I tried with all my might to cry out. . . . But even then, I could manage no more than a groan. [Japanese student]

Some respondents described footsteps, apparitions, unexplained lights or other anomalous phenomena which occurred during their paralysis. Night paralysis episodes sometimes take on the character of a conflict between spiritual forces:

Once a demon visited me. I was lying in bed paralyzed and I began to pray the Lord's Prayer and then, and only then, did the thing vanish. [African-American student]

Two years ago, when I was sleeping on a bed in the studio, I felt a strange pressing and perhaps heard a person talking to me. I was sleeping lightly. I didn't know the language. It wasn't English or Chinese. It sounded like somebody upset, and I heard murmuring when I felt the weight.
   I couldn't move or speak, but there was no actual weight. I woke up and tried to get up. It lasted about one minute. I tried to think of Jesus Christ, but then the force was actually stronger. It calmed down when I thought about a Buddhist god. The force left me gradually. I could get up then. [Chinese respondent in Emmons, 1982: 145]

Some people regard their experiences as the most terrifying events in their lives. Some report demonic images and impressions. Hufford's (1982a) analysis of night paralysis events refutes the cultural source hypothesis. He found common features in firsthand accounts from two distinctly different cultures. The narratives in my collection replicate his findings. These experiences can produce belief but are not fully products of it.

Out-of-Body and Near-Death Experiences

Out-of-body experiences (OBEs) entail the feeling of being exterior to one's body. Experiencers often conclude that their souls had left their bodies. Several sample narratives illustrate the universality of these episodes:

I was mentally "out of it" and saw myself standing with two friends. I felt I was seeing this several feet off the ground—not "in my body." [Caucasian-American student]

I was in my bedroom . . . [when] I begin to feel my body lift off the bed and begin to float, but my physical body was still on the bed; yet I was up in the air looking at my body on the bed. . . . I floated around the room for about two minutes. [African-American]

Often, I thought as if I were not me. I am another person who is looking at "me." I can feel what "she" or "he" feels. I don't know what was the reason of this sense. . . . I don't think it is possible, perhaps, it is better to say that I don't wish it is possible. [Chinese student]

Once when I was meditating, I had the fleeting feeling that I was seeing myself from outside my body. [Japanese student]

A family member was ill and hospitalized. I "kind of went into a trance" [and] "traveled" in my mind four hundred miles to the hospital where I had never been, looked down into the operating room, saw her there at the beginning of the surgery. As the surgeon prepared to make the incision on the right side, I said to him (in my mind) "No—it's on the left side." The surgeon changed over, made the incision. . . . When I received information about the surgery, I asked, "Which side was involved?" I was told, "They finally decided it was on the left side." I understand that this kind of ethereal travel is possible. [Elite American scientist]

Some narrators describe events or images at a distant location which they believe they could not have perceived through normal means. Such experiences led them to accept the episodes as valid. Some people claimed their attitude toward life changed as a result of their OBE. They felt more certain that people had souls and that there was life after death.

Near-death experiences (NDEs) have similar but more complex features. Moody (1975) lists elements within the NDE: ineffability (an inability to describe one's perceptions in words), hearing news (of one's own death), feelings of peace and quiet, the noise, a dark tunnel, out-of-body perception, meeting others, encounters with a being of light, reviewing one's life, perceiving a border between normal life and the afterworld, and coming back. He also discusses "telling others" and "corroboration." Most experiencers return to their bodies before reaching the advanced stages. Only 28 percent within Sabom's (1982) sample of nonsurgical cases encountered "the being of light." Ring (1980) hypothesizes that five stages exist in a near-death experience: a feeling of peace, separation from the body, entering the darkness, seeing the light, and entering the light. Experiencers often evaluate NDEs as "more real" than normal reality and many attempt thereafter to live more selfless lives.

Various respondents claimed to have had no knowledge of other NDEs, yet their reports coincide with the primary features in NDE literature. For example, one respondent spent years wondering about the following experience, eventually categorizing it as an NDE after seeing a program about them on television:

When I was on the operating table . . . some figures came . . . and they took my spirit up to the upper part of the ceiling and I watched the doctors working on my body, and I said to myself, "What am I doing up here and I'm down there." . . . There was this kind of bright light but not hot. It was real pretty and quiet . . . there was water that was flowing so smooth you couldn't tell that it was moving, seems like it was wider than the earth. . . . And there was a figure across the water . . . and when I heard the doctor say, "Okay, we're closed now" . . . this figure from way across the water reached his hand out all the way across the water and touched my hand, and said, "You can go back now, and everything will be all right." When he said that, the figures took me back down and the spirits were around my body again. [E177, "Resuscitated man relates visions of beyond"; E481.2, "Land of dead across water"; E720, "Soul leaves or enters the body"]

Although researchers have sought to uncover the nature of OBEs and NDEs, many issues remain unresolved. These episodes share a common form even for people from different cultures. The experiences have the capacity to transform belief, having direct impact on religious faith. The data strongly support the experiential source hypothesis.

Synchronistic Events

Synchronistic events are cases in which two seemingly unconnected incidents appear to be related. The "synchronistic" grouping includes various miscellaneous reports that do not fit into previously defined categories. Many of these can be categorized using Virtanen's (1990) classification of "signs in nature—simultaneous experience." Various stories link a loved one's death to a symbolic or psychokinetic event. An event preceding a death may be labeled an omen. Corresponding items are often symbolic and are specific to a society's folklore (a bird's activity coincides with a human's death, for example). Other episodes involve anomalous coincidences that do not involve death. Although my narrative collection lacks a Japanese case, I hypothesize that synchronistic events are perceived within all large populations. The examples that follow illustrate various synchronistic event patterns:

Mrs. Perkins and her husband put their house up for sale to move to the country. The house she would be moving into was a large two-story house . . . weekends were devoted to stripping wallpaper and paint. Mrs. Perkins stated that one Saturday afternoon her husband was stripping the layer of wallpaper in the dining room . . . he pointed to some writing. . . . There was a name and a date of January 23 on the wall and the name written on it was theirs, Perkins, and the date January 23 was her birth date. [African-American student]

One morning a couple of years ago, a bird flew into (hit the glass of) our bathroom window. I mentioned to my parents that a teacher I had in high school once stated that an old myth says that when a bird hits your window a relative is supposed to die. Later on that day we received a phone call telling us that one of my father's uncles had died that morning. [Caucasian-American student]

Two days before my mother's death, in the morning, a lot of flies flew into the kitchen of our house. There were very many. I felt very curious. . . . Two days later, my mother passed away. I feel this was very strange. [Chinese student]

Some synchronistic episodes are thought to indicate the existence of an all-encompassing structure within reality. When a synchronistic event coincides with or follows a death, narrators may assume that the deceased person caused the episode; for example, a clock stops at the moment of the owner's death. Omens have a synchronistic quality

(D1812.5, "Future learned though omens"; B147, "Animals furnish omens").

Déjà Vu

Déjà vu is the feeling of previously having had an experience when this was not the case. In some narratives, déjà vu is accompanied by an extrasensory perception or precognition whereby the individual can describe places, events, and so forth before visiting them or before they occur (Neppe, 1983). Since déjà vu is often attributed to physiological factors, it is not surprising that this experience has cross-culturally common features:

Several times I've felt [that I've been in a situation with] the same people . . . in the same place, with the same thing happening, with the same feelings occurring. . . . The smell was even the same; of course, this could not be, unless it was another dimension, time, space. [African-American student]

O. was escorting a couple through this house [as a tour guide]. Suddenly, the woman stopped dead before entering the kitchen. Excited, she described the entire arrangement of the kitchen: the pantry, positioning of windows, et cetera. She swore she had been there before. The couple was visiting South Carolina for the first time. [Caucasian-American student]

Often, when I'm talking to people or doing something, I have the strong feeling that I've done exactly the same thing before. [Japanese student]

I often have this experience: for example, something happened today. I knew clearly this had never happened before or could never have happened, but I felt as though I had once had such an experience. This experience was not from a dream. This phenomenon often makes me puzzled. I can't understand this. [Chinese student]

Although no respondent claimed that déjà vu has a religious explanation, the notion of reincarnation may have evolved, in part, from its incidence. The extrasensory elements within some déjà vu reports have the same social effects as ESP. In some instances, déjà vu supports belief in life after death (Neppe, 1985/86).

Psychokinesis and Other Forms of Anomalous Experience

A variety of other forms of anomalous experience probably have universal features. Psychokinesis (PK), simultaneous dreams, and some varieties of mystical experience are examples of these other forms. Although my samples of Japanese and Chinese firsthand accounts are insufficient to support this argument, folklore from many regions seemingly reflects primary features within accounts derived from such experiences.

Five percent of my North Carolina narrative collection entailed apparent PK. Such effects differ from apparitions in that PK is clearly not hallucinatory. Anomalous rapping sounds, for example, are heard by all present (E402.1.5, "Invisible ghost makes rapping or knocking noise"). PK narratives can include events such as a light going off, a clock stopping, or a picture falling, yet respondents cannot discover the cause. If they learn later that a relative died at that exact time, the episode might be considered synchronistic. When a PK event is attributed to a deceased person, it contributes to belief in life after death:

My grandmother lives by herself now that my grandfather has died. She says that since his death, strange things have happened. My grandfather loved to watch wrestling on his television. My grandmother said that she had returned home to find her remote-control television on during wrestling matches. She believes my grandfather has come back to watch television. [African-American student] [E337, "Ghost reenacts scene from own lifetime"]

During my study, I witnessed various cases of alleged psychokinesis (one must consider the possibility that I was deceived). On one occasion, with six witnesses present (on August 6, 1982, at Walter Uphoff's residence in Oregon, WI), I saw a previously bent spoon unbend very gradually without anyone touching it. The Japanese psychic Masuaki Kiyota was attempting to direct energy at it. The spoon was propped up in such a way that it would have fallen over if touched. Observers agreed that it was clearly unbending. I felt around the spoon for hidden wires and then took it into another room. The spoon continued to unbend while in my possession.

American, Japanese, and Chinese parapsychologists described experimental PK events equivalent to those I observed. Professor Soji Otani of the Japanese National Defense Academy has videotaped psychokinetic feats by Kiyota (McClenon, 1989). His video portrays Kiyota attempting to "direct energy" at a spoon on which Otani had glued a special tag to prevent substitution. The spoon, with tag visible, slowly twists without being touched.

In connection with psychokinesis, I interviewed Drs. Chen Shou Liang, of Beijing University, Lin Shu Huang, of the Beijing Normal Institute, and Hsu Hungchang, of the Institute of High Energy Physics in Beijing. They and many other Chinese researchers have witnessed and recorded similar anomalous performances by Chinese subjects (Eisenberg, 1985; Zha and McConnell, 1991). Subjects have seemingly caused objects to move paranormally and to pass paranormally through solid matter. Many Chinese researchers gathered at a conference in Beijing observed psychically gifted children holding flower buds which opened before their eyes and then closed anomalously. I have observed and photographed a rosebud gradually open during a half-hour period while it was being held by a psychically gifted American (D2195.1: "Flower blooms when touched").

Occult Experiences and Practices

Some respondents described anomalous experiences associated with occult practices and their narratives have common features. Thompson's *Motif-Index* devotes an entire chapter to magic. The types of experience within this category are not different from those discussed previously; they constitute a separate category because they are not spontaneous but result from occult practices (many of my previous accounts of psychokinesis overlap with this grouping). Some methods of occult practice harness subconscious muscular energy, as in using a Ouija board. Visiting a psychic practitioner, such as a healer, is an alternate theme in these narratives.

Me and some friends of mine have communicated with many dead people through a television tray spelling out words by rocking. One of my hall mates is somewhat of a medium. [Caucasian-American student]

In 1974, I visited a fortune-teller and he told me about my future life. Twelve years have passed now and what he told me seemed to have been true. In many ways, my experience has been the same. [Chinese student]

[In past days, an occult healer] was the sole medical help for blacks and Indian people because white doctors would not see them. . . . He used all kinds of plants, spices, and incantations to make short work of whatever was wrong with his patients. [African-American student]

Occult practices are typically rooted in folk beliefs. They involve a kind of performance (a secondary wondrous event) and sometimes stimulate further experiences (tertiary events). For example, using a Ouija board can result in apparitional and psychokinetic experiences:

Janice began the ritual, chanting and praying for hours. Then she asked the board questions and nothing happened. She went through the process for about a week with no success until Friday. Then when she started the chants, she swore she heard a strange humming noise. She started the prayer and she heard a moan and she asked the board a question and the arrow responded without her even placing her hands on it. . . . She asked the board to send her a guardian spirit. The board asked her to identify who she was and what right did she have to ask for anything. Janice demanded a guardian because she had become master of the board and could do anything she wanted and it had to please her. She heard a loud shriek and the light bulb above her head burst. She crouched in the corner, and before her eyes she witnessed an apparition with a hideous form. It stayed for a period of fifteen seconds, then vanished. The next day, Janice burned the Ouija board. [African-American student]

Secondary and tertiary wondrous experiences reflect cultural shaping. African-Americans consult root doctors, Caucasian-Americans describe psychics, Japanese and Chinese respondents visit shamanic practitioners. Yet cross-culturally consistent features exist within these episodes. For example, all societies have individuals who are thought to have paranormal or supernatural powers to predict the future (D1825.1, "Second sight. Power to see future happenings") and cure ailments (D2161.5, "Magic cure by certain person").

Certain exercises have a universal capacity to stimulate wondrous experience. Sensory deprivation and overstimulation increase the potential for anomalous episodes (D1733.3, "Magic power through ascetic practices"). Those reporting frequent anomalous experiences sometimes gain reputations for having special abilities. They may undertake training and initiation so that they can perform wondrous demonstrations and create wondrous experiences for others.

Culturally Specific Features within Some Experience Narratives

Some narratives revealed culturally specific features. A few Americans described born-again experiences in response to the survey request for a "very unusual experience." African-American ministers in North Carolina reported special "calling" experiences as being instrumental in their becoming preachers. Chinese and Japanese respondents furnished no equivalent religious reports. Some Chinese respondents described nightmares that they considered "very unusual experiences." These cases indicate that only certain types of anomalous experience harbor universal features; some narrative elements are culturally specific.

Analysis

The cultural source theory states that all wondrous stories are products of the narrator's socialization. The experiential source theory argues that this is not always the case, that some types of anomalous events have features that transcend culture. The data in the present study refute the cultural source hypothesis and support the experiential source theory. These findings coincide with Hufford's (1985b) predictions. The cultural source theory cannot explain the existence of natural categories of anomalous experience, such as apparitions, precognitions, extrasensory perceptions, night paralysis, out-of-body experiences, synchronistic events, and déjà vu, all of which have cross-culturally consistent features.

The argument that these episodes reflect religious needs associated with fear of death does not explain the prevalence of mundane forms of experience in each of the categories. Some forms of experience, such as precognitive dreams, waking ESP, synchronistic events, and déjà vu often do not directly support religious doctrines.

The data indicate that people's interpretations of their perceptions *are* shaped by culture, and that some perceptions have culturally specific elements. Yet only a minority of experiencers—less than one-quarter of those interviewed—claimed that an anomalous episode affected their religious faith. Many of the respondents who reported only a few experiences were relatively unaffected by them. Yet those who reported frequent anomalous episodes displayed robust beliefs. They perceived themselves as having special capacities, and their narratives indicate belief in spirits, souls, life after death, and anomalous abilities.

Individual wondrous experiences provide the building blocks for more complex narratives. Miraculous healings, for example, are attributed to particular individuals, objects, or places. As we will see in the next chapter, haunting and poltergeist cases consist of sequences of wondrous experiences associated with a particular individual or location. Complex folk traditions appear to have evolved from collections of such accounts.

Chapter 4
Haunting and Poltergeist Cases: Constructing Folk Belief

Haunting and poltergeist cases foster belief in spirits, life after death, and contact between the living and dead. They consist of a series of wondrous events, most frequently apparitions, sleep paralysis, and psychokinesis. The word "poltergeist," a German term for "noisy spirit," refers to episodes wherein objects seem to move about paranormally. Unlike individual anomalous experiences, haunting and poltergeist narratives often involve multiple witnesses. The rhetorical quality of these stories is frequently based on correspondences between independent narrators' accounts. In the following, I present evidence gathered through participant observation of twenty cases in order to illustrate their common features and the processes by which they contribute to folk belief.

Although the incidence of claims of ghost sightings has apparently remained about the same over the last decade (about 10 percent of the United States population professes experience), the percentage of people believing in ghosts has increased. In 1978, 11 percent of the American population accepted the existence of ghosts, while in 1990, 25 percent regarded them as real (Gallup and Newport, 1991). This change is probably a consequence of media coverage of haunting and poltergeist reports.

As with individual experiences, aesthetic qualities within group haunting accounts determine, in part, the degree to which each narrative is disseminated. During the modern era, reports are published in weekly tabloids or portrayed on television, a process contributing to popular culture and contemporary folk belief.

My collection of twenty cases is consistent in form with the huge body of literature produced by psychical researchers (Gauld and Cornell, 1979; Roll, 1977). My orientation differs from theirs in that I do not attempt to authenticate paranormal claims. I hypothesize that haunting and poltergeist narratives contain universal features that contribute to cross-cultural similarities in folk belief. The correspondences between elements in the firsthand accounts in my collection and the classifications in Thompson's *Motif-Index of Folk-Literature* (1966) support this argument.

Psychical Research Findings

Gauld and Cornell's (1979) computer analysis of features evident in five hundred cases found two overlapping groups. One cluster, equivalent to the folk category of *hauntings*, contained a larger number of events that were long-lasting, nocturnal, concentrated in houses, and characterized as raps, imitative noises, voices, phantasms, or luminous effects. The second category, labeled within folklore as *poltergeists*, included more short-lived cases that are centered around specific individuals. In these cases, more objects were displaced, thrown, or carried through the air. Because the two categories overlap, some cases are difficult to classify. I sometimes use the term *haunting* as a matter of convenience, even when referring to cases with poltergeist-type events.

Although interpretations of haunting episodes are culturally shaped, these cases reveal universal features. Gauld and Cornell's narratives originated in such diverse locations as Turkey, Eastern and Western Europe, South America, the former Soviet Union, Scandinavia, Canada, the United States, Iceland, China, Indonesia, Jamaica, India, South Africa, Madagascar, and Malaysia. The authors noted categories that transcend culture: some phenomena are closely related to specific people; some are highly destructive, even involving physical assaults; other narratives feature entities uniquely capricious in an intelligent manner; still other forms produce a belief in demons. Some cases include recurrent phantasms who visit specific sites. Cases often include intermixed forms of phenomena. Emmons (1982) collected haunting narratives in Hong Kong; his accounts are equivalent to those of Gauld and Cornell and the rest of the psychical research literature.

Some psychical researchers argue that humans produce paranormal effects with their minds, a theory that does not require the existence of disembodied spirits. They suggest that haunting effects are a special, robust form of ESP and PK. I do not attempt to resolve this issue but to test social science hypotheses regarding the origin of folk belief.

Poltergeists may be affiliated with special forms of pathology. Certain individuals, termed *poltergeist agents*, often are central to psychokinetic outbreaks. Palmer (1974), Roll (1976), Rogo (1982b), and Bender and his associates (Mischo, 1971) have described this sort of agent as frequently an adolescent having "low tolerance for frustration but possessing the ability to repress or deny feelings of aggression and hostility from consciousness" (Rogo, 1982b: 233). Rogo hypothesized that, in cases with no central agent, poltergeist outbreaks are precipitated by dysfunctions experienced by an entire family rather than by individual problems suffered by particular family members.

Psychic practitioners, clergy, shamans, and mediums have employed a variety of methods to terminate haunting and poltergeist phenomena. These include exorcism, the reburial of a body, proper execution of a will, or a suggestion offered by a psychic practitioner to the haunting spirit that leaving the earthly plane is a good idea. No strategy is uniformly effective. Roll (1977: 404) analyzed twenty-nine cases in which exorcism was attempted; he found that the phenomena ceased after four cases, abated temporarily in four cases, and was unaffected in twenty-one cases.

During recent years, I have devised a treatment strategy for reducing negative haunting experiences. Those witnessing the most phenomena within a particular case generally report previous anomalous experiences. The resolution of a case is often dependent on the thoughts and feelings of these individuals. My approach, while not adequately evaluated, appears to have been effective in five test cases. I hypothesize that those experiencing frequent anomalous events have lowered the unconscious, skeptical barriers that normally prevent such episodes (Batcheldor [1984] and see Chapter 11). Experiencers can develop mental strategies to control the forms of event they perceive. The incidence of negative experience often declines when people (1) discuss and acknowledge the phenomena's nonthreatening and "unreal" qualities; (2) attempt to increase their "mental strength" through connection with powerful spiritual forces; (3) examine the possibility that anxieties shape group anomalous experiences and that future experiences can be controlled by individual and group attitudes; and (4) treat the phenomena as real and create nondestructive directions for occult forces to express themselves. I sometimes invite an amateur psychic, who is also skilled in family counseling, to assist with my inquiries. I also teach meditation and self-hypnosis techniques. The cases described in this chapter were investigated prior to my developing this counseling strategy.

Hauntings as Collective Behavior

Theories within the study of collective behavior, including contagion, emergent norm, and value-added theories, can be used to interpret haunting and poltergeist accounts. Although no single orientation fully explains haunting phenomena, an eclectic use of these theories provides insights regarding the social processes surrounding such events.

Social contagion theory, for example, argues that individuals within crowds lose their sense of self-consciousness, causing increased group conformity. Contagion theory has fallen out of favor with modern researchers since more recent studies have indicated that people in crowds demonstrate great variation in attention and focus (Miller, 1985: 17–23). My use of the term "contagion," however, carries a special connotation, since haunting experiencers need not be part of a group for phenomena to occur. Some people claim no previous knowledge of a given haunting yet report perceiving apparitional images that coincide with prior reports. Such perceptions correspond with folk belief: a spirit residing at a particular location is thought to affect paranormally the perceptions of its occupants. Some people appear more susceptible to "contagion" from paranormal agencies, subconscious cues, or the anomalous transmission of images from other experiencers.

Emergent norm theory specifies that people interacting among themselves will, in time, evolve common standards of behavior and belief. This theoretical orientation views collective behavior phenomena as governed by the same rules as other forms of human interaction (Miller, 1985: 23–30; Turner and Killian, 1957/1972). Haunting experiencers, for example, typically compare notes regarding their perceptions. They seek to determine "what really happened." Speakers and writers shape accounts to coincide with their audiences' expectations and needs. This process can be explained using emergent norm theory, whereby supernatural beliefs are socially constructed. What is written as having "really happened" is constructed through the interaction of narrators, writers, and their audiences. The present chapter illustrates this process. A book published by an academic press requires a style different from that desired by a tabloid newspaper. This process can even influence the memories of participants and shape later oral reports of their experiences. I hypothesize that my memory of the events I witnessed would be different if I were writing for a tabloid newspaper.

Hauntings can be analyzed using a variation of Smelser's (1962) *value-added theory*. Smelser's approach portrays collective behavior as a series of stages, each of which is necessary, but not sufficient, for the next step. Smelser's orientation can be applied to the cases at hand to the degree that hauntings follow overlapping developmental stages: (1) experiencers seek normal explanations for anomalous perceptions; (2) they frame these episodes within the context of belief in spirits, ghosts, and life after death; (3) they act to reduce negative effects; and

(4) transmission of narratives contributes to folk traditions. Smelser hypothesizes that generalized belief, the shared evaluation of a situation, is required in order for precipitating factors to mobilize participants for action. Because haunting experiences can occur prior to generalized belief, my collection of cases refutes strict adherence to Smelser's theory.

I summarize five sample cases drawn from twenty haunting and poltergeist cases I investigated between 1979 and 1992. The episodes occurred in Maryland (three cases); Virginia (three cases); North Carolina (five cases); California (one case); Illinois (one case); Okinawa, Japan (five cases); and Taipei, Republic of China (two cases). I hypothesize that:

1. Haunting cases follow progressive stages, evolving as information is gathered about the nature of the phenomena (value-added theory).
2. Haunting narratives are based on experiences that exhibit universal features, contributing to a belief in spirits, souls, and life after death (experiential source theory).
3. Collective behavior processes shape experiencers' narratives, contributing to the social construction of folk belief. During modern times, the media disseminate accounts that encourage belief in spirits, souls, and life after death, within the context of culturally specific ideologies (contagion and emergent norm theories).

The Baltimore Haunting

On September 30, 1979, I interviewed nine members of a family in Baltimore. The married homeowners, Mr. and Mrs. M., were 62 and 63 years old; their two unmarried sons, Mick and Robert, were 36 and 27; their two divorced daughters, Manny and Nancy, were 33 and 30; and each daughter had a son (ages 9 and 7). Mrs. M.'s retired sister, Ms. R. (age 72) also lived with the family.

The family moved into the house in April 1979 and began hearing unusual knocking sounds almost immediately. Mick assumed that rats were the culprits. He set out poison, which had no effect. About a month later, Manny experienced a strange nightmare that woke her. While awake, she felt paralyzed, yet saw a bright yellow orb of light on the wall (*Motif-index*: F471.1, "Nightmare. Presses person in dream"; D2072, "Magic paralysis"; E530.1, "Ghost-like lights"). This began a series of nightmares involving images of herself in demeaning, sometimes sexual, situations with unusual and misshapen individuals.

Unaware of Manny's experience, Nancy and Mrs. M. had separate experiences in which they each saw a large orange orb of light on their bedroom walls. Manny, Nancy, and their mother discussed their similar experiences and developed the hypothesis that something paranormal was occurring in their house (E421.5, "Ghost seen by two or more persons; they corroborate the appearance"). The family's narratives reveal a form of contagion. They reacted by devising a collective explanation (emergent norms).

The family decided to evaluate the authenticity of the phenomena by staying up all night in the room where the most events had occurred. Their efforts led to many unusual experiences. Manny tried to photograph the strange light orbs they witnessed. The lights appeared stimulated by her efforts, but the developed photographs revealed nothing unusual. In later incidents, the lights took the form of "an orange ball the size of a tennis ball," and of "an orange zigzag, snake-like light on the floor."

The disturbances began occurring on almost a daily basis and were sometimes experienced as a feeling on the face or ankles (numbness, itching, tingling or burning sensations). The disturbances also manifested themselves as unexplained knocks, voices, whistling, music, and the sound of percussion instruments (F473.5, "Poltergeist makes noises"). Family members claimed to be paralyzed in a peculiar fashion, sometimes while seeing apparitions (night/sleep paralysis). On one occasion, while Nancy felt paralyzed by the phenomenon, Manny saw Nancy, and the air surrounding her, turn strangely misty and orange. On another occasion, Manny and Mick simultaneously heard an apparitional, distorted voice, whose tone was experienced differently by each.

Family members reported various episodes of bed shaking. Mr. M. decided to investigate by spending the night in the bed that was the focus of many incidents. He made a special effort to keep alert and planned to signal Mick if anything unusual occurred. During the night he experienced a "funny feeling," as if someone were physically pushing his feet. Then he heard a knocking noise. He became paralyzed and was unable to gesture to Mick, who was resting nearby on the floor. A short time later, while Mick was watching, the entire side of the mattress under Mr. M.'s feet spontaneously raised about eight to twelve inches (D2072, "Magic paralysis"; F473.2, "Poltergeist causes objects to behave contrary to their nature").

Concerned and upset, the family asked Methodist, Pentecostal, and Catholic religious leaders to alleviate the disturbances. Their efforts caused only temporary abatement. Family members also consulted psychics and fortune-tellers but did not gain convincing or consistent information. The apparitions and nightmares provided few clues beyond providing images of people in "old-timey," nineteenth-century clothing.

On October 5, 1979, I spent the night in the room where much of the unusual activity had been experienced. Mick, Manny, and Nancy joined me in waiting for phenomena to occur. We experienced the contagious "itching and burning" feeling on our faces and heard an unusual "rap" on the wall (E402.1.5, "Invisible ghost makes rapping or knocking noise"). I fell asleep at approximately 3:30 A.M. At 6:30 A.M., I woke and observed, for approximately thirty seconds, an elliptical red light on the wall by a window. Although I heard no sound, I assumed that the light was created by a car on the street outside. As the light faded, Mick began moaning as if having a nightmare. A rap sounded within the wall beside my head. I alerted Mick, Manny, and Nancy, hoping that they would witness whatever further events might occur. Mick later stated, "I was having a dream in which I was crawling over the floor toward your bed. It [the spirit] wanted you out of the bed. It felt you had to wake up, to get up."

The others had heard the rap but were not in a position to observe the elliptical red light. I attempted to duplicate the light but could not devise an explanation for it. A heavy shade was drawn over the window, making it impossible for light to enter. We all went back to sleep.

At about 7:30 A.M., I woke when the bed I was sleeping on started vibrating; the vibrations were equivalent to those of a minor earthquake yet I observed no lamps or pictures swaying in the room. This experience continued for half a minute.

I felt that the phenomena in the house warranted further investigation. Although Mick, Manny, and Nancy agreed with me, Mrs. M. wished to ignore the incidents because she felt the events were demonic. Mrs. M. prevailed. I was allowed to visit and interview whenever I wished, but I was not permitted to spend the night again. Although I assured the family that they appeared psychologically normal, they were afraid they would be judged mentally incompetent in some way if information about their experiences became public.

Originally, the family wanted desperately to leave their house, but were prevented by the financial loss they would incur from selling. As they stayed, however, their experiences gradually became more subjective (unusual dreams and apparitional voices) and less dynamic (movement of objects and bed shaking no longer occurred). This illustrates a typical progression within haunting cases. Belief occurred after the phenomena began; it was not required for its incidence. Hauntings are not equivalent to panics, riots, or other collective behavior phenomena. Instead, hauntings are more like detective stories: People assemble clues while seeking a solution because the causes of the phenomena are unknown. Experiencers logically attempt to evaluate the evidence they gather.

The family in this case revised their beliefs as a result of their perceptions. Prior to the haunting, only the owner of the house had firm religious opinions regarding life after death. Because of their experiences, however, the other family members came to believe in the reality of an afterlife. One daughter noted, "Although it has been truly inconvenient to have had all these things happen, in a way I feel blessed. Not many people have the kind of certainty that I do. You just can't doubt when you have experienced it so many times."

Yet no clear relationship exists between their experiences and the "life after death" of any known person. In this case, narrators framed their reports within the context of folk ideologies after they concluded that their house was haunted. Seeing apparitions in nineteenth-century clothing apparently contributed to this process.

The media are important during modern times in constructing folk beliefs regarding hauntings. After I presented a paper regarding this case at a regional parapsychology conference (McClenon, 1981), two tabloid newspaper writers sought telephone interviews with me. I refused, believing that media exposure would violate the interests of the family. One writer asserted that his articles regarding hauntings required no fabrication since his tabloid's readers found factual reporting of actual haunting accounts to be interesting.

In order to gain an understanding of the nature of media treatment of hauntings, I read the *National Enquirer* over the course of several years. I also talked with tabloid reporters about their craft. The Baltimore case would require reshaping before a suitable tabloid article could emerge from it. Tabloid reporters must develop plots, narrative tension, and conflict to market their stories. Many articles also cite an authority of some kind. One freelance reporter told me, "All I need is to quote two witnesses and someone with a Ph.D. and I can sell the story." Conflicts between skeptical and occult positions are acceptable and can increase an article's value. On the other hand, because too much ambiguity ruins a "good" ghost story, tabloid writers may embellish people's accounts to create more marketable products.

The Alexandria Haunting

On June 14, 1981, I interviewed three residents of a house in Alexandria, Virginia. Gary, his wife Sue, and their friend Bruce claimed numerous poltergeist experiences. All were in their late twenties and employed in stable, white-collar jobs. They had previously lived as neighbors in another part of Alexandria.

They claimed to have heard unusual walking and banging sounds soon after they moved into the house on March 1, 1981. Their glass possessions also began breaking inexplicably. Sue found her unlocked Volkswagen parked unusually, pointed toward the house and blocking the road. She had left it in the driveway with the emergency brake on. On another occasion, many decorative balloons suddenly burst. These events were puzzling but, at the time, they did not seem paranormal. Later, Bruce saw Sue's papers flutter out of a cabinet and levitate; since he was drunk at the time, he refused to evaluate this event (F1083.0.1, "Object floats in air"). The bathroom was also found anomalously disordered on various occasions (F473.1, "Poltergeist throws objects").

On March 22, 1981, Bruce was told by a neighbor about a woman, Mary, who had committed suicide by hanging herself in the house in 1973. Since he was highly skeptical of paranormal claims and did not wish to stimulate superstitious beliefs, he did not share this information with Gary and Sue. They continued hearing unexplained sounds and finding mirrors and glasses broken inexplicably.

In early May, Sue dreamed that a woman spoke to her. The woman stated that while Sue was at work, she remained at home with Sue's husband. After waking, Sue felt the dream was meaningful, but did not believe her husband had been unfaithful. In early June, Bruce shared the tale about Mary, the woman who had hanged herself. Sue believed that the description of Mary fit that of the woman in her dream (E334.4, "Ghost of suicide seen at death spot or nearby"). Gary and Sue decided that their house was haunted and contacted a representative of the Institute for Parapsychology who notified me of this case.

As with the Baltimore narrative, the participants had anomalous experiences prior to classifying their case as a haunting. They later reframed their conceptions, attributing the unusual episodes to Mary. Gary heard the unexplained noises on a daily basis and ceased attempting to seek normal causes for them. One night, a woman's apparition appeared at a window. On another occasion, Bruce and Gary heard an unexplained explosion from a can they used as an ashtray. Once, a smoke alarm went off for no apparent reason.[1]

I questioned Gary, Sue, and Bruce regarding previous occult experiences. Gary reported many incidents, Sue described a few, and Bruce had no prior history of anomalous experience. He found the events troubling because they challenged his skeptical attitude. Each participant's past frequency of experiencing such incidents corresponded to his or her number of haunting accounts.

In July, the group decided they would urge Mary to "go toward the light" so she could satisfactorily reach the "other side." (As specified by the emergent norm theory, these people, interacting among themselves, had evolved common standards of behavior and belief.) Following this phase, the glass-breaking activity in the Alexandria house ended, although unexplained noises continued throughout the summer. Later, Bruce, Gary, and Sue reported seeing strange smoke in the kitchen, a phantom-like whirlwind, and unusual shadows (E421.4, "Ghosts as shadow"). Bruce moved out of the house for unrelated reasons and eventually two male roommates moved in. In April 1982 Gary informed me that nothing had occurred since Christmas. He stated that since "Mary was gone," the case was resolved.

The decision to interact with Mary seemed to reduce the rate of incidents (E451.4, "Ghost laid when living man speaks to it"). Before July 1981, approximately nine major incidents had occurred at the house during a four-month period (at the rate of 2.25 incidents per month). This does not include numerous, ambiguous glass-breaking incidents. After July, three incidents occurred during a six-month period (0.5 incidents per month). At one point, Sue contacted a local newspaper reporter, who wrote an article about the case. The article, published in the *Alexandria Journal* on Halloween, attracted little attention (Donovan, 1981).

I interviewed a police detective regarding Mary's death. Their documents indicated conclusively that her death was by suicide rather than by murder. My activity, at this point in the case, can be viewed as an attempt to provide further clues for the haunting mystery. If the police report had suggested homicide as a possibility, the narrators may have linked the phenomena to an unsolved murder (E231, "Return from dead to reveal murder"), thereby increasing the dramatic features within the unfolding story.

On June 27, 1982, Gary and Sue died of smoke inhalation during a two-alarm fire originating in the kitchen of their house. The two male occupants escaped unharmed. Fire investigators classified the blaze as "undetermined, accidental" (F473.2.4, "House burns for no apparent reason"). Reporter Rose Marie Donovan discovered that Sue had remarked to a friend the day before her death that "Mary was kicking up again." A bathroom door had mysteriously opened three times. One of the male occupants reported an anomalous noise that sounded like a "bull or an elephant in a tin can factory" a noise he had heard a few days before the fire (Donovan and George, 1982).

To ensure factuality, Ms. Donovan checked with me before she published her article. I remarked to her that I had no reason to believe that the fire had a paranormal origin. I noted that, since the residents smoked, they might have improperly disposed of cigarettes.[2] Fire investigators also felt this was a likely possibility. I also remarked to her that haunting cases occur more frequently than most people realize. I emphasized that one study of a random sample of Charlottesville, Virginia, residents indicated that 7 percent believed they had lived in a house they felt was haunted (Palmer, 1979). Because of the prevalence of hauntings, we would expect that some people who died from fires would also have experienced hauntings, even though the two events may be unrelated.

Although Ms. Donovan's article, published in the local newspaper, *Alexandria Journal*, noted my skepticism regarding the paranormal origin of the fire, the article also included statements from an amateur psychic who had parked his car beside the charred house. The psychic claimed to have felt "waves of evil" emanating from the property, a sensation supporting the argument that the fire had a supernatural origin (Donovan and George, 1982).

The *Alexandria Journal* article was summarized by the Associated Press, whose synopsis was carried by newspapers throughout the country. The *Weekly Mirror*, a supermarket tabloid, featured the case on its front page with the headline "GHOST KILLS A YOUNG COUPLE." The article was preceded with the subhead: "The most terrifying story of the year!" and subtitled: "Evil spirit wanted their home—and murdered them to get it" (Cooke, 1982: 1). I was quoted as saying, "This case is not as uncommon as you might think" (a statement derived from Donovan's article referring to the Charlottesville, VA, survey).[3]

The tabloid's narrative supported an ecumenical, universal folk belief: ghosts are real and have the power to bring about severe misfortune (E200–299, "Malevolent return from the dead"). The Alexandria case therefore became suitable as a ghost story for a mass audience.

This chronology illustrates the manner in which tabloids use personal narratives to support folk religion. Tabloid reporters need not fully fabricate oral accounts; they can simply shape them to fit the desires of mass audiences. The Alexandria haunting had no deeply malevolent tone until the deaths of Gary and Sue. Reporters created the connection through investigation, fabrication, ambiguity, and quotes from a psychic. Although less factual, the *Weekly Mirror*'s article is more suitable as oral literature than the narrative I include here. Aesthetic features, sometimes gained through retelling, grant some haunting narratives the capacity to affect folk traditions and mass culture; reports lacking such features have little impact. "Good" stories gain greater circulation.

Academics sometimes ignore the ability of the mass media to formulate and disseminate folk ideologies. While relatively few people read books published by academic presses, weekly tabloids have the largest circulations of all types of newspapers in America. Some academics believe that a clear distinction exists between the sacred and the profane. Folk belief, supported by tabloid journalism, blurs this boundary. The miraculous is as close as the nearest grocery store; at the checkout counter, one can learn about spirits, souls, life after death, and wondrous capacities as experienced by normal people.

The Hot Cross Case

On February 14, 1982, I interviewed eight family members involved in a haunting/poltergeist case in Southern Virginia. Frances, a thirty-six year-old widow, had three children: Robert (age 16), Deanna (age 12), and Scott (age 11). Her widowed sister Cheryl (age 32) also had three children: Susan (age 13), Donna (age 12), and Danny Ray (age 6).

Cheryl, who had been separated from her husband for seven years, had had recurring dreams that the police would notify her of his death in a car accident. In 1979, she found his body along the roadway. He had been killed by a hit-and-run driver. As might be expected, these events had a powerful impact on her.

In March 1980, Cheryl moved into a house in Virginia with her children, her nephew Greg, and his wife Denise. Two weeks later, they began experiencing vivid, terrifying dreams, seeing apparitional images, and perceiving unusual cold sensations. Using a Ouija board, they contacted Cheryl's dead husband, who informed them that a treasure was buried in their front yard (E371, "Return from dead to reveal hidden treasure"). Later in the evening a threatening entity thwarted communication with the husband and sexually propositioned the females present through Ouija board messages. Although Frances and her children later moved into the house, no one had a metal detector, which they felt was required to search efficiently for the deeply buried treasure.

In December, Cheryl discovered writing in lipstick on the outside of a window (inscribed backward so it could be read from the inside). The message read, "I will get you" (E557, "Dead man writes"). She noticed that objects were being disarranged. For example, a crucifix disappeared from one wall and was found beneath the covers in the center of her bed, with the its base turned toward the head of the bed (F473.2.2, "Spirit hides articles in strange places"). On one occasion, as Denise bent over to pet their cat, the shadow of a cross hanging from her neck passed over her foot. The shadow burned her, causing a slight blister. She handed the cross to Robert and it burned his hand. He threw it across the room. When Frances touched it, she found it to be strangely cold. After Denise became pregnant, she and Greg departed for South Carolina.

The remaining group perceived many apparitional figures, voices, and sounds which radiated an evil, foreboding quality. On one occasion, an image of Cheryl's husband warned the family to move away (E363.3, "Ghost warns the living"). Robert attempted to defend the family against a series of apparitional prowlers who seemed to mock him. He shot one with his .22 rifle; it fell to the ground and disappeared. Once he was knocked to the floor by a mysterious force.

After a particularly frightful winter night in 1981, the sisters decided to abandon their house and take their children to North Carolina. A strange demonic dog appeared seemingly from nowhere; it sat outside the front door and watched them drive off. Cheryl decided to sell her house and signed a contract with a real estate agent.

On February 26, 1982, I accompanied the sisters and their children to their unsold, haunted house. Frances had purchased a metal detector and, after we arrived, Robert used it to search for the treasure. To my surprise, his device located metal in exactly the area indicated by the Ouija board message. Robert began digging for the treasure. As evening approached, Cheryl and Frances were alarmed by a vision. I stood beside them while they described a hallway widening and extending anomalously before them. The hall appeared normal to me.

As it became dark, Robert struck a hard object with his shovel. He shouted for my help. We discovered a large slab of concrete about three feet below the ground's surface. It was more than three feet in diameter and flat on top. We would need to dig extensively to discover what was beneath it. Because of the darkness, we abandoned the project, intending to continue work in the morning.

Late in the evening, I left the group huddled fearfully in the living room and went to sleep in the room where the most haunting incidents had been reported. The family woke me before sunrise, demanding that we leave immediately. During the night, Frances and Robert saw an apparitional shape of a little girl going into my bedroom. They also saw a dark, demonic figure. It was snowing, and they were terrified of becoming snowbound. We left before dawn.

Although the family never returned to the house, they continued to report sporadic anomalous experiences in their North Carolina apartment, some of which included poltergeist events. On one occasion, a terrarium overturned inexplicably and various objects in the room were rearranged. Family members twice reported hearing the phantom girl crying. On another occasion, Susan went on a rampage, seemingly in the control of an outside power. She refused to take baths or to leave the apartment. Cheryl consulted a psychiatrist, who argued that Susan's behavior was not extremely unusual. I surmise that he considered severe conflicts to be normal in families with adolescent children and thus rejected a paranormal explanation.

In May, the real estate agency found a buyer for Cheryl's house, removing any need for her to return to it. Cheryl's fear of spiritual forces was greater than her desire for the treasure that she had left behind. In July 1982, I telephoned Frances and Cheryl but discovered their numbers had been disconnected. I also attempted to contact them by mail. Both had moved, leaving no forwarding address.

Although it lacks resolution, this case illustrates a progression typical of hauntings. "Minor" psychic experiences, dreams, and Ouija board communications contributed to labeling the case as a haunting. Eventually, archetypical images of malevolent, ghostly figures became prevalent, and the experiencers came to believe they were haunted by demonic forces.

Except for Cheryl's husband's messages, no experience was clearly related to a deceased individual. Cheryl, Frances, and their children merely assumed that otherworldly forces were active in the house since they could not otherwise explain their perceptions. People placed in this position often interpret their experiences within a religious context even when they are not particularly religious. The beliefs that evolve have very real effects. In this instance, economic decisions were based on anomalous perceptions. The teenage children privately informed me that they planned to convert to Catholicism when they became adults. They hoped to protect themselves from future incidents.

With shaping and fabrication, this account could have been sold to a tabloid. A reporter could interview a psychic to discern the reasons for the haunting and establish a suitable conclusion. With quotes from an "expert," such an article could be completed.

The Military Police Station Haunting

A newspaper article describing a military police station haunting appeared in a U.S. Army post newspaper in Maryland in March 1980. The article reported that "at least a dozen men, all entrusted by the government to carry weapons, are convinced that 'there's something going on out there.'" The ghost, nicknamed "Gwendolyn," haunted a headquarters building constructed in 1885. The article gave the names of seven men who had reported haunting experiences. None knew of any violence associated with the building. The experiences included seeing an apparition of a young female on numerous occasions, hearing footsteps on the upstairs floor, finding lights and water turned on without explanation, the inexplicable movement of furniture, and doors and windows opening, even after being secured by the MPs (F473, "Poltergeist, invisible spirit").

I gained permission from military authorities to investigate in November 1980. Only three of the original twelve experiencers still worked at the station; the rest had been routinely rotated to other posts or duty stations. The three reported that the newspaper article was factual. Although no other MPs reported experiences, two of the three individuals had experienced further phenomena. One, who had expressed a skeptical opinion, experienced more convincing phenomena and now placed credence in the reports.

On one occasion, a trained German shepherd police dog was brought to the house in an attempt to locate the female intruder. The dog's handler was amazed to find that the dog refused to go into the station's basement (E421.1.4, "Ghost visible to dogs alone"). No intruder was located. This event was one of many occasions when multiple observers simultaneously experienced anomalous events, after which authorities attempted—unsuccessfully—to devise normal explanations for the episode (E421.5, "Ghost seen by two or more persons; they corroborate the appearance").

Based on interviews, I constructed a chronology of events associated with the haunting. Sergeant G., who served on the day shift, had his first experience in the spring of 1979. For a long time, this sixty-five-year-old man was the only experiencer. Later, the night desk sergeant, who originally had been highly skeptical, heard pounding noises, witnessed doors open and close by themselves, and, on one occasion, observed a heavy typewriter spontaneously move about eight inches. Sergeant G. was not present during these events. As noted previously, hauntings can have a contagious quality, a capacity to infect others in a particular environment.

One experiencer, PFC M., reported four specific events, the first of which was in the company of Sergeant G. Later, PFC M. shared another sergeant's single experience. At the time of my interview (December 1980), PFC M. had not had an experience for many months.

Neither Sergeant G. nor any of the other men were thought to be under tension or to have any personality disturbances. All were considered dependable and capable individuals. Moreover, the desk sergeant's job was not stressful since the base was small and the duties routine.

Unlike the other experiencers, Sergeant G. reported a history of paranormal perceptions and beliefs. Earlier in his life, he had seen an apparition and heard poltergeist-like rapping in a recently built house that he owned. He visited a psychiatrist who advised him not to worry, stating, "You'll be the only one who hears it." After two or three experiences, the rapping stopped.

I sporadically visited the military police station to interview personnel. Sergeant G. reported about one experience each week. He claimed to be able to sense the presence of Gwendolyn and was not concerned or afraid of her. Once, while alone, Sergeant G. observed Gwendolyn standing on the station staircase; he dashed up the steps, but she vanished before he reached her. Other military policemen accepted the existence of Gwendolyn and jokingly referred to her as Sergeant G.'s girlfriend.

No individuals other than Sergeant G. reported experiences after September 1980. I spent the night at the station in December 1980, but had no unusual experiences. Sergeant G. was routinely transferred in the spring of 1982, after which all haunting experiences at the MP station ended.

During the twenty-four months of the station haunting, approximately fourteen major incidents occurred (0.58 incidents per month), yet the haunting ended with Sergeant G.'s transfer. Sergeant G., the individual with the greatest history of paranormal experience, reported the most haunting events. The case was "resolved" when he departed. Individual or group tension appeared not to be a factor. Other aspects of this case are consistent with patterns found in Roll's (1977) collection: when the central figure moved away, the poltergeist phenomena ended.

The MP case stimulated no further media interest. The building was later demolished and the military police headquarters relocated without incident. MPs at the new station had no knowledge of Gwendolyn. The lack of ongoing experiences reduced the capacity of narrators to shape accounts worth retelling.

The Haunted C-130 Case

During 1985, many marines at a U.S. Marine air station on Okinawa reported paranormal experiences surrounding a particular C-130 Hercules transport plane. I interviewed six men who performed maintenance on the airplane. Respondents reported that there were "about a million stories" regarding C-130 #800, which they nicknamed "BOO." (When stenciled on the side of the craft, "800" resembles the word "BOO.")

Respondents reported seeing an apparitional figure on a cargo ramp, seeing lights inside the airplane when the main battery was disconnected during maintenance, hearing apparitional footsteps on the wings and outside the aircraft, and observing psychokinetic movement of objects such as coffee cups and tools inside the aircraft. On numerous occasions, groups of people saw psychokinetic effects (F473, "Poltergeist, invisible spirit").

Mechanics repairing the aircraft discovered undiagnosed malfunctions that sometimes disappeared without explanation. In the summertime, the plane was thought to smell like a morgue. On several occasions, mechanics pulled up all the floor panels and cleaned the plane thoroughly, but they were unable to alleviate this problem.

Various explanations for the haunting were offered. BOO had transported dead and injured men during the Vietnam War. A marine had been asphyxiated while working on BOO at El Toro Point; he had used a cleaning agent without wearing a respirator (E334, "Non-malevolent ghost haunts scene of former misfortune, crime, or tragedy").

Unlike the previous military police station case, BOO's haunting had an ongoing existence, independent of any single experiencer. Like the MP station case, experiences occurred among personnel who lacked both occult beliefs and knowledge of other paranormal reports. Although the events within the MP station had been better verified, BOO's episodes functioned better for supporting folk belief, since the aircraft was associated with violent deaths and ongoing experiences. This narrative combines robust phenomena with ambiguity—characteristics that encourage the production of rumors and folk belief. The experiences had real effects; the unit's commander was aware of the stories and allowed those who did not wish to perform services on the aircraft to do alternate tasks. Later, I was told that BOO had been featured in a tabloid, but was unable to locate the article.

Other Cases

The typical haunting attracts little publicity, such as the following three cases investigated in Okinawa: (1) A local family reported a long series of anomalous noises. Although they felt that a small cave behind their property might be responsible, they developed no evidence supporting this hypothesis. (2) An American wife in Okinawa experienced poltergeist phenomena while her Air Force husband was absent. Eventually, her husband and neighbors shared her experiences. (3) Okinawans and American military personnel saw ghosts dressed in traditional Okinawan clothing walk toward an ancient village marker on various occasions. Cases with sufficient aesthetic qualities gain publicity: An Okinawan man wrote a book about his paranormal experiences, attributing them to spirits. In my interview with him, he told me of many anomalous lights, apparitional images, and unexplained sounds in his residence. Other people sometimes shared his perceptions. Although he advocated belief in local spirits, he also noted universal features within his experiences.

I uncovered similar cases in other areas: (1) A temple in Taiwan contained a bench thought to be haunted. Those sitting on the bench were sometimes shoved off paranormally. (2) Residents of a house in Warrenton, Virginia, thought it to be haunted. After they moved out, the new residents reported no equivalent incidents. (3) Taiwanese taxi drivers discovered that their fares sometimes disappeared when they drove through a particular tunnel (parallel to the vanishing hitchhiker motif; Brunvand, 1981; *Motif-Index* E332.3.3.1). These reports resulted in a small article in a Taiwanese newspaper containing interviews with taxi drivers. (4) A family in Illinois saw apparitional images of a child and perceived anomalous sounds. After a psychic attempted to communicate with the spirit, the haunting ended.

Discussion

These cases reveal a progression of events that shape belief. Respondents in the Baltimore, Alexandria, and hot cross cases originally expressed puzzlement regarding their experiences. Later, they concluded that their residences were haunted. The MP station and the C-130 cases followed similar patterns. Authorities originally sought normal interpretations but, after investigation, acknowledged unexplained effects. The typical progression is not from generalized belief toward experience but rather from experience to belief. People report equivalent experiences, perhaps through contagion. They then discuss their perceptions, seeking to determine "what really happened."

People often report perceiving unknown forces rather than deceased individuals. Through discussing their experiences, they personalize the phenomena, developing consensus as to "what it really was." They often create accounts that correspond to folk beliefs regarding hauntings. The assumption that most people fabricate these narratives to deal with death anxiety or to gain publicity is not borne out by the cases I investigated. Many accounts are ambiguous rather than directly related to death. Only one of the respondents (Mr. M. of the Baltimore case) was deeply concerned with religious issues. None of the respondents expressed unusual anxiety regarding death. Few sought publicity.

Subconscious processes apparently shape group experiences, perhaps reflecting social or psychological tensions. The dysfunctional family of the hot cross case reported highly negative images. Well-adjusted, easy-going individuals, such as Sergeant G., suffered no ill effects. Groups who came to accept their anomalous perceptions (as in Alexandria and Baltimore) experienced a declining rate of incidents. Some episodes reflect unvoiced anxieties. Anomalous events made skilled personnel appear incompetent since they were unable to discover the causes of irregularities (the haunted miliary police station and C-130 cases). Women were exposed to undesired sexual messages (the Baltimore haunting, Alexandria haunting, and hot cross case).

Hauntings seem organized like collective dreams that are perceived by groups rather than by individuals. As in dreams, haunting perceptions have symbolic features that may express subconscious forces. Sometimes, as in precognitive dreams, symbolic events foretell misfortune (images of smoke and explosions preceded the Alexandria fire). Hauntings direct people's attention to spiritual matters since religion provides a framework for explaining the unknown. Elements support belief in both positive and negative spiritual forces.

Haunting entities often reveal special qualities. Spirits sometimes write backward, or leave whimsical and ambiguous evidence of their existence (Chapter 11 provides further examples). Unexplained forces can act capriciously, as if they wish to resist complete verification. This characteristic sometimes contributes to scientific skepticism regarding paranormal claims (a feature discussed in Chapters 10 and 11).

Haunting accounts with appropriate aesthetic qualities are suitable as oral literature and therefore gain wide circulation. Narrators tend to humanize the phenomena by attributing personalities to whatever forces are thought to produce the anomalous effects. Modern media selectively broadcast accounts that support existing folk beliefs, fusing folklore with mass culture.

Haunting cases have had a major impact on religious ideology. Throughout the ages, people have been perceived to return from the dead. Accounts of these episodes shaped beliefs regarding life after death. Some Biblical scholars use the term "apparition" to describe Jesus' Resurrection (Mitchell, 1991: 64; Vermes, 1986: 19). Indeed, Jesus' reappearance after death can be seen as the most important haunting case in history.

New Testament accounts of Jesus' return contain features equivalent to the narrative elements of modern hauntings. The arisen Jesus was seen by groups, appeared and vanished before people's eyes, gave precognitive information, and withstood close inspection by the skeptical Saint Thomas (John 20:26–28; Luke 24:39). Modern apparitions reveal similar features. They have been viewed by groups (Gauld and Cornell, 1979), twenty to thirty people at a time (Emmons; 1982: 4 [E421.5, "Ghost seen by two or more persons; they corroborate the appearance"]). They appear, disappear, and pass through solid objects (E572, "Ghost walks through solid substance"). Respondents have closely inspected them, finding them to be solid forms (McClenon, 1984: 216). Like Jesus, ghostly visitors have supplied information that was unavailable to any living person, demonstrating extrasensory perception (Gauld, 1982; D1810.13, "Magic knowledge from the dead").

The Gospel writers Luke (24:30, 43) and John (21:15) indicate that the resurrected Jesus consumed food (E341.2, "Dead grateful for food"; E541, "Revenants eat"; F473.6.4 "Spirit eats food"). Many Asian traditions include setting out food for hungry ghosts.

Discrepancies in Jesus' Resurrection accounts can be explained by the apparitional nature of his return. The earliest existing written reference to the Resurrection is found in Paul's first letter to the Corinthians (15:6), written during the winter of A.D. 53–54. Paul states that Jesus appeared to more than five hundred brethren at one time, most of whom were still alive. Although such an occasion should be highly memorable, the four Gospel writers do not mention this event. The earliest existing Mark Gospel, written between A.D. 60 and 80, includes no Resurrection story. An account appears appended as an afterthought in later versions (Vermes, 1986: 19). Resurrection narratives that are not consistent appear in Matthew, Luke, and John, written between A.D. 80 and 120.

These discrepancies may have evolved from Jesus' apparitional nature. Specters produce variations in perception and interpretation. Typically, some witnesses are not convinced by such experiences and some perceive no image whatsoever. Jesus' appearances may have had a similarly uneven quality. Indeed, the Gospel narratives hint that this was the case. Disciples sometimes had trouble recognizing the resurrected Jesus (Matthew 28:17; Luke 24:16; John 20:14, 21:4) and skeptical traditions developed regarding the Resurrection (Matthew 28:11–15). A normal return from a journey would seemingly leave more consistent accounts, unlike the contradictory narratives in the New Testament.

Historians such as Crossan (1991) maintain that the Resurrection probably never occurred. In the case of apparitions, skeptics argue along parallel lines. They feel that the evidence for ghosts is inadequate to compel belief in an afterlife. Yet factors related to the incidence of apparitions, especially as portrayed in the psychical research literature, support the argument that major Christian traditions originated with people who saw Jesus' apparition. His apostles, a cohesive group, had been exposed to many anomalous events. On various occasions, Jesus implied that he would return. Such factors provided preparation for, and increased the probability of, later apparitional episodes. More importantly, Jesus' violent and unjust death would be expected to be followed by ghostly perceptions. Famous people who die violently are likely to be seen as specters. Abraham Lincoln, for example, has appeared to many reputable White House visitors. Given the existence of the many elements favorable for apparitional incidence, it would be surprising if Jesus had not been perceived as returning to life after his death. As with all such narratives, the Resurrection story would be subject to cultural shaping through distortions of memory, oral transmission, and written transcription. The Resurrection account contains many aesthetically powerful features, contributing to its wide dissemination.

Recently, a Christian scholar at a conference argued that I placed insufficient emphasis on the theory that haunting cases have supernatural origins. This scholar believes that both ghosts and Christian claims are authentic supernatural phenomena. Her argument is difficult to test within a scientific context. I merely present a hypothesis: the patterns within hauntings allow predictions regarding future returns from the dead. For example, an unjust, gruesome execution of a charismatic religious leader would have a high probability of being followed by apparitional experiences. The impact of each case will depend on the collective behavior processes following the original experiential reports. During the modern era, the media are closely involved in this process. The successful dissemination of such narratives depends on their capacity to resonate with cultural needs, aesthetic factors, and media requirements. Apparitional sightings of the singer Elvis Presley, and anomalous healings surrounding these events, illustrate this process (Moody, 1989).

The existence of universal features within these narratives supports the experiential source theory. Many firsthand narratives contain elements that are consistent with those found in Thompson's *Motif-Index of Folk-Literature* (1966). It is logical to hypothesize that folkloric patterns emerged from common features within personal experiences. The argument that original experiences are wholly cultural products does not explain the prevalence of certain motifs in these experiences.

Hauntings are one of the many types of collective wondrous events. People who report frequent wondrous events play primary roles within these processes. The Christian apostles, Nancy and Manny in the Baltimore case, Gary from Alexandria, Cheryl in the hot cross case, and Sergeant G. in the military police station case demonstrated high capacities for anomalous experience. Such people provide a necessary ingredient for hauntings, miracles, spiritual healings, and ritual magic. The special labeling, recruitment, and socialization of those with high capacities for wondrous experience will be discussed more fully in the next chapter.

Chapter 5
Psychic Practitioners and Wondrous Events

As with hauntings, universal features within the life stories of psychic practitioners contribute to cross-cultural uniformities in folk belief. Although most haunting experiencers have little control over the chaotic anomalous phenomena they perceive, psychic practitioners claim to detect and manipulate occult forces at will. The present chapter focuses on factors related to the self-selection and recruitment of contemporary shamans, mediums, psychics, and spiritual healers.

Psychic practitioners' lives are shaped by wondrous experiences. Like haunting experiencers, they often follow rational processes in evaluating their perceptions. Three developmental stages are present in their life stories: (1) During a preliminary stage, spontaneous anomalous experiences (primary wondrous events) shape their self-concept and belief. They then try to adjust to the social reactions stimulated by their anomalous claims. (2) During an intermediate stage, some practitioners learn to perform secondary wondrous events for audiences. Many solicit expert assistance to attain special mental states. Some demonstrate fire immunity, pain denial, psychokinesis, ESP, or unusual physiological effects. (3) Finally, mastery of performance skills allows the practitioners to create tertiary wondrous experiences in others. Spiritual healing is the most common objective.

The experience-centered approach is more problematic when applied to psychic practitioners' narratives than it is for spontaneous wondrous perceptions. Psychic performers are more likely to fabricate stories, since their careers depend on their reputations. The experience-centered approach cannot measure these informants' sincerity. Yet false stories, which audiences believe to be true, have real social effects.

Universal features within these life stories are of interest to social scientists because they contribute to recurring motifs within folk belief.

Various scholars have provided personal accounts of secondary and tertiary wondrous experiences (Eisenberg, 1985; Stoller and Olkes, 1987; Turner, 1992). I describe my own performances in Chapter 6.

The Sample

Between 1978 and 1990, I observed and interviewed more than thirty-three Asian spiritual healers and seventeen American psychic practitioners, some of whom provided written autobiographic material (Table 5.1). I interviewed the practitioners who seemed most noteworthy in each area I visited. No attempt was made to gather random samples of healers from each country. I also include in my study data written autobiographies of Western healers who have been tested under laboratory conditions (Kraft, 1981; Manning, 1974; Tanous, 1976; Worrall, 1970). Of these, only Olga Worrall was interviewed for this study.

Participant observation often involved multiple visits and in-depth discussions, especially in Sri Lanka, the Philippines, Taiwan, and the United States. I visited Chakara C., in Thailand, and various Okinawan practitioners only once. My Korean research was limited by translation difficulties. When presenting healers' life stories, I refer to individuals using abbreviations of their surnames except in cases where the name is extremely common or the person's biography has appeared in print. By custom, Japanese and Chinese surnames precede what in the West is labeled the "first" name.

Previous Studies as a Basis for Comparison

Winkelman (1992) defines three types of magico-religious practitioners: shamanic healers, priests, and sorcerer/witches. According to this system, the practitioners in my sample would be categorized as shamanic (or shamanistic) healers. Previous researchers have portrayed the nature of shamanic and spiritual healing (Eliade, 1974; Frank, 1973; Kakar, 1982; Kiev, 1964; Kleinman, 1986; Krippner and Welch, 1992; Weatherhead, 1953). Spiritual healing is linked, in these sources, with persuasion, religion, faith, and altered states of consciousness. My observations support the general thrust of these studies.

Many of the healers I interviewed described ideologies and methodologies coinciding with those portrayed by Ahern (1973), Covell (1983), Heinze (1984, 1990), Jordan (1972), Jordan and Overmyer (1986), Kleinman (1980), Lebra (1966), and Wolf (1974). A larger percentage of the respondents in my sample were urban and often less traditional in comparison to the practitioners described in this litera-

TABLE 5.1. Summary of Spiritual Healer Study

Country	Methodology	Example Cases
Korea	Observation of three ceremonies (kuts); interviews with shamans and clients; videos of Christian healer.	Mrs. Kim
Philippines	Interviews with eleven psychic surgeons; observation of more than one thousand "psychic surgeries"; interviews with six folk healers on Siquijor Island; observation of treatments; interviews with clients.	Eleuterio Terte Alex Orbito J. Escandor-Sisson David O. Wilhelmina S. Mrs. A.
Okinawa	Interviews with two traditional shamans, four nontraditional folk healers, one Christian folk healer, three Okinawan psychotherapists (familiar with Okinawan folk-healing practices), and many clients.	K. Higa T. Shizuko Dr. U. C. Toshihiko Reverend N.
Thailand	Interviews with two folk healers and their clients; a visit to a meditation "healing" center.	Wilasinee W. Chakara C.
Sri Lanka	Interviews with three traditional folk healers, one nontraditional healer, many clients, and participation in a firewalking ceremony at Kataragama.	Piyadasa K.
Taiwan	Interviews with three Taoist shamanic healers, various clients, and observation of numerous ceremonies.	Li Ch't-ts'e
People's Republic of China	Interviews with herbalists, qigong master, acupuncturist, and clients at Northwestern Polytechnic Institute Medical Center.*	
United States	Interviews with and observation of ten New Age healers, three Protestant fundamentalist healers, and four Spiritualist mediums, 1980–1982 and 1986–1991; participation in firewalking "workshop."	Matthew Manning The Worralls Dean Kraft Alex Tanous

*Due to political considerations, I do not discuss a specific example case from the People's Republic of China in the text.

ture. This was probably a result of my tendency to seek individuals who had attracted widespread attention. My sample is more suitable for revealing the adaptability and longevity of shamanic practice than for portraying traditional methods.

Cooperstein (1992), in his evaluation of Western transpersonal healers, noted a universal shamanic complex. He quotes Noll's (1983: 444) argument that inherent psychobiological predispositions contribute to this pattern: "[T]ranspersonal healing appears to be a contemporary adaptation of the shamanic complex, a core process from which the variety of transpersonal healing methods evolved" (p. 125). Winkelman's (1992) findings are consistent with this conclusion and my data support their arguments; I found that similarities exist within the shamanic life narratives collected from many localities.

Krippner (1989) describes five methods by which Brazilian spiritualist healers are "called." These include (1) anomalous experiences, (2) coming from families where mediumship is practiced, (3) attending ceremonies and then volunteering services, (4) being identified as a potential medium by a spiritualist healer, and (5) attending lectures or reading books.

Although my data coincide, to a degree, with Krippner's findings, the capacity for anomalous experience was a key element in the socialization of all the psychic practitioners I interviewed. Many respondents followed pathways 1, 2, or 4 in Krippner's system (psychic experience, mediumship family, identification by practitioner). Some New Age and Protestant fundamentalist Americans, whose roles were established by organizational structures, attained status through social interaction. They followed pathways 3 (attending ceremonies) and 5 (lectures or books). Even in these cases, however, personal experiences were important. Most in my sample described anomalous experiences (pathway 1) *and* meeting occult experts (pathway 4) as most important to their socialization process, but this may be a result of my seeking out individuals who were famous and successful. I did not focus attention on less prominent healers who were merely members of religious groups.

Self-Selection of Psychic Practitioners

Certain psychological variables related to wondrous experience predispose some individuals to having anomalous experiences and to becoming psychic practitioners. These variables include hypnotic suggestibility (Nadon and Kihlstrom, 1987; Pekala, Kumar, and Cummings, 1992; Wagner and Ratzeburg, 1987; Wilson and Barber, 1983; Wickramasekera, 1988), fantasy- proneness (Wilson and Barber, 1983), and dissociation (Richards, 1991; Ross and Joshi, 1992). Pekala, Kumar, and Cummings (1992) found that about 10 percent their subjects who exhibited high hypnotic suggestibility were especially likely to report anomalous experiences.

The factors related to wondrous experience are also associated with spiritual healing. Heber et al. (1989) found the incidence of dissociative experiences to be far higher among alternative healers than among traditional therapists. Ninety-two percent of Wilson and Barber's (1983) fantasy-prone subjects saw themselves as psychic or sensitive (compared to 16 percent of the control group). More than two-thirds of the fantasy-prone subjects, and none of the comparison controls, felt that they had the ability to heal someone spiritually.

My study suggests that wondrous experiences activate a social process by which potential practitioners attempt to adjust to the reputations they acquire. They come to believe that they have extraordinary faculties or special connections to spiritual powers. Their anomalous experiences sometimes increase their capacities for compassion, making them more effective as healers.

The narratives also reveal two patterns related to dissociation, mental state, and belief: (1) All Asian practitioners believed special states of consciousness contributed to wondrous experiences. The use of altered states is not unusual. Bourguignon (1973) found that 90 percent of the 488 societies in her sample employed institutionalized forms of altered states of consciousness. Winkelman's (1992) cross-cultural analysis reveals a decline in the deliberate use of altered states in societies with more complex political organization. Correspondingly, I found that most Western practitioners in my sample placed less emphasis on altered mental states. (2) All practitioners attempted to verify their anomalous perceptions during early developmental stages. The results of these efforts contributed to their belief in occult forces.

In what follows, I present sample cases that confirm these patterns. I invite others to test and adjust my assertions by analyzing alternate cases. Further narratives in Chapters 6 and 7 focus on performance techniques and audience reactions.

Matthew Manning

Matthew Manning's (1974) autobiography, *The Link*, illustrates his progression from poltergeist agent to psychic practitioner. At the age of eleven, in February 1967, Manning was at the center of a poltergeist outbreak. He and his family heard numerous anomalous knocks and other sounds. Lightweight ornaments, chairs, cutlery, ashtrays, baskets, plates, furniture, and scores of other articles in his home moved paranormally. The incidents ended by Easter of that year.

In April 1971, more powerful paranormal effects began to occur in his house which included the appearance of pools of water and other liquids; he also witnessed objects in flight, the disappearance of objects, and paranormal writing on walls. Manning found he could interact with the phenomena, willing or requesting missing objects to return.

His life was severely disrupted when the phenomena followed him to boarding school, where, as a result of these unusual events, his headmaster threatened to expel him.

Manning found he could communicate with a spiritual entity by passing into a self-induced altered state of consciousness. From that point on, the poltergeist outbreaks began to decline. He engaged in automatic writing about which he remarks, "It appeared that the energy I used for writing had previously been used for causing poltergeist disturbances. . . . I discovered that I could switch myself 'on' or 'off' like an electric light switch" (p. 86, 87). Manning's autobiography provides a prototypical account of a person who experiences frequent anomalous episodes but gains control over his or her psychic faculties.

Manning saw apparitions and found that he could perceive information paranormally. He began to create drawings while in self-induced trance, adding the signatures of famous deceased artists. He would spend one or two hours to produce a drawing that would normally take an artist six to eight hours to create.

Manning gained control over the incidence of his experiences, avoided the negative social reactions to them (expulsion from school, for example), and eventually became a professional spiritual healer. Scientific investigations seemingly verified the paranormal quality of his abilities (Braud, Davis, and Wood, 1979).

Ambrose and Olga Worrall

Wondrous events were a central impetus within Ambrose and Olga Worralls' (1970) socialization as practitioners. Olga states,

> By the time I was three years old it became very apparent to my parents that they did indeed have a child with a frightening and undesirable trait that caused her to claim the ability to see and hear those who had died. . . . To further complicate matters I would describe people whom my parents had known in the old country and who, unknown to my parents, had died. These phenomena greatly disturbed my parents. . . . I was the one child of the eleven who saw things that no one else could see, and made prophecies that were laughed at, but that came to pass, much to their consternation and alarm. (p. 85)

Her reputation as a psychic healer, gained at an early age, attracted requests for aid from neighbors and relatives.

In 1927, at the age of twenty-one, Olga and her family heard loud knockings from various locations in her room. A psychic identified her as a "sensitive" and made many accurate predictions about her future. The rapping phenomenon lasted a week but ceased on the day she met her future husband, Ambrose.

At the age of six, Ambrose Worrall also began seeing apparitional images. One was of a man who was later identified as having died ten years prior to Ambrose's birth:

The episode was particularly significant in my life as an example of my own dawning realization that I was in some way different. I did not want to believe I was different; I did everything I could to deny it in my own mind. I brushed it aside. I was simply a boy like all other youngsters. . . . Still, the awareness was there. I had learned, for example, not to speak of the people—the visitors—who came at night to my room. It was wiser, I found, not to talk of these things. (p. 32)

As an adult, Ambrose on one occasion felt compelled to touch his sister's neck, causing her to recover immediately from a paralysis. A psychic identified him as having unique abilities and assisted him in testing and verifying these capacities. He developed the capacity to experience OBEs, telepathy, and contact with the dead. People asked him for "psychic treatments," and he states,

To my astonishment, people began to report to me that they were getting better, or were actually healed, and very often they had real evidence to show me, including some interesting medical reports. This gave me encouragement to go on with these experiments. (p. 68)

After they married, Olga and Ambrose experienced poltergeists in their first apartment. They moved to a new one and attempted further healings. People began seeking aid in large numbers. Olga's paranormal capacities have been tested and verified by various scientific investigators under controlled conditions (Dean and Brame, 1975; Rauscher and Rubik, 1980, 1983).

The Worralls' accounts illustrate the central role that wondrous events played within their socialization process. Both overcame resistance from those around them, perceived themselves as unique because of their anomalous experiences, and felt compelled to heal those seeking aid.

Dean Kraft

Dean Kraft (1981), the product of a middle-class Jewish family, had not been exposed to particularly strong religious beliefs. He was not interested in healing, spiritualism, or the occult. Yet, at the age of twenty-four, he became the center of a strange psychokinetic phenomenon. He and other observers watched as all four electric door locks in a rented car began clicking rapidly up and down in a systematic pattern. He and the passengers devised a code, allowing the phenomenon to answer the questions they asked. Kraft was advised by the messages to use his powers carefully and to help others. He began experiencing clairvoyant and other unusual visions and found he could move objects psychokinetically. He also felt compelled to attempt spiritual healings. His success in healing his father, who had had a chronic, debilitating back condition for more than twenty years, powerfully affected his beliefs. His narrative illustrates the experiential element within the shamanic complex:

> I can still remember the sudden and tremendous feeling of warmth, of oneness, that overwhelmed me. I felt an intense desire to help relieve my father's pain, to give of myself to him. It was an overpowering sense of love. This was my first realization that healing is love, as corny as it sounded, even to me. . . . I began to understand and accept what I had done. For the first time, I considered the possibility of healing as a serious endeavor. Doubts and questions lingered, but my journey into a new way of life had begun. (pp. 18, 21)

As Kraft continued his attempts at healing, many other people reported alleviation of medical problems as a result of his efforts. He sought to have his abilities tested under controlled conditions and produced results that ostensibly exceeded what might be produced through normal means (Kmetz, 1981). He presently works as a professional psychic healer.

Kraft's story again illustrates a progression from anomalous experience to controlled production of anomalous effects. Requests from observers, as well as inner urgings, compelled him to become a psychic practitioner.

Alex Tanous

From the time he was eighteen months old, Alex Tanous engaged in psychometry, the ability to gain paranormal information about an object merely by touching it. At the age of four, he predicted the sickness of a childhood friend. A few days later the playmate fell sick and died soon afterward. At five, he had his first out-of-body experience and was in frequent contact with spirits of the dead. A school teacher remarked to him in an interview, "You'd go off on a walk in the middle of the day, then come back and tell us that something was going to happen—and it would! We didn't know what to make of it" (Tanous, 1976: 12).

Tanous's ability to know in advance that a person would die, to see paranormally events in the past and the future, to locate lost objects, to relay information from the dead, to stop watches paranormally, and to create paranormal photographic and electrical effects led him to become a psychic practitioner. His out-of-body abilities have been investigated by researchers at the American Society for Psychical Research; he activated a strain gauge at the location of his OBE projections during experimental trials (Osis and McCormick, 1980). He also spontaneously provided clairvoyant information about an attempted Presidential assassination during one laboratory session (Osis, 1981).

Chakara C.

Chakara C. was a prosperous, middle-aged Thai chemist working for the Bangkok branch of a multinational oil company. His account indicates that wondrous experiences can affect people with scientific orientations. His narrative portrays features that are universal among psychic practitioner accounts.

While an infant, C. related information about people he claimed were his parents in a former life. Research by his actual parents revealed that this information coincided with existing people and events. They believed he could not have obtained this knowledge through normal means.[1] As he matured, C. sometimes found he "knew" information through means other than his normal senses. Friends and neighbors began to visit him, seeking help, information, and healing.

C. told me that, like most young Thai males, he had served for a time as a Buddhist monk. During that time, a woman asked an older monk's advice about her frequent sleep paralysis experiences. Although she had moved from house to house, trying to escape what she thought was an evil spirit, the problem continued. The monk felt C. had mediumistic abilities and asked him to empty his mind so that the spirit might enter it. When C. attempted to do this, the spirit's voice came from his mouth and he felt a surge of hatred for the woman. The monk demanded that the spirit explain himself. The entity replied that he had been killed by the woman in a previous life and was seeking revenge. After lengthy negotiation, the spirit agreed to forgive the woman, in exchange for the merit he would obtain by her dedication of a worthy deed to him. The monk suggested that the woman buy a Buddhist novice his first monk's robe, a typical method for Thais to acquire merit. After she did this, her sleep paralysis episodes ended.

This was the first of many situations in which C. used his meditative ability to benefit others. As reports spread of his psychic proficiency, people increasingly sought C.'s help. Initially, he was puzzled by his experiences and remained skeptical. During my interview with him, he speculated that the woman's beliefs, in the case just mentioned, may have led to her recovery. He was ambivalent regarding the possibility that spirits exist but was certain that meditation contributes to paranormal effects.

At the time of my visit, he had set aside time in the evening to talk with those seeking assistance. He charged no fee and wished to avoid publicity. He told me that people often asked him about the source of his ability. In response, he has fashioned an ideology fitting his scientific occupation. He believes that meditation is analogous to physical processes. Mental "energy" is typically dispersed by individuals in many directions; by closing off the normal outlets, meditators channel this force. By halting "normal" internal mental activity, an individual increases the probability of receiving communications from outside spiritual entities.

C. perceives himself as deviant in relation to Thai Theravada Buddhist teachings. Theravada Buddhists argue that people are completely responsible for their own physical and spiritual states. The healing of one person by another is impossible. Yet C.'s experiences, and the fame he acquired as a result, led to the evening-time treatments. I hypothesize that all societies have special people like C. who attract clients because of their reputations for producing wondrous events.

Wilasinee W.

Wilasinee W., a Thai shamanic healer in her fifties, was originally a school teacher. On one occasion, she spontaneously envisioned an accident associated with a scheduled school trip. She was so troubled that she did not go on the excursion. Her decision prevented her from being injured in the serious bus accident that followed. This and other precognitive experiences caused W. to perceive herself as having wondrous abilities.

W. began visiting mediums, hoping to understand her special capacities. Although she found that most mediums were fraudulent, some seemed to be authentic. They knew detailed information about her family which they apparently gained paranormally.

Later, she discovered that she could go into a trance herself and that, during this trance, spirits would speak through her. She began a trial-and-error process, testing different methods for treating medical problems. When her own children were sick, she attempted to cure them with the help of the divas (powerful spirits) that spoke through her. The healings were most effective when she touched the afflicted area with her feet.[2]

Stories of her "miracles" spread and local people began asking for help. Initially, she cured ailments such as facial tics, cardiac distress, paralysis, and even gallstones. Eventually, she came to believe that she could cure rheumatism, insomnia, suicidal depression, and even the

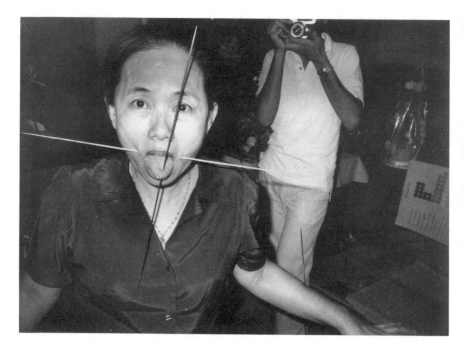

Figure 1. Thai healer Wilasinee W. demonstrates pain immunity (photo by J. McClenon).

early stages of cancer. She also developed the ability to remove curses and to do exorcisms. Afflicted people come from all over Thailand, seeking healing (I noted approximately forty people on each of my visits to her in 1985).

As part of her ceremony, W. performs a ritual devised by her divas. She goes into trance and inserts silver needles through her cheeks, tongue, arm, and hand while delivering a humorous dialogue (see Figure 1). Later, she extinguishes a bundle of burning incense on the palm of her hand. Family members, including her sister and brother-in-law, also demonstrate heat immunity and trance dancing. W. gives a thirty-minute sermon, emphasizing the Buddha's precepts and the reality of heavens, hells, and reincarnation. At the end of the ceremonial performance that follows, which includes various symbolic healing procedures, W. dips her heel in coconut oil and touches it on a red-hot iron plate; she then places her foot on the client's afflicted part. Although I observed no instantaneous healings, many patients claimed that their pains were subsequently alleviated.

This narrative differs from those of the other healers described thus far in that W.'s early socialization contained fewer anomalous incidents. She described no apparitional sightings, psychokinesis, OBEs, or spontaneous contacts with the dead. She reported no medical problems that might be labeled psychosomatic nor other indications of fantasy-proneness. Her choice to leave the teaching profession was based, in part, on financial considerations and the excitement of a new career rather than on a paranormal compulsion or "calling." W. does not merely meditate or pray silently, as did C., Manning, Kraft, Tanous, or the Worralls; she uses elaborate performances to effect cures. The capacity for trance and drama, rather than for spontaneous experience, is central to her life story. My narrative collection suggests that informants with fewer intense spontaneous experiences place greater reliance on rituals in order to perform spiritual healings.

Eleuterio Terte

Many shamanic life stories fit the following pattern: An individual suffers from what Western-style medical doctors might diagnose as a psychosomatic disorder. By following shamanic advice, the sick person becomes well, and, as a result, learns healing techniques. He or she then begins treating others.

Some individuals experience spontaneous healings without the guidance of another practitioner. For example, a Filipino named Eleuterio Terte became a healer in 1925 after two angelic children appeared to him when he was seriously ill.

The two apparitions asked him to accept the healing power which would be given to him and he would be free from his illness. When he accepted his mission, he was cured the next morning, and has since been healing people from all walks of life. (Licauco, 1982: 8)[3]

Valla and Prince (1989) hypothesize that many religious experiences reflect the psyche's healing mechanisms. The anthropological literature regarding shamanism supports their argument. Troubled people can be restored to wholeness through dissociative experiences. Shamanic training in altered states of consciousness entails spiritual healing, allowing the individual to aid others (for Korean examples, see Youngsook, 1978).

K. Higa

K. Higa's life story presents a variation on the "calling-through-wondrous-healing" theme. K., a successful Okinawan business man, suffered from severe illnesses that medical doctors could not alleviate. He became completely disabled, perhaps near death. As a last resort, he attempted intense meditation and successfully cured himself.

Afterward he experimented, using the same method to heal others. His first success was with a woman suffering from a mental disorder. As he discovered successful procedures, his fame spread, and, at the time of my interview, he claimed his healing practice generated more income than did his profitable business.

K. argues that those who consult *yutas*, traditional Okinawan shamanic healers, delude themselves. He believes there is no spirit world or afterlife. His treatments are based on a doctrine that combines physics, chemistry, psychology, and secular elements of Western occult lore. Like the Thai chemist C., he attempts to direct "energy" from his own mind to his client's body. K. suggests that his clients attend weekly lectures regarding his complex pseudoscientific theories. His formal treatments often cause clients to pass into a therapeutic unconscious state. His ideology is vaguely parallel to the eighteenth-century theories of Franz Anton Mesmer. Mesmer hypothesized the existence of "animal magnetism," a force that could be used to cure medical disorders (Podmore, 1965/1909).

Among the life stories I collected, K.'s was the only one lacking spontaneous anomalous episodes. Yet many elements in his narrative are parallel to those of the Okinawan *yutas* he derides. *Yutas* are typically "called" by being cured of a severe illness by another *yuta*. In a parallel fashion, K.'s experience of self-healing caused him to try healing others. Had he been a woman, he probably would have been directed toward becoming an Okinawan shaman, who are generally female.

K.'s account supports the argument that a shamanic complex transcends culture. His self-developed strategies parallel those of other shamans. His belief evolved through the experience of healing himself, through observing the anomalous faintings caused by his treatments, and from noting the success of his methods.

Jesus of Nazareth

We might arrange psychic practitioners on a continuum according to their cultural impact. A stereotypical notion regarding such practitioners is that they are of marginal importance, accepted only in primitive societies or among disadvantaged groups. Although many shamans practice in developing nations, various psychic healers have had widespread influence. People came to Olga Worrall's healing services from all over the world. Wilasinee W. attracts clients from all parts of Thailand.

Other psychic healers have founded significant movements. Franz Anton Mesmer (1734–1815) staged exhibitions of an alternative treatment, later known as mesmerism, which stimulated metaphysical imaginations for decades afterward. His methods evolved into what is today termed *hypnosis*. Mary Baker Eddy, who was spiritually healed in 1862, went on to found Christian Science, one of the five largest religious denominations to emerge in American history (Fuller, 1989). Esoteric cultures have had important and continuing influence on modern society (Tiryakian, 1974).

Jesus of Nazareth has had the most profound impact of all spiritual healers. Belief in his miracles is pervasive in modern Western societies. Indeed, Christian history refutes the assumption that all spiritual healers are of limited importance. Jesus' life essentially established Christian healing traditions which have survived for two millennia (the impact of spiritual healing by medieval Christian saints will be discussed in Chapter 8.)

We may analyze Jesus' life story by examining the wondrous events in the Gospels and related texts. The features within his development as a healer coincide with recurring patterns in the lives of modern psychic practitioners. Biblical scholars have sough to understand the historic Jesus through analysis of ancient Christian, Jewish, and pagan sources. His primary biography has survived in the Gospel of Mark, thought to be the oldest of the existing canonical Gospels. Written about A.D. 75, the Gospel of Mark was used in the eighties or nineties by both Matthew and Luke, who also consulted an early source or sources, now lost (Smith, 1978: 11).

Scholars such as Mitchell (1991) and Smith (1978) interpret religious traditions as reflecting both documented and undocumented events. They argue that Jesus' childhood experiences led him to become a psychic practitioner. Since the virgin birth concept did not exist within his culture, they contend that it arose later as an explanation that would counter accusations regarding his parentage. These critics suggest that Jesus was viewed by his community as illegitimate and that this stigma contributed to his leaving Nazareth, and to his wondrous perceptions and conversations with demons. (One wonders if he was told about his divine conception and, if so, how this affected his personality.)

Some traditions indicate that Jesus' early life was marked by wondrous events. Miracles surrounding his birth are described in the Gospels. Other documents also report miraculous healings, exorcisms, and even malevolent tantrums of the Christ-child. Jesus was said to produce blindness and death in those offending him. The violence of these narrative may have caused them to be rejected by Augustine's bishopric in Hippo in 393 and in Carthage in 397 (Schepps, 1979). Traditional narratives regarding Jesus could be categorized in Thompson's *Motif-Index* V221.0.3, "Miraculous healing power of saint as child."

Modern informants report equivalent experiences. People with high capacities for wondrous experience sometimes perceive that their childish desires for blessing or revenge are fulfilled paranormally. The anthropologist Paul Stoller describes a "curse," that resulted from his own magical practices (Stoller and Olkes, 1987).

In addition, the Gospels portray Jesus' relations with his family and neighbors as somewhat cold (Mark 3:33; John 7:5; Luke 14:26). Family tensions increase the tendency for children with exceptional wondrous capacities to dissociate. Miraculous claims can cause friction; children who acquire reputations as miracle workers stimulate hostile reactions from skeptics who demand proofs of alleged events. But those who adjust to their fame may use their dissociative skills to counsel others.

Evidence in the Gospels suggests that Jesus' biography fits the shamanic pattern. His behavior during his early ministry was so erratic that his friends believed he was possessed. They tried to put him under restraint for his own protection (Mark 3:21). Yet his visions were apparently therapeutic. Following his baptism by John the Baptist, Jesus heard a divine voice call him a "beloved Son" (Matthew 3:17; Mark 1:11; Luke 3:22). The Gospels relate that the spirit he received caused him to wander in the desert, a common shamanic practice (Matthew 4:1–11; Mark 1:12, 13; Luke 4:1–13). His conversations with desert demons suggest a capacity for special psychological states. The troubled Jesus then seemingly healed himself through dissociative experience. He attained a certainty of the existence of spiritual dimensions and later opposed the Sadducees, who denied life after death.

After visionary experiences there, he returned to Galilee where his new spiritual power manifested itself in exorcism, in cures of types familiar in magic, in teaching, with magical parallels and authority, and in the call of disciples, who, like persons enchanted, were constrained to leave their families and belongings and follow him alone.

With these disciples he lived the predictable life of a travelling magician and holy man. . . . The company was supported by his success as exorcist and healer, which increased and was increased by his fame. His fame was such that other magicians began to use his name as that of a god in their exorcisms. (Smith, 1978: 137)

Elements in Jesus' early life, development, and career are consistent with those of the shamanic complex. Childhood difficulties probably contributed to his dissociative capacities which led, thereafter, to his wondrous perceptions. He demonstrated the performance skills required for spiritual healing, but later antagonized religious authorities so much that they had him crucified. This event was followed by apparitional experiences of Jesus that continue to the present (Wiebe [1991] has collected modern accounts).

Analysis

Although some practitioners may have embellished their life stories, this factor does not pose a methodological problem since the narratives reveal cross-culturally consistent patterns. If respondents consider anomalous episodes to be significant, then reports of such incidents have real consequences.

The narratives indicate that psychic practitioners are socialized, in part, through wondrous events. Most report numerous spontaneous psychic episodes in their early lives. An alternate, but not exclusive, pathway involves experiencing an unusual instance of self-healing. Spontaneous wondrous experiences often stimulate a belief in spirits, souls, life after death, and anomalous capacities. These beliefs provide the foundation for most spiritual healing.

Potential practitioners then pass through a transitional stage in which they learn or devise treatment strategies. The potential healers build confidence by observing which methods prove successful. A later stage entails regular use of these methods to generate wondrous experiences in others. The accounts thus indicate that the practitioner's progress is driven by rational analysis. Anomalous experiences provide the certainty required to fulfill the healer's role.

My findings do not dispute the argument that cultural factors influence healing ideologies and methods. Trance behavior, ritual practices, and healing ideologies are shaped by the practitioners' native cultures. Yet commonalities within shamanic experience also reflect universal features of human physiology and psychology.

Persistent experiential features in these narratives have contributed to recurrent motifs in folk literature. Many of the accounts suggest that altered states of consciousness and spiritual possession provide benefits. In many societies, certain individuals are believed to have magical skills (for example, Thompson's *Motif-Index* includes D1817.0.1.6, "Wizard detects thief by trance"; D1810.13, "Magic knowledge from the dead"; D1821.8, "Possession by spirit of dead person gives second sight"; and D2161.5, "Magic cure by certain person.")

This chapter has focused on the spontaneous wondrous events that contribute to psychic practitioners' socialization. Some of these individuals also learned performance skills so that clients would accept them as authentic (Wilasinee W. demonstrated resistance to the effects of pain and heat.) In Chapter 6, I present results from participant observation of similar secondary wondrous events (ESP, psychic surgery, and firewalking). As with primary wondrous experiences, secondary wondrous events also reveal universal features. Although such performances are shaped by culture, secondary wondrous events have elements that affect folk traditions in common directions in societies all over the world.

Chapter 6
Performing Wondrous Events: ESP, Psychic Surgery, and Firewalking

Numerous sociologists distinguish between "illness," the subjective sense people have that they are not well, and "disease," an objective pathology of the body. They note that spiritual healing most successfully deals with illness rather than disease. Its practitioners declare success when a client is psychologically oriented toward well-being (Danforth, 1989; Kleinman, 1980).

I suggest that wondrous performances help alleviate illness by contributing to clients' psychological well-being and that this in turn can create physiological effects that aid in healing disease. My evidence, which is not conclusive, was gained through participant observation of three types of wondrous performances: ESP demonstrations, psychic surgery, and firewalking. My observations indicate that recurring features within wondrous performances (for example, altered states of consciousness, subterfuge, and showmanship) contribute to producing placebo effects which amplify healing.

The Latin word *placebo*, meaning "I shall please," was used in the nineteenth century to describe medicines adapted to please rather than to benefit the patient (Mumford, 1983: 184). Yet investigators have found that placebos can produce real effects, depending on the social and psychological settings of their administration (Wickramasekera, 1988). Both active and inert agents have been found to stimulate placebo effects. Placebos are as effective with educated patients as with uneducated ones.

Some wondrous performances *may* produce paranormal results. Such psychic healings could involve active (paranormal) agents rather than placebos. I have collected many stories from people claiming miraculous cures; likewise, studies have found that some subjects can anomalously affect living organisms under laboratory conditions (Braud, 1990; Grad, 1965; Grad et al., 1961; Rauscher and Rubik,

1980, 1983; Watkins and Watkins, 1971). Benor (1990) and Murphy (1992: 257–283) provide overviews of this literature.

As a field observer, I have no means to determine if an event is paranormal. The effects I saw could be explained as psychosomatic. As Shakespeare noted, "Our remedies oft in ourselves do lie, which we ascribe to heaven." Perhaps because a large proportion of patient complaints have psychosomatic components, spiritual healers' clients tend to be more satisfied with their treatments than those visiting conventional medical practitioners (Glik, 1986). By regarding wondrous performances as placebos, rather than as supernatural events, we can better study their effects on belief and health.

Placebo effects have been conceptualized as resulting from social influence, self-fulfilling prophecy, and conditioned response. They occur across a wide range of treatment modalities (drugs, surgery, psychotherapies, biofeedback) and in relation to many physical and mental symptoms (pain, anxiety, edema, tachycardia, emesis, fever, vasoconstriction, phobias, depressions [Wickramasekera, 1988: 99]). Although the results of hypnotic suggestions differ from placebo effects, the limitations of my data prevent me from making clear distinctions between these influences within field settings.[1]

A growing body of evidence indicates that emotions, attitudes, and beliefs are related to chemical responses in the brain (Mumford, 1983). Faith, persuasion, and imagery, it is argued, can therefore affect health (Frank, 1973; Kiev, 1964; Weatherhead, 1953). What is "in the head" influences what happens "in the body." Optimism, for example, can be considered biologically adaptive, while adversity, pessimism, and feelings of helplessness can contribute to illness (Seligman, 1991; Tiger, 1979).

From a traditional medical perspective, it appears that viewing wondrous performances can also influence brain chemistry, causing healing rates to increase. The question of whether such events are equivalent to "active" agents need not be resolved, since both active and inert agents produce placebo effects.

There is a plausible chain of events that starts with bad life events and ends up in poor health. The chain begins with a particular set of bad events—loss, failure, defeat—those events that make you feel helpless. As we have seen, everyone reacts to such events with at least momentary helplessness, and people with a pessimistic explanatory style become depressed. Depression produces catecholamine depletion and increases in endorphin secretion. Endorphin increases can lower the activity of the immune system. The body is at all times exposed to pathogens—agents of disease—normally held in check by the immune system. When the immune system is partly shut down by the catecholamine-endorphin link, these pathogens can go wild. Disease, sometimes life-threatening, becomes more likely. Each link of the loss-pessimism-depression-catecholamine depletion-endorphin secretion depletion-immune suppression-disease chain is testable, and for each we already have evidence of its operation. (Seligman, 1991: 182)

The notion of what constitutes a psychosomatic disorder is made complex by the relationship between mental and physiological states. Medical problems often trigger psychological stress, a condition that can reduce the body's capacity to respond. At the same time, psychological dilemmas can contribute to the development of disease. Psychological and physiological conditions are, in all likelihood, intertwined; placebo effects consequently contribute to alleviating a variety of pathological conditions.

Wondrous performances may contribute to health by alleviating feelings of helplessness and stimulating optimism; spiritual healing typically entails a reformulation of attitudes. By manipulating symbols, psychic practitioners replace their clients' images of illness with models of health (Kleinman, 1980). One method adopted by such healers entails inducing altered states of consciousness in their clients and then instilling therapeutic conceptions of the future (Achterberg, 1985).

Wondrous performances thus stimulate belief and provide placebos for healing. Long (1977) located almost one hundred descriptions of psychic phenomena in the literature, most of them secondary wondrous events. Eisenberg (1985), Stoller (1989), Turner (1992), and Winkelman (1982) provide additional accounts and references. The phenomena involved demonstrations of ESP, psychokinesis, apparitions, feats of strength, weather control, unusual creative abilities, protection from the cutting action of blades, and immunity to pain, heat, cold, and poison.

Wondrous performances often have striking impacts on their observers' beliefs. Wilasinee W., described in the previous chapter, convinced clients that she had paranormal mental powers. She pierced her body apparently without feeling pain and touched her foot to a red-hot iron plate without burning it. Dr. Jamal N. Hussein, of Paramann Programme Laboratories in Jordan, provides photographs of similar performances (see Figures 2–4). Sufi dervishes of Tariqa Casnazaniyyah seek to demonstrate the validity of their faith by piercing their bodies (Figure 2), placing hot coals in their mouths (Figure 3), and allowing poisonous snakes to bite their tongues (Figure 4).[2] Such exhibitions coincide with *Motif-Index* classifications D1766.1.4, "Pain stopped by prayer," D1841.3.2, "Fire does not injure a saint," and D1840.1.2, "saint invulnerable to poison."

The connection between secondary wondrous events (performances) and tertiary events (typically spiritual healing) can be explained within

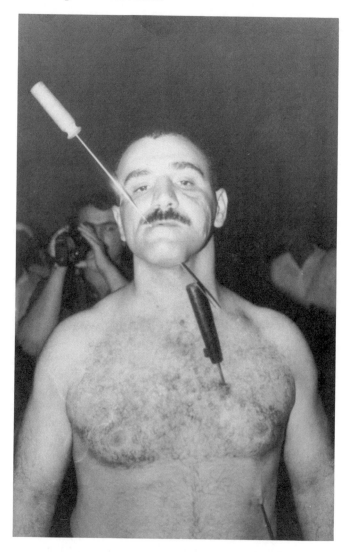

Figure 2. Sufi dervish of Tariqa Casnazaniyyah demonstrates
pain immunity (photo courtesy of Jamal N. Hussein).

various paradigms. My analysis is based on the assumption that mind-
body interactions, related to either inferred hypnotic suggestions or
placebos, can link wondrous performance with spiritual healing. The
hypothesis that many wondrous events have physiological components
does not preclude other explanations. Religious people often pre-

Figure 3. Dervish demonstrates resistance to effects of heat (photo courtesy of Jamal N. Hussein).

sume that psychic phenomena are produced by supernatural forces and that such episodes verify their own beliefs or the power of certain individuals.

Philosophically, anomalous events do not confirm one religion as better than another. As early as 1764, Rousseau (1972) argued that

Figure 4. Dervish demonstrates resistance to poisonous snake bite (photo courtesy of Jamal N. Hussein).

miracles were inadequate proof for Christian beliefs. He reasoned that miracles, defined as exceptions to nature, cannot be established. First, he argued, no one knows all the natural laws; therefore no one can determine which events constitute reversals of them. Today's miracle may tomorrow be explained scientifically as a natural event. Second,

Rousseau pointed out, we cannot separate delusions from actual miracles because we cannot be certain of the basis of any particular wondrous account. Third, Rousseau argued, Jesus discouraged people from seeking miraculous proofs and hesitated, at times, to reveal his miraculous abilities.[3]

Folk religious systems do not employ Rousseau's arguments. Believers continue to make use of wondrous performances to increase their belief and to effect cures. Rather than struggling with skepticism, religious healing systems often compete against each other. Folk traditions even describe magic contests (D1719.1) in which spiritual practitioners duel to determine which religion is better (V351). Performers who stimulate greater wonderment and effect more cures are deemed victorious. Those with greater "magic healing power" (D2161) attract their opponent's followers. (Chapter 8 describes Christian and Buddhist wondrous performances used to convert people from other faiths.)

To serve as placebos, wondrous performances must include either direct or inferred therapeutic suggestions. This process typically entails more than merely uttering a simple hypnotic command. Traditional wondrous performances take place within a symbol-laden environment. They have been shaped over time to reflect the needs and expectations of the audiences that benefit from them.

Schechner (1985) discusses the transforming quality of ritual performances and the way that performances can be transformed through enactment. His formulations are valuable for my analysis of wondrous events. An anomalous incident may be described verbally, creating a story. The tale may be transcribed and then delivered orally, becoming a literary performance. These alternate forms reflect the original event, yet differ from it. Each permutation transforms its audience, supports their belief, and contributes to further wondrous experiences. For example, the New Testament was transcribed, edited, copied, translated, and distributed over many centuries. It furnishes the basis for literary performances. Although interpretations of the New Testament are culturally shaped, some readers report that reading it can cause miraculous transformations. For example, an Okinawan Protestant minister, described in Chapter 7, reported a personal healing associated with reading the Bible.

Modern wondrous performances have similar effects. People perceive wondrous events; they experience healings; and they then tell others of their perceptions. Stories of wondrous events become oral performances that, afterward, attract new audiences. Folk religious traditions are shaped, in part, through this process. These traditions reveal universal features as a result of the recurring elements in wondrous performances.

To illustrate the patterns within secondary wondrous events, I will discuss three performance forms:

1. *Psychic phenomena*. Practitioners seemingly demonstrate extrasensory and psychokinetic abilities. They often couple belief in supernatural forces with trance performances.
2. *Deception*. Shamanic healers often simulate paranormal events (Hansen, 1992). I discuss psychic surgery as an example. Even practitioners who engage in subterfuge, however, present biographies that fit the shamanic complex and can trigger psychosomatic healings with their performances.
3. *Physiological feats*. Some practitioners demonstrate unusual physiological skills; these include demonstrations of strength, perceptive capacities, artistic or mental abilities, and immunity to pain, heat, cold, poison, and the cutting action of blades. I describe firewalking, using an experience-centered approach.

The "psychic," "deception," and "physiological" classifications just described are merely categories of convenience rather than rigid demarcations. Consider the following narrative, given by a Protestant minister:

I'm in the church service and you come in. Now I never laid eyes on you before. You don't know me. You never talked with me. I'm preaching, Holy Spirit preaching. But I'm gonna stop and tell you your thoughts in your mind. Hey, it's to let you know that somebody knows your prayers, what you've been praying for, asking God in your secret closet. Make you believe something, don't it? And you might have a bad knee, an infected eardrum, or whatever. Doctor say you need an operation. Maybe God say it's not time for your deliverance. Or maybe I shout, "Well, that knee's gonna heal tonight!" People get up, hollering, and screaming. . . . Then you walk up and God makes a miracle and you're healed just like that, but it's not the man, never the man [that deserves] the glory, always God. . . . I learned a long time ago, it's not the man. But people get healed!

This performance might be diagrammed within a traditional medical paradigm. In this schemata, the healing takes place through a symbolic conversation between practitioner and client, illustrating the placebo effect:

Healee: I believe in Jesus but my mind has not released the chemicals required for my inflamed knee to heal.

Preacher: While in an altered state of consciousness, I will utter the thoughts that come into my mind. These correspond with your prayers. I attribute this ability to God and reason as follows: If God can reveal to me your thoughts, then he can heal your knee. I'll give a suggestion that your knee will heal.

Healee: Your ability to know my thoughts causes me to wonder. I allow myself to get caught up in the emotional atmosphere and respond to your suggestion. I perceive that my knee heals spontaneously.

Preacher and Healee: We will tell this story to others, attribute the healing to God, and create a foundation for future wondrous performances.

Although the minister quoted above claimed his performance was a psychic feat produced by God, we cannot be certain that he gained his knowledge paranormally. If he had agents secretly supply him with information about his audience, his demonstration would have been based on deception. If he were highly observant, he might have noticed cues that revealed his participants' psychological and physical concerns. The preacher's statements regarding audience members may be broad enough to fit a variety of clients, making correspondences coincidental rather than extrasensory. The preacher, in trance, may have been unaware of his method.

Many of the elements that comprise a wondrous performance are socially constructed. Performers and their audiences tend to ignore ambiguities. They make performances work by becoming caught up in wonderment. Although skeptics are rarely convinced by descriptions of wondrous performances, such events function as placebos for believers. Some performances work on such a subconscious level that even self-professed nonbelievers are sometimes healed.

Various folk traditions have arisen from the patterns within wondrous performances. For example, the preacher's narrative couples *Motif-Index* classification V223.3, "Saints can perceive the thoughts of another man and reveal hidden sins," with D2161, "Magic healing power." In the following, I attempt to portray the way that audiences, including myself, have been changed by such linkages. Through participant observation, we can gain a greater understanding of the universal features contributing to spiritual healing.

Extrasensory Perception

One motif within folk literature is "magic knowledge of another's thoughts" (D1819.1). This tradition has experiential roots which I previously discussed in the example of the preacher knowing his parishioners' secret prayers and using this ability to heal them.

In order to better understand ESP performance, I conducted a remote viewing experiment with Professor Ray Hyman of the University of Oregon (McClenon and Hyman, 1987, 1989). Remote viewing requires a subject to "view" psychically the site that another person, termed the "agent," is visiting. The researcher records the subject's description of mental images and impressions while the agent is at the site. The degree of correspondence between the subject's narrative and the target image is evaluated statistically by having judges rank order a set of possible target sites by their similarity to the subject's narrative. The remote viewing procedure has been found by some parapsychologists to be particularly successful for producing ESP effects (Duanne and Bisaha, 1979; Hansen, Schlitz, and Tart, 1984; Schlitz and Gruber, 1980; Targ and Puthoff, 1977).

Overall, the subjects' data from our eight trials did not produce statistically significant results. At the time of this experiment, I was not aware of the need to select subjects on the basis of their meditative ability or frequency of anomalous experience (subjects were student volunteers.)

Yet one aspect of the experiment, which had nothing to do with the subjects, produced interesting results. I acted as the agent in all of the trials. Photographs of the possible targets had been numbered (1–8) for each day. Prior to each session and acting on my own, I attempted to visualize the number corresponding to the day's target. Each day, I wrote down the number that popped into my mind while I meditated. Afterward, I picked up the randomly selected target number from a supervisor at the University of Oregon computer center and evaluated my forecast. At the end of the series, the overall probability of my guessing these numbers as accurately as I did was 12 out of 1,000. Statistician refer to this result as *statistically significant*, since it would occur by chance less than once out of every twenty times ($p < .05$).

In our analysis of this experiment, Ray Hyman and I correctly concluded that, since my experiment was not part of the planned procedure, my results do not provide formal evidence for the existence of ESP. Yet this episode shares elements with the preacher's ESP performance described above. People sometimes experience astonishing correspondences between their thoughts and information they (seemingly) could not have gained through normal means.

My experience affected my beliefs. I know that I did not cheat. The experimental conditions precluded my gaining the numbers through sensory cuing. Yet I perceived correct numbers coming into my mind. Were I to find that I was never able to gain similar experiences, I would regard these results as coincidental. Yet within other, similarly controlled experimental sessions conducted at parapsychological laboratories, I again perceived accurate information through similar means.

Overall, remote viewing experiments have attained statistical significance relatively frequently. Hansen, Schlitz, and Tart (1984) compiled all available reports of remote viewing experiments conducted between 1973 and 1982. They note that "more than half (15 out of 28) of the published formal experiments have been successful, where only one in twenty would be expected by chance" (p. 265). Honorton and Ferrari (1989) analyzed 309 precognition studies reported by sixty-two investigators who together conducted nearly two million individual trials by more than 50,000 subjects. Meta-analysis reveals an overall level of statistical significance of $p = 6.3 \times 10^{-25}$. Thirty percent of the studies were significant at the 5 percent significance level.

Parapsychologists have conducted laboratory experiments investigating the relation between altered mental states and ESP. Some conclude that restricting or reducing sensory input increases the potential for receiving extrasensory information (Braud, 1974, 1975; Honorton, 1977). This finding has led to skeptical attacks (Hyman, 1985), researcher response (Honorton, 1985), consultations between skeptics and believers (Hyman and Honorton, 1986), and further replications by parapsychologists (Honorton et al., 1990; Schlitz and Honorton, 1992). From a social science perspective, I have noted that those who perform such experiments tend to increase their belief in ESP.

In a parallel vein, many psychic practitioners find that the information that comes into their minds during a trance state is sometimes valid. They do not reject their experiences as false merely because others cannot duplicate their feats. They assume that those who fail at paranormal tasks lack extrasensory ability or a suitable environment. As Honorton and Ferrari (1989) note, specific people and procedures are more successful than others.

Commonalities exist in a broad range of folk accounts regarding psychic capacities. Indian yogis, Chinese Taoists, and mystics from many traditions "still" their minds and slow their bodily functions. Early texts describe their procedures. For example, the ancient Indian Patanjali transcribed the oral traditions of yoga, noting that practice leads to the development of psychic powers, called *siddhis* (Prabhavananda and Isherwood, 1953). These include ESP, clairvoyance, and the ability to leave one's body. Since many ancient practitioners experienced similar events, they concluded that meditation and other altered states of consciousness were means for discovering the nature of spiritual realms and for gaining paranormal skills. Some individuals were thought to have innate capacities to perform extrasensory feats, while others gained such abilities through mental exercise (*Motif-Index*: D1737, "Magic power inherited," and D1733.3, "Magic power through ascetic practices").

Many people who meditate regularly report perceiving information through extrasensory means. Most teachers of meditation are familiar with such reports. Famous meditation masters have the reputation for knowing the thoughts of others. They sometimes reveal this knowledge during counseling sessions by answering questions before they are asked. As with the Protestant preacher mentioned previously, their demonstrations can trigger spiritual healing.

One parapsychological theory is that extrasensory information is like a signal lost in the noise of normal human consciousness. If a person reduces this noise—through sensory restriction, for example—the signal is received more clearly (Honorton, 1977). In this instance, the findings of meditators such as Patanjali coincide with those verified experimentally by parapsychologists. Although skeptics are correct in arguing that there is a tendency for believers to focus on observations that reinforce their beliefs (Marks and Kammann, 1980), meditators from many societies, over the course of thousands of years, have reached common conclusions regarding ESP and mental states.

Recognizing ESP as a performance method allows for a better understanding of religious history. For example, Smith (1978: 115) notes:

[T]he belief that Jesus knew the minds of people he met may be founded on fact. Some people are uncannily (or cannily?) able to read the minds of others. To those who do not have the gift it looks like magic. (Calling it "mental telepathy," "extrasensory perception," or "divine omniscience" adds little to our ignorance.) This gift is almost necessary for a successful magician; therefore most of them must have had it, as the gospels say Jesus did.

Although I cannot test hypotheses regarding past events, I predict that future occult practitioners will perform (or believe that they have performed) similar extrasensory feats.

Some parapsychologists believe that ESP is linked with creative subconscious skills. ESP performances are similar to artistic creations in that both artists and performers appear to retrieve material from their unconscious minds. Researchers have found the belief in ESP, and the incidence of ESP experience, to be related to creativity (Davis, Peterson, and Farley, 1974; Moon, 1975; Murphy, 1963, 1966; Schlitz and Honorton, 1992). Unconscious processes seem more conducive to extrasensory faculties than conscious means. Spontaneous ESP experiences, occurring during altered states of consciousness such as sleep and the hypnogogic state, tend to convey more information than episodes occurring during normal consciousness (Virtanen, 1990).

The trance state may also facilitate counseling. Many practitioners show greater intelligence in trance than during normal consciousness. Although none of the shamanic ESP performances I observed were clearly paranormal, many practitioners demonstrated skill in dealing with audience concerns. Successful ESP performances grant a practitioner's therapeutic suggestions greater weight.

Psychic Surgery, a Sleight-of-Hand Performance

Licauco (1981: 4) defines psychic surgery as "painless, barehanded, surgery-like interventions into the human body, the removal of diseased tissues or tumors or growths and the closing of the incision leaving hardly any trace of the operation at all." Psychic surgery is practiced mainly by the Union Espiritista Cristiana de Filipinas (Christian Spiritists Union of the Philippines), concentrated in Pangasinan Province, north of Manila. Although many foreigners visit psychic surgeons, most Filipino people are unaware of this relatively small sect. Numerous alternate types of Filipino psychic practitioners also exist.

Many observers have expressed certainty that psychic surgeries are genuine (Lava and Araneta, 1982; Licauco, 1978, 1981, 1982). Licauco (1981) furnishes accounts of observers inserting their hands into the patient's incision, proving to themselves that the opening is authentic. They then perceive the opening to close magically. While in the Philippines, I heard similar reports. Various Western writers have suggested that some of these events defy scientific explanation (Krippner and Villoldo, 1976; Meek, 1977; Sherman, 1967; Stelter, 1976; Valentine, 1975).

At the same time, Filipino psychic surgeons have been exposed as fraudulent on many occasions (Hansen, 1990; McClenon, 1985). Perhaps the first debunking was produced by Joe Pyne in 1967 (Rogo, 1976). The surgeon/writer W. Nolen (1974) described many fraudulent practices. Magicians James Randi (1987) and David Hoy (1981; see also Meek, 1977: 107–110) have duplicated psychic surgeons' feats through sleight-of-hand. They conceal small bags filled with red liquid in their hands, or within false thumbs, and secretly break them at the proper moment to create the appearance of blood; they dexterously bend the joints of their fingers, making them appear to penetrate the fleshy parts of their patients' bodies. These demonstrations appear much like the Filipino psychic surgeries I witnessed.

Some Filipino psychic surgeons remove minor tumors after making true incisions. I suspect in these cases that they conceal small blades in their fingers, giving the appearance that they use only their bare hands. Such "real" operations are rare, and, in this respect, Filipino psychic surgeries differ from those in Brazil, where incisions are made without anesthesia using unconcealed instruments.

Anthropologist Philip Singer has produced a videotape documenting the methods of Filipino psychic surgeon Phillip Malicdon (Schlitz,

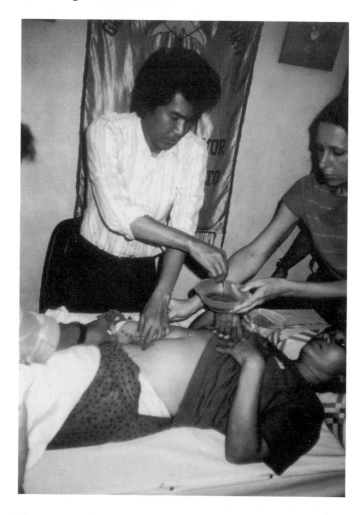

Figure 5. Psychic surgeon performs operation in Manila (photo by J. McClenon).

1991). Although Malicdon agreed to perform psychic surgery, causing human body substances to materialize paranormally under controlled conditions, he and his wife purposely violated the experimental protocol and were caught engaging in suspicious behaviors by video cameras that recorded their actions.

During December 1982, I observed and interviewed more than a dozen Filipino psychic surgeons. I returned later for two months in 1983 and five months in 1984 and 1985. I watched more than one

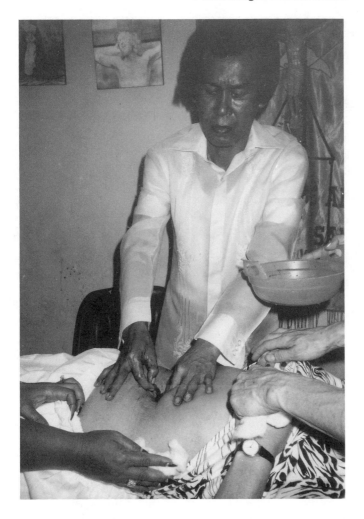

Figure 6. Another demonstration of Filipino psychic surgery (photo by J. McClenon).

thousand psychic operations (Figures 5 and 6) and interviewed many of the psychic surgeons' clients. I even had an "operation" on myself (Alex Orbito offered this "treatment" after I told him I felt tired.) I suffered no ill effects (see Figure 7). Although some investigators, such as Licauco (who has witnessed far more performances than I), are convinced that some psychic surgeries are authentic, my observations lead me to assume that most are done through sleight-of-hand.

Although the movements of these practitioners are, in my experi-

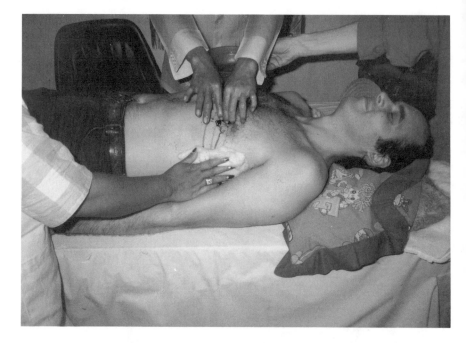

Figure 7. Alex Orbito performs psychic surgery on the author (photo provided by J. McClenon).

ence, generally more fluid and "natural" than those of magician James Randi, their motions always allowed for the possibility of concealing material in their hands which could then be "materialized" as if it were extracted from patients' bodies. Sometimes their hands would brush towels that had been strategically placed over the client's body, a motion that would allow them to "load up" their fingers with fresh organic material (probably small pieces of raw chicken). Their fingers then appeared to intrude into the clients' "incisions" in a manner that could be duplicated by bending the joints. "Surgeries" on the stomachs of obese people were particularly dramatic. The surgeon could make his or her entire hand disappear into the "incision" (actually a pool of red liquid surrounded by flesh) by bending his or her wrist and concealing the hand from the observers' line of sight. Western magicians are often amazed by the dexterity demonstrated in many of these exhibitions (see for example, Hoy, quoted in Meek, 1977: 107–110).

Sleight-of-hand magic is a part of the healer's art throughout the Philippines. For example, on Siquijor Island I observed a practitioner treat an anthropologist's infected thumb by blowing through a bamboo

Figure 8. Filipino spiritual healer treats an infected thumb (photo by J. McClenon).

tube into a glass of water held by the patient (Figure 8). The water magically clouded, and a bone with a cross carved on it "materialized" in the glass. The bone's appearance symbolized the removal of the infection. When the healer blew through the tube again, the water magically cleared, indicating that the "evil" from the infection had been removed. The practitioner received only one peso for providing this treatment.

The history of psychic surgery reflects the impact of Western medicine. With modernization, Filipino psychic practitioners became more aware of Western surgical procedures and adopted methods that imitated its appearance. In the 1950s, foreigners "discovered" Eleuterio Terte, a healer who appeared to do surgeries with his bare hands. Sherman's book, *Wonder Healers of the Philippines* (1967), contributed to popularizing the phenomenon, attracting both writers and wealthy clients. During the 1970s, healers such as Antonio Agpaoa, Jun Labo, and Alex Orbito earned huge sums from grateful foreigners. Today Alex Orbito regularly visits the United States and, although he has encountered legal difficulties, he locates many clients willing to pay hundreds of dollars for brief operations. The poverty that exists in the

Philippines, the tradition of sleight-of-hand performance there, and the willingness of tourists to pay huge sums for psychic surgeries virtually guarantee that hoaxes will occur.

Psychic surgeries can be viewed as psychosomatic treatments in which anomalous images trigger therapeutic, sometimes physiological, effects. Dramatic scenes of blood and organic material reorient the client's outlook to such a degree that medical improvements may result. In my inquiries, I found it easy to locate people who claimed to have been healed. Some declared they had been cured of extremely grave illnesses, such as cancer. Although various respondents asserted that their disease had been closely monitored by Western physicians and that their recovery was clearly paranormal, most success stories involved disorders that probably had psychosomatic components. I did not attempt to verify these claims.

Many practitioners gave special attention to the attitudes and orientations of their clients' families. The patient and his or her relatives were "treated" by exposure to an environment rich in images and emotionality. Observers and clients left with recollections of red, streaming blood and open wounds, coupled with an intensely sacred atmosphere in which the "problem" was removed. Family members were encouraged to photograph and video tape operations, preserving images that reinforced the original effect.

Yet psychic surgery is often ineffective, providing no benefit at all. Meek (1977: 66) notes that within some tour groups of afflicted people "not even one patient considered his trip was worthwhile." In the cases I monitored, psychic surgery treatments produced no immediate results, merely feelings of excitement and expectation. I would expect these emotions to be therapeutic over time. I contacted various American and Canadian psychic surgery patients after they returned to their homes. A few claimed that their medical problems were "cured." For example, one woman who had suffered from bladder control difficulties had no current problems. Others found that their medical condition continued to deteriorate. Most typically, clients evaluated their experiences as positive, though their physical problems were not alleviated. One man, who had cancer, died within the year.

The life stories of psychic surgeons illustrate elements common to the shamanic complex. Most claimed to have encountered a spiritual entity who assisted them in developing as a trance medium. Healings and other wondrous events occurred as a part of this process. The healer then eventually gained the ability to perform psychic surgeries.

Alex Orbito's biography is typical (Licauco, 1978, 1981). After dropping out of high school, Orbito had recurrent dreams of healing people with a Bible in one hand. Alternate dreams involved a wise old hermit in a white garment who became his spirit guide. The hermit gave him a secret word that allowed him to pass into a trance state almost at will.

A neighbor's mother, who lived some distance away and had been paralyzed for ten years, had a vivid dream in which Orbito healed her. The neighbor asked Orbito to visit the woman. When he complied, she was healed, and this event caused his fame to spread rapidly throughout the province. Because psychic healers receive little compensation within the Spiritist community, Orbito worked at various menial jobs under an assumed name, seeking to avoid his notoriety. While working as a photographer's assistant, he was accused of stealing equipment and was jailed as a suspect. As he languished in his cell, voices in his head redirected him to the profession of healing. After the true thief confessed, Orbito was released, but he still avoided the healer's role. He became seriously sick, however, and again experienced voices ordering him to begin his mission. When he returned home and followed the directives of the voices, his sickness abated. Before long, his psychic surgeries attracted many clients. His fame spread throughout the Philippines and, later, the world. He has performed healing services in the United States, Europe, Australia, New Zealand, Nigeria, and Saudi Arabia, accumulating great wealth.

Although elements in this account may be fabricated, it reveals themes common to the shamanic complex. Orbito's progression toward the role of psychic surgeon was similar to those of the practitioners described in Chapter 5. Spirit guides, the "calling," spiritual sickness and healing, and spontaneous psychic experiences are typically part of the psychic practitioner's development process.

I frequently visited Orbito's clinic, which is adjacent to his house in Quezon City (north of Manila). His weekend public healings attracted dozens of clients, their family members, and spectators. Before Orbito's psychic surgeries began, assistants preached sermons and offered prayers. The preachers reminded the audience that Jesus never stated, "I am healing you." They argued that people healed themselves by their own faith. Their emphasis on this point led me to suspect that they were aware of Orbito's deceptive methods. If fraudulent, his performances require conspirators.

The healing operations are performed on a table covered by a white sheet. Orbito maintains an intense air of sanctity, visibly going into trance before the surgeries begin. Each operation requires only a few minutes. Orbito asks the client for a diagnosis, explains his own interpretation of the problem, and then quickly gropes about with both hands, creating a slight popping sound as blood gushes forth. He extracts pieces of organic material as he pokes his fingers into the apparent incision. After wiping the area with a swab of cotton, the "incision" disappears.

He washes his hands after each operation and wipes them with a fresh cloth. This would allow him to load his hands with new packets of liquid "blood" and animal parts to extract from his next client. His movements, although appearing spontaneous, prevent viewers from seeing hidden aspects of the performance.

On one occasion, I waited behind Orbito's house because the operations were delayed. I saw a man deliver a plate of meat scraps, probably poultry. I assume kitchen personnel prepared the "surgery materials" by folding them into Orbito's towels. The operations began after an appropriate interval.

Orbito's persona has been shaped by his capacity to reach deeply altered mental states. He often acts as if he were in a trance even during his everyday life, contributing to the "sanctified" atmosphere surrounding him. I believe that he would pass a lie detector test on the subject of his honesty.

The coupling of trance with fraud is a common feature of shamanic performances. In her autobiography, psychic surgeon Josephina Escandor-Sisson (1987) described numerous demanding pilgrimages during which she perceived many mystical and psychic events. In one vision, a saint granted her special abilities to perform "mind cleaning" operations. This procedure has become part of her standard healing practice. With the saint's aid, she makes pieces of cotton disappear into her clients' ears. She then removes the cotton from the other ear. Although clients claim benefits from these performances, I have often noticed the "vanished" cotton wadded up between her fingers while she pulls a new piece from the other ear.

The fantastic quality of the psychic surgeons' biographical narratives suggests fantasy-proneness and dissociative abilities. They simply block out perceptions or activities that contradict their beliefs. They appear to be in trance, gracefully perform fraud, and in the process they reveal no guilt. Of those I interviewed, all denied engaging in any form of deception.

By attending remote spiritist churches less frequently visited by tourists, I gained a greater understanding of the process by which Spiritists become psychic surgeons. Rural practitioners often described spontaneous experiences equivalent to those of their more famous peers. For example, the rural healer David O. became sick at the age of eighteen. After medical doctors could not help him, he was forced to rely on his childhood faith and the guidance he received in his dreams. At night, he experienced trances in which he found himself fully awake and levitating. Sometimes he saw bright lights in his room and heard voices instructing him to preach the word of God and to lay his hands on the sick. He was puzzled by his experiences until his wife, too, began to see the lights. She assured him they were real.

O. followed a common shamanic pattern. As is common in these life stories, his medical problems disappeared when he became a healer. The validity of his experiences was further confirmed when he found that people were healed by his treatments. He too claimed to have performed psychic surgeries, but these sporadic episodes occurred while he was in trance, making their ontological status unclear.

O. supports himself through farming and does not wish to become an urban spiritual healer because, he says, there is "too much temptation." His most common form of therapy, performed at the chapel by his house, involves casting out demons while the person seeking aid is in trance.

Members of small rural churches often perform symbolic psychic surgeries. In trance states, they wave their hands about the church members as if pulling out disease without resorting to sleight-of-hand procedures. No incision or blood appears. Practitioners, who are in trance, may perceive that real operations are occurring and clients sometimes report astonishing benefits, reinforcing the potential practitioner's visionary perceptions. In some cases, clients and practitioners may simultaneously perceive apparitional images of incisions. Anomalous physical effects can result from this conjunction (some of Krippner and Villoldo's [1976] narratives support this argument). However, in order to create consistently powerful images for clients, the practitioner must learn sleight-of-hand techniques.

Psychic surgery has a sinister face. Practitioners sometimes exploit dying wealthy patients, receiving large amounts of money while providing few benefits. Although such dishonesty is morally repulsive, I know of no psychic surgeon who has ever expressed remorse. The dissociation in evidence during such performances may protect performers from experiencing guilt.

Firewalking, a Physiological Feat

Firewalking entails traversing a bed of hot coals without injury. Although firewalking has been explained within various paradigms, it is most typically labeled by scientists as a physiological feat. When observers regard it as anomalous, however, it becomes a wondrous event.

Heat immunity demonstrations have affected folk traditions. Examples from Thompson's *Motif-Index* include D1382, "Magic object protects against cold or burning"; D1733.1, "Magic power by jumping into fire"; D1841.3, "Burning magically evaded"; D1841.3.2, "Fire does not injure saint"; D1841.3.2.2, "Saint walks through glowing coals without harm"; D1841.3.2.3, "Red hot iron carried with bare hands without harm to saint"; D2158, "Magic control of fires"; H221, "Ordeal by fire"; H221.1.1, "Test of sanctity: carry of live coals in a robe or a cloak without harm to the garment or injury to the bearer"; H331.1.5, "Suitor contest: riding through fire"; H412.4, "Chastity ordeal: passing through fire"; J2411.6, "Imitation of jumping into fire without injury; dupe burned up"; V21.2, "Woman confesses murder: unharmed by execution fire"; V222.8, "Holy man passes through fire for his faith."

Many heat immunity reports seem to defy attribution to normal causes. Saint Catherine of Siena was observed to have lain in a fire while in an ecstatic trance without even her clothes being burned. Eight witnesses report seeing Saint Francis of Paula enter a blazing furnace and return unharmed (Fodor, 1974: 138–140, provides many other examples). Daniel Dunglas Home (1833–1886), whose paranormal performances are discussed in Chapter 10, held burning coals in his hands and was able to grant this immunity to others (Coe, 1958; Fodor, 1974: 139). Gaddis (1967) cites reports of people transferring heat immunity to others and to shoes, socks, and clothing. Various observers note that some heat immunity feats defy physiological explanation (Gaddis, 1967; Inglis, 1986; Karger, cited by Doherty, 1982; Rogo, 1982a). (For bibliographies of firewalking accounts, see Truzzi [1983] and Vilenskaya and Steffy [1991]).

Scientific studies of firewalking provide various theories. H. Price (1936, 1937) concluded that nonblistering was a matter of low thermal conductivity and brief time of contact between foot and coal bed. Coe (1958) and Walker (1977) argued that heat immunity could be explained by the Leidenfrost effect, that is, the propensity for water droplets to dance around on a vapor cushion while on a hot skillet, thereby surpassing the normal longevity of liquid at high temperature. Coe held red-hot iron bars in his bare hands, refuting the "low thermal conductivity" hypothesis advocated by Price. Later, after he discovered that his heat immunity feats involved trance, Coe (1978) came to believe that the Leidenfrost explanation was inadequate. Apparently unfamiliar with Coe's and other's demonstrations, various skeptical scientists argued that physical theories were satisfactory (Frazier, 1985; Leikind and McCarthy, 1985; McCarthy and Leikind, 1986).

Anthropologists have provided explanations that fit my observations (I have not witnessed the more astonishing feats). Kane (1982) proposed that many heat immunity feats are associated with hypnotic suggestions. Inferred suggestions cause the body to mobilize peripheral vasoconstriction in the area exposed to high temperatures. This prevents blisters from forming, even though the cells have been exposed to high temperatures. Studies conducted by Ullman (1947) and Chapman et al. (1959) support the argument that hypnotic suggestion can repress inflammatory response.

Danforth (1989), in his ethnography of the firewalking Anasternaria of Greece, links firewalking with spiritual healing. The Anasternaria reveal elements common to the shamanic complex; many suffer from medical disorders that are resolved when they join the firewalking group.

I firewalked more than a dozen times as part of my participant observation of this phenomenon. My first firewalk was with the Buddhists of the Shingon sect at Mount Takao, Japan, in March 1983. Shingon firewalking rituals are thought to contribute to world peace, to sustain the health of those walking over the coals, and to reduce the number of automobile accidents in the prefecture during the coming year. The firewalk I attended was preceded by a dramatic ceremony that involved colorful costumes, lengthy chanting, and shooting arrows to drive away evil spirits. *Nadegi* (literally, "rubbing boards") are pieces of wood that the Buddhists rub against infirm parts of their bodies before the ceremony. During the ceremony the *nadegi* were thrown on the fire. After the fire burned down, the priests walked across the coal bed. Lay people were then allowed to follow (Figure 9 shows a firewalk in 1984). The symbolic dynamics were straightforward: people walked over the hot coals, demonstrating victory over their infirmities.

I joined the lay people waiting to cross the coal bed. The first firewalkers had trampled out a pathway, and it appeared that I could walk on the ashes without stepping on burning coals. As I waited behind an old woman, a priest raked out the coals and this pathway disappeared. I followed her as she walked at a terrifyingly slow pace. I felt a wave of excitement. I knew I was stepping on red-hot coals, yet walking safely! After completing the walk, I found I was not burned.

Later, I participated in the July 1983 Esala Festival at Kataragama, Sri Lanka. Firewalking is one of many masochistic activities participants perform there. Pilgrims, many of whom are Tamil Hindus, thrust skewers through their tongues, cheeks, backs, and arms, and roll on the ground for great distances. Entranced individuals put hooks through their backs and hang from scaffolds. Onlookers ask the hanging men questions, as it is believed that a deity speaks through them. In Kataragama, pain denial is a wondrous event that gives the speaker's words special importance.

Sri Lankan firewalking requires special preparations. Firewalkers vow to forgo eating meat, drinking alcohol, and engaging in sex for the

Figure 9. Lay people firewalk at Mount Takao, Japan (photo by J. McClenon).

week prior to the event in order to gain divine protection. Hindu participants seek to fulfill religious vows made in return for a favor the deity Murugan, Shiva's son, has granted (Feinberg, 1964). For example, a father might vow, "If my son recovers from his sickness, I will walk over the coals at Kataragama!"

I interviewed several swami firewalkers who claimed knowledge of magical feats. One swami, who had been chief of the firewalkers on three previous occasions, explained the process. "Just forget that fire can burn and you will be protected," he told me. Yet he admitted being burned slightly on his third firewalk. "I do not know why the fire is hotter some years," he remarked.

Belief systems regarding firewalking are not uniform in Kataragama since both Hindus and Buddhists participate together. Most firewalkers expect to be protected by the Lord Murugan, a Hindu deity. Others rely on the Buddha. "You can call on any religious figure since all religions are one," a swami informed me. At the time, I believed I would be protected by whatever processes allowed such demonstrations (articles by skeptics made it seem easy and I assumed that the feat involved normal physical processes). Through interviewing successful firewalkers, I formed the impression that those who stepped off the side of the fire pit, or who fell down, risked serious injury, but that those who demonstrated their faith by successfully completing the feat could walk safely.

More than fifty individuals made up the firewalking group. On the day before the event, we danced from temple to temple within the Kataragama complex, receiving special blessings. We then danced to the Buddhist stupa, a ceremonial structure, for additional ceremonial rituals. We participated in the evening parade and later danced before the fire. Finally, early in the morning, we walked, one by one, over a twenty-foot-long, red-hot bed of coals.

My first step on the fire was extremely painful and I proceeded as quickly as possible. Afterward, we walked from temple to temple to receive further blessings. The Buddhists invited me to a ceremony of thanks at the stupa. I was something of a celebrity, the first Westerner to firewalk at Kataragama. People called me "Swami," one of the brotherhood of "those who had done it."

More than an hour after the firewalk, I discovered that my feet were blistered. I suspect now that the excitement of ritual activity prevented me from thinking about my pain. I went to the first aid station set up for such emergencies. Attendants there told me that approximately one-third of the firewalkers had been similarly injured. At the station, I talked with some of the most religious Hindus who had also been blistered.

Later, a master firewalker explained my error. "If you had walked evenly and lightly, you would not have been harmed," he stated. "My feet get hot, but afterward, they are okay." The locations of blisters on my feet were consistent with the hypothesis that I had exposed myself to excessive heat by walking too rapidly over the coal bed.

My blisters required three weeks to heal. As I recovered, Sri Lanka erupted in ethnic violence. Buddhist Sinhalese mobs burned Hindu Tamil shops throughout the country. Hundreds of Tamils were slaughtered by mobs. Although the firewalking swamis emphasized that "all religions are one," many Sri Lankans do not accept this doctrine. Firewalking ceremonies, however, seem to provide an ecumenical ritual contributing to Sri Lankan unity.

Walking, in the weeks afterward, was extremely painful. I had much time to think about performance techniques. Meanwhile, with only a Bible to read, I found various passages referring to heat immunity. Isaiah 43:2 states, "When you walk through fire you shall not be burned, and the flame shall not consume you." Shadrach, Meschach, and Abednego were thrown into a furnace, but were not harmed (Daniel 3:21–27). Their success was attributed to belief. Why were some of the most religious Sri Lankan firewalkers injured? All demon-strated faith by walking across the coals, yet about one-third were blistered!

Filipino psychic surgeons recommend particular biblical verses that they feel justify their performances. "[A]nyone believing in me shall do the same miracles I have done, and even greater ones," Jesus stated. "Yes, ask *anything*, using my name, and I will do it!" (John 14:12, 14). These passages provide insight into trance logic, which is a part of the shamanic complex. Jesus told his followers that their powers were limitless. Many people, however, recognize this claim as absurd and feel that no modern human has unlimited magical abilities. Special logic is required to accept this belief.

Belief in unlimited powers is often aided by dissociation and trance logic. Folk religions often encourage believers to act as if hypnotized. Hypnotized people reveal special capacities for accepting contradic-tion (Orne, 1959). Through dissociation, they refuse to acknowledge that certain thoughts or perceptions are logically inconsistent. At the same time, a "hidden observer" within the unconscious mind remains aware of all dissociated elements and generally protects subjects from harm.

I hypothesize that believers apply trance logic while evaluating won-drous events. Performers, in trance, generally attempt only limited feats, ones explainable through normal processes. Yet they and their audiences attribute *all* wondrous feats to occult forces even though extremely anomalous events are rare. By believing in *unlimited* super-natural forces, the faithful expand the potency of less wondrous per-formances, increasing the probability that they will experience placebo benefits.

Aspects of the shamanic practitioner's socialization often parallel the induction of hypnosis. Shamans seemingly act without volition, as if under the control of exterior forces. Hypnotic suggestions need not be stated directly; they can be imbedded within the context of a situation. Hypnotic suggestibility, coupled with religiosity, fulfill functions for so-cieties; suggestion and dissociation enhance wondrous performances, which in turn support unifying religious beliefs and spiritual healing. Experiential religious systems thus are particularly well suited for those capable of self-hypnosis.

Many elements of religious ceremonies act as hypnotic inductors. Chanting, praying, singing, dancing, and preaching contribute to hyp-notic trance. Yet the capacity to achieve a hypnotic state varies from person to person; some are better at this mental feat than others.

My inability to achieve trance analgesia limited my performance as a firewalker. (I have scored a nine on the twelve-point Harvard Group

Scale of Hypnotic Susceptibility, placing me in the moderate to high range.) The pain I experienced when taking my first step in Sri Lanka prevented me from walking evenly. My rapid, lengthy steps probably increased my exposure to the heat, since my feet dug more deeply into the coals. People with shamanic propensities would be more likely to feel no pain, walk evenly, and emerge unburned.

Hypnotic suggestibility, particularly autohypnotic suggestibility, may be a source of religiosity (Schumaker, 1990). I hypothesize that those who respond to hypnotic suggestions are more likely to experience tertiary wondrous events. The Christian experience of being "born again" (a tertiary wondrous event) is more profound for those more suggestible to hypnosis. All the "high-susceptibles" who professed having been "saved" in Gibbons and Jarnette's (1972: 152) sample of 185 undergraduate volunteers reported "profound experiential changes" while none in the low-susceptible "saved" group reported such phenomena.

After my Sri Lankan firewalking experience, I read Julianne Blake's (1985) study. She polled American firewalking workshop participants about their beliefs. She had medical personnel inspect their feet after each firewalk. She found that heat effects were significantly correlated with the type of belief system firewalkers used. Those relying on outside factors (such as spiritual forces) blistered less than those depending on their own internal abilities. Although critics may be correct in arguing that "typical" firewalks do not require paranormal capabilities, these skeptics often ignore the role of belief and mental states.

I hypothesize that people's conscious declarations of belief are less important for experiencing and producing wondrous events than their subconscious mind/body relationships. Drawing from the observation that some of the most religious firewalkers were severely burned, I theorize that the capacity to firewalk safely is dependent on mind/body states rather than on outward expressions of belief. This argument is parallel to a finding presented in Chapter 2: frequency of wondrous experience was rarely highly correlated with expressions of religiosity.

My next firewalk was at Mount Takao, Japan in March 1984. I had been successful there before and wished to restore my confidence. Unlike the previous year, the weather was clear and a huge crowd was present. I could not push to the front of the multitude. The priests did not even out the firebed as they had done the year before, and I walked on a trampled-out hot ash pathway rather than the glowing coals. Although the risk was far less than it had been before, heaps of red-hot coals lay beside the pathway, obscuring the nonparticipants' view of the safe pathway. The audience was amazed at our bravery. Firewalking, like psychic surgery, can involve showmanship and pretense.

After this experience, I decided to firewalk on my own to gain better data. Members of a meditation group in Okinawa were interested in firewalking and wanted me to lead a workshop. I devised an ecumenical ceremony for the Westerners, Indians, and Okinawans who wished to participate. I had people describe their motivations, fears, and aspirations. Some participants harbored scientific orientations; others held Hindu beliefs. We practiced breathing exercises and chanted mantras. I led a hypnotic induction and gave the suggestion that when they saw me walk across the coal bed, they would become certain they could follow safely. I suggested that by walking across the coals they would increase their capacity to overcome fears in their everyday lives.[4]

We chose an isolated Okinawan beach for our ceremony. The night was still and the glowing fire flickered beside the shoreline. I hid my personal fear from the other participants.

I had brought Omegalabel temperature monitors from the Omega Engineering Corporation and glued a number of them to the bottom of my feet. These small pads, which have adhesive material on one side, are designed to change color immediately on reaching their designated temperature. By using a variety of pads, each with different designated temperature, I could determine the approximate temperature on the bottoms of my feet. I also measured the coal bed temperature using an Omega 871 Digital Thermometer.

I led the group across the coals without problem. Everyone walked across the five-foot coal bed, taking two or three steps. One woman, who had declared previously that she was just an observer, had been swept up by the hypnotic induction. She followed me across the coals. "You said I could do it, so I did," she explained.

The group was ecstatic. For weeks afterward, members described their profound experiences, some claiming that it was the most remarkable event in their lives. I had played a shamanic role, creating a special setting so that my followers could experience personal victories. They experienced a wondrous event.

The surface of the coals had been approximately 355 degrees Fahrenheit, not particularly hot. Although the scattered glowing coals were frightening, they were far less dangerous than a solid red-hot bed of embers. The temperature monitors revealed that my foot temperature attained only 200 degrees Fahrenheit, a safe level.

This was the first of seven experiments in which I glued temperature labels on my feet, measured the fire-bed temperature with the digital thermometer, and walked across the coals. On four occasions, I organized groups that followed me across (Figures 10 and 11). Although no participants in any of my workshops were blistered, one suffered minor heat effects. On two occasions, I walked alone after making the coal

Figure 10. Okinawan participant firewalks at the author's second workshop (photo by J. McClenon).

beds as hot as I could get them (more than 1,000 degrees Fahrenheit). Each time I felt pain and some of the temperature monitors on my feet bottoms registered higher levels (300 and 325 degrees Fahrenheit). These findings indicate that the higher the firebed temperature, the greater the heat transfer to foot bottom, and the greater the skin trauma. Although my feet did not blister, my observations reflect normal heat transfer processes.

On three occasions, I glued heat monitors to the bottoms of an old

Figure 11. The author firewalks (photo provided by J. Mc-Clenon).

pair of shoes. After firewalking barefoot with monitors, I walked again wearing the shoes. The "barefoot" and "shoe" conditions revealed no significant differences in the monitors' response (Figure 12). Although unusual skin conditions may have contributed to my firewalking success, there is no reason to believe that, within my experiments, a special force came out of my bare feet to protect the monitors on the skin surface.

I often found that some of the high-temperature monitors had

Figure 12. The heat sensitive monitors after a firewalk (photo provided by J. McClenon).

changed color, leaving low-temperature monitors unaffected. Typically, only a portion of a temperature monitor would change color. These results indicate that heat enters the bottom of the foot in a highly sporadic fashion, reflecting varying temperatures of the firebed. The position of the heat monitor on the foot bottom had little bearing on which monitor would show heat effects. This may indicate that I distributed my weight evenly as I walked over the irregularly heated surface. Although firebed temperatures vary from point to point, people walking over coals are probably exposed to approximately the same maximum temperatures since they take more than one step. I base this argument on the fact that monitors on my shoes and feet showed similar effects.

I hypothesize that differences in heat damage reflect, in part, variations in people's ability to tolerate high temperatures. Firewalking seemingly tests physiological capacities influenced by hypnotic suggestion. Those unable to produce analgesia or to control blistering following exposure to heat have a higher risk of injury. When skeptics firewalk safely, I argue that mind/body processes provide them a degree of protection. My explanation does not pertain to more anomalous feats of heat immunity where people hold red-hot metal for extended periods.

Witnessing or participating in heat immunity feats may trigger further placebo effects. Japanese sect members believe firewalking influences their health and the number of automobile accidents in their province. Sri Lankan firewalks validate faith; some Sri Lanka participants also report seeing deities during the ceremony. Westerners use firewalking as a form of psychotherapy. In all cases, the act is imbedded within a set of latent suggestions, effective for both participants and audiences (McClenon, 1988b).

Wondrous Events and the Placebo Effect

ESP exhibitions, psychic surgery, and firewalking exemplify wondrous performances that stimulate placebo effects. Audiences respond to suggestions embedded within these rituals. The success of a performance is often facilitated by dissociation, subterfuge, and showmanship. The anomalous qualities of feats performed in trance are thought to exceed those possible during normal consciousness. Dissociation also supports deception. Although most performers stress belief in supernatural forces, their actual feats are limited. This paradox is permitted by trance logic. Trance performers maintain a sense of wonderment since they remain uncertain, on a conscious level, of what "really happened."

Psychic performers do more than treat specific clients; their demonstrations also support religious beliefs. Spiritual healing is not simple. Some healing rituals merely manipulate symbols; these can be effective if clients accept the existence of the occult forces thought to create a healing effect. Healing ceremonies typically reformulate people's interpretation of their sick condition, thereby moving them from illness to health (Danforth, 1989: 56).

ESP, firewalking, and psychic surgery are merely some of the many wondrous events that psychic practitioners use to stimulate placebo effects. Korean shamans dance on the blades of metal choppers. Indian yogis demonstrate extraordinary control of the breath and muscles. Chinese *qi gong* masters break huge rocks with their hands and resist the cutting action of blades.

Effective performances require suitable audiences. Successful practitioners must attract clients who respond to their suggestions. Because of this requirement, spiritual healing often takes place within small, alternative religious groups. Skillful groups attract people whose requirements are met by the assembly's practices and beliefs. The following chapter presents a variety of performance strategies, each of which serves the needs of a unique audience.

Chapter 7
Wondrous Events and Audience Attraction

In modern societies, spiritual healing is often a form of cult behavior. Sociologists define *cults* as small religious groups whose ideology comes from outside their society's cultural mainstream. Spiritual healing is cult-like because its ideological foundations differ from that of modern medicine.

Cults have been important in religious history. Jesus was a psychic healer, the leader of a small cult that eventually grew into a religious movement. Muhammad was a trance speaker whose message contributed to the success in warfare of local tribal groups. During his lifetime, the Buddha's preaching drew only local interest. If we wish to understand how religions begin, we must study cults and the ways they attract members.

The word *cult* carries negative connotations which impede conceptual clarity. More powerful groups employ the word to demean and marginalize smaller groups. I use the term cult when reviewing other's theories, but refer to "small, alternative religious groups" in my own discussion.

Sociologists have devised various theories to explain cult structure and recruitment. Bainbridge and Stark (1980b) distinguish among three types of cults: *Cult movements* are fully developed religions in a deviant religious tradition. *Client cults* are groups that dispense magical services such as astrological readings, fortune-telling, and magical therapy. *Audience cults* provide esoteric entertainment by dealing in myth and weak magic, thereby attracting consumers through the media to lectures, fairs, discussion groups, and so forth. Some client cults evolve into cult movements (Bainbridge, 1978; Bainbridge and Stark, 1980b; Wallis, 1976). Spiritual healing often entails client cult behavior since those with medical and psychological problems are served by psychic practitioners. Jesus was the center of a client cult that evolved into a cult movement.

One theoretical orientation supported by many sociologists argues that cults recruit people who suffer from deprivations. "To understand whom a particular group recruits, it is necessary to see to whom its ideology offers the most" (Stark and Bainbridge, 1980: 1377). The deprivation-ideological appeal orientation hypothesizes that a congruence exists between the ideology of a group and the deprivations of those who join. Deprivation refers to "any and all of the ways that an individual or group may be, or feel, disadvantaged in comparison either to other individuals or groups or to an internalized set of standards" (Glock and Stark, 1965: 246). Participation in a cult allows its members to transcend their feelings of deprivation by replacing them with feelings of privilege. Deprivation is viewed as a necessary, but not sufficient, condition for a person to join any organized social movement.[1] Studies supporting, in part, the deprivation-ideological appeal orientation include Balch and Taylor (1977), Cohn (1957), Glock and Stark (1965), Hobsbawn (1959), Linton (1943), Lynch (1977), Richardson and Stewart (1977), and Wilson (1959).

This orientation is pertinent to understanding spiritual healing. Audiences are attracted most readily, and cures occur most frequently, when the psychic practitioner's ideology coincides with the psychological needs of the client population. Along these lines, one practitioner may fail to cure a particular client while another is successful. Successful practitioners are those whose suggestions are so skillfully embedded within their performances that a large percentage of observers benefit.

People from all societies suffer from ailments that have psychological components. Some find that modern medical practitioners cannot aid them. Within modern societies, those suffering from psychosomatic problems often generate thick medical files without gaining relief (Wickramasekera, 1988). These people may benefit from psychic treatments. Although Bainbridge and Stark's (1980b) notion of the client cult has been criticized (Jorgensen, 1992), many groups associated with spiritual healing derive their ideological inspiration from outside of the mainstream culture. Their methods of attracting patients are like those of client cults (small, alternative religious groups that serve clients).

The social networks paradigm argues that people are often attracted to a cult through their friends and relatives (Stark and Bainbridge, 1980). They also must be free from temporal and ideological commitments so that they are available to take part in group activities (Snow et al., 1980). Such networks of faith are particularly powerful in shaping an individual's beliefs.

These theories coincide with my observations. People often learn of spiritual practitioners through friends, neighbors, and relatives. At the same time, they must be ideologically disposed to seek spiritual healing. Yet other factors influence recruitment and survival of small, alternative groups. A experiential factor is also involved. Practitioners who aid a high percentage of their clients stimulate "good" stories about their miraculous healings. This attracts new clients so that the cycle continues. Small, alternative religious groups exist within a spiritual marketplace, offering a variety of options to those with religious needs. Each spiritual practitioner provides a particular treatment method, with some attracting larger audiences than others.

Stark and Bainbridge (1985) explain how some client cults become cult movements and eventually churches. Established churches are subject to secularization. They sometimes fail to provide religious compensators for their members. In response, sects and cults seek to fulfill this demand. People who find established doctrines or medical procedures ineffective are more likely to seek relief from client cults. Cults can be viewed as free enterprise, in competition with more traditional groups. They are subcultural groups that evolve over time, having the potential to become established churches.

Many theories regarding religious proselytizing encompass forms of Jesus' "sower model." Jesus described recruitment as being like a sower scattering seeds, some of which sprout after falling on fertile soil; other seeds fail to germinate due to poor conditions (Matthew 13:3–8). In this model, both the sower, symbolizing the spiritual practitioner, and the resting place of the seed, representing the potential member's environment, are important. Symbolic interactionists, and similar theorists, portray potential converts as actively involved in their own recruitment (Straus, 1976). Within this paradigm, the seed selects its environment, creating its conversion to a particular small alternative group. My studies coincide with both these formulations. "Seekers" work for (or against) their own cures and both consciously and unconsciously respond to (or resist) suggestions.

Spiritual healers cannot alleviate all psychosomatic disorders. Many people erect subconscious barriers that thwart their recovery. They have devised subconscious "locks" protecting their infirmities. Psychological situations lead to physiological changes in the body which contribute to disease. Western doctors are often unable to find active agents to resolve their patients' problems. Such clients often go from doctor to doctor seeking a "key" that will open their special psychological "lock."

Spiritual practitioners vary in ideology, procedure, and style. These features provide a variety of "keys," differing from those offered by traditional medicine. When a healer's "key" coincides with the client's psychological "lock," the individual's mental problem is resolved and the person's physical situation may also be cured. This process seems miraculous because clients find that one procedure is suddenly successful after many others have failed.

Although interpretations vary, people from all cultures relate stories of spontaneous, miraculous cures. They have experiential foundations for their beliefs (Hufford, 1983b, 1988, 1993; McClenon, 1993). I have collected more than sixty accounts of spiritual healing in northeastern North Carolina. For example, one informant reports:

I was in the hospital room the night before my surgery was scheduled. The doctor had informed me that my situation was grave since I had cancer of the uterus. I was only thirty-two and frightened. My family had been to visit me but had left and I was in the room by myself. Suddenly, a woman appeared at the door. The woman told me that she was not sure if she was supposed to be there or not, and asked me if she could pray with me. I agreed, and the woman prayed over me and laid her hands on my stomach. I had my eyes closed and when I opened my eyes, the woman had vanished. The next morning I went up to surgery, but the doctors could not find one trace of cancer anywhere. The doctor told me that my uterus was like that of a normal young woman. I believe that the person that came to me was an angel of mercy.

More frequently, someone with a reputation as a healer is consulted:

In 1952, my brother and I were playing with some reeds we had cut and were using them as spears. We were trying to see who could throw them the highest. He threw one and yelled for me to look up. When I did, the spear pierced my right eye. I was taken to an eye specialist in Berea, Kentucky. The doctor told my mother there was nothing he could do but sew up my eye. My mother told him not to sew it up. I was taken home and my Aunt Barbara prayed for me and put a prayer cloth over my eye. When she was through praying she took the cloth off and I could see at once. I was taken back to the doctor and all he could find was the scar. I have had 20/20 vision ever since.

Some parapsychologists believe that psychic practitioners may actually affect physiological processes. Psychic healers have produced anomalous effects under laboratory conditions (Benor, 1990; Braud, 1990; Braud, Davis, and Wood, 1979; Grad, 1965; Murphy, 1992: 257–283; Watkins and Watkins, 1971). I do not argue that spiritual healing does not have mysterious qualities. However, because I did not witness any clearly paranormal cures, I believe that spiritual healing generally functions on a psychosomatic level. I hope to reveal the elements that attract and satisfy psychic practitioners' clients.

My data portray a social process in which "good" performances create "good" stories, thereby attracting new audiences. Successful psychic practitioners generate a cycle by benefiting a sufficient percentage of their audiences so that stories worth retelling are created. Psychic practitioners and their groups operate in a spiritual marketplace, in competition with each other. Those generating the "best" stories prosper most.

I offer below some sample narratives that illustrate how "good performances" produce "good stories" and how some practitioners fail or have limited success. Healing depends not only on dispositional susceptibilities and social networks, but also on aesthetic qualities within wondrous experiences and within the stories of such experiences.

Wilhelmina S.

During my stay on Siquijor Island in the Philippines, I sought out *mananambals*, practitioners who remove sorcery curses. A former local court judge, attorney Anastacio L., suggested that I interview Wilhelmina S., whom he considered the most famous *mananambal* on the island. Crowds had come to her house after stories spread of her precognitive dreams and remarkable treatments. Many who came to see her experienced miraculous cures.

Attorney L. then told me a "good story," the kind that attracts clients. He had suffered from an unusual, severe illness. His doctor could not diagnose the problem and advised him to consult S. because he had heard of her prophetic dreams. When L. talked with her, she stated that a man involved in one of his recent court cases had placed a curse on him, causing his medical problems. Since the case had been tried on the other side of the island, her accurate description of the man amazed L. He was even more astonished when her herbal remedies proved to be an effective cure.[2]

When I visited S., she was suffering from a severe head cold. She and her husband had no work and no one was visiting her. She looked extremely depressed. It appeared that her charisma (or magical abilities) had vanished. She reported no new precognitive dreams. I saw no wondrous events or clients. As I departed, she asked for money, saying that she was hungry and had none.

Psychosomatic healing is not as easy as armchair theorists might presume. The situations triggering placebo responses vary from client to client. Professional psychic healing is a business in which the practitioner must appeal to a wide a spectrum of clients while, at the same time, satisfying individual needs. S.'s guiding spirit, or the subconscious forces playing that role, apparently could not continuously meet audience expectations. She expressed puzzlement. Her story illustrates how market forces can affect a healer's career. Practitioners who do not continue to create "good stories" attract few clients.

The Slow Practitioner A.

In 1985, I sought to interview Mrs. A., a rising star in the world of Filipino psychic surgery. A. was a doctor's wife who had experienced visions that led her to become a spiritual healer. People said that, using her psychic skills, she had magically removed a bullet from a gunshot wound and that the wound healed miraculously.[3] This, and other "good" stories, attracted the multitudes. I arrived at her center early one Saturday morning and joined a huge crowd. I waited outside for hours while she treated only a few clients in an inner room of the building. The sun grew very hot. It became clear that most of those waiting would be turned away.

Late in the afternoon, I talked with a group of her supporters. They told me of the miracles that had attracted them to her. They had suffered from stomach ailments, skin disorders, and headaches, problems often having psychosomatic origins. Although medical doctors could not help them, she had attributed most of their ailments to witchcraft. She cured each using her psychic powers.

While I waited in the hot sun, surrounded by crippled children, crying babies, and extremely sick and disabled people, I realized the pressures that famous healers face. They must deal with people they cannot help. Most of the people waiting appeared to have organic problems.

Successful healers must devise ceremonies that are effective for treating many forms of psychosomatic disorders. By providing suggestions effective for a broad spectrum of people, those most open to suggestion respond and "good" stories spread regarding the healer's abilities. Meanwhile, those who are not healed maintain hope.

I never got the opportunity to interview A. Instead, I observed spiritual healing's pathetic side. Many came, but few were healed. Mrs. A. apparently had no procedure for offering rapid treatments for the masses.

Mrs. Kim

In 1985, I attended a meeting of the Japanese Society for Parapsychology. Dr. Tosio Kasahara described his investigation of Mrs. Kim, a Christian psychic healer in Seoul, South Korea. Kasahara brought back a videotape supplied by her organization (the "Seeing-Hearing-Feeling Church"), as well as tapes he made during his visit.

The organization's tape showed Mrs. Kim making barehanded incisions into patients' bodies in a way that would seem to harm them. She tore out cancerous growths with her hands and afterward squeezed fluid from the remaining lesions. She vigorously rubbed flaking skin from the bodies of clients with severe skin disorders. The video documented their wonderful progress toward recovery over several weeks. Although Kasahara could not determine the medical value of her interventions, her organization claimed a high cure rate.

Kasahara's private videotape provided different images. As a congregation fervently sang hymns, she symbolically treated a multitude of people simply by applying small adhesive bandages to their infirmities. The atmosphere appeared highly conducive to psychosomatic results.

Perhaps Mrs. Kim still gives lengthy treatments to some clients. I suspect that she had more time for prolonged performances at the beginning of her career. Unlike the "slow practitioner" A. discussed above, she demonstrated methods for treating the crowds her reputation has attracted.

Mrs. Kim's movement has apparently prospered. She has many followers in both Korea and the United States. Even if the frequency of her extremely anomalous healings declines, it seems likely that her public demonstrations will generate additional cures. Her videotape has captured her previous miraculous performances, allowing the continuous presentation of "good" stories.

Technology provides new media for recording performances. The practitioners of earlier eras relied on oral narratives, some of which were eventually transcribed and became sacred texts. Various modern practitioners make use of electronic media, capturing miraculous images to attract audiences and stimulate tertiary wondrous events.

Dr. Li Ch't-ts'e

Li Ch't-ts'e's life history illustrates a case in which a medical doctor was transformed by his wondrous experiences into a psychic performer. Dr. Li was born in 1907 in China where he was trained in Western-style medicine. He left mainland China for Taiwan in 1949 and continued his medical practice. Although he meditated regularly from the age of eighteen, it was not until he was thirty-two that he felt an unusual power affecting him. He was able, sometimes, to diagnose his patients' medical problems without examining them.

Although he had little knowledge of Chinese painting, Dr. Li began expressing himself, in trance, using brushes and paints. He painted very rapidly, left-handed, with the paper turned sideways, though in his non-trance state he was right-handed. The two spirits who he claimed helped him were Tsi Gong (Buddha Tsi), a Chinese Buddhist monk of the Sung dynasty, and Quan Yin, the Goddess of Mercy, a Buddhist deity.

Dr. Li's performances were among the most impressive of all that I observed in Asia. He rapidly created paintings in trance which constituted "solutions" to his clients' problems. He performed twice a month under the auspices of a nonprofit Buddhist charity that supports all religious faiths. Dr. Li is a Protestant Christian.

Those who seek Dr. Li's assistance need not tell him their problems, since Buddha Tsi is thought to be able to read people's minds. Hundreds of people pay a fee equivalent to U.S.$12.50 to have their names added to a list of those seeking a painting. Dr. Li seems impervious to those around him while he works (Figure 13). In trance, he creates a colorful painting and adds a calligraphic inscription thought to apply to the client's problem. Dr. Li is not informed of anyone's problem or question. Two psychic "interpreters" later explain each painting's symbolism for the benefit of clients.

Although no one claimed that Buddha Tsi, using Dr. Li, was perfectly accurate, virtually everyone I spoke with felt he had supplied valid advice through extrasensory means. Some noted that he had previously diagnosed medical disorders before their discovery by traditional methods. Most frequently, however, his paintings alleviated believers' anxieties about common problems.

In order to portray Dr. Li's ability, I present a summary of all ten of my interviews conducted during one visit, with no selection regarding the quality of stories. I also describe Dr. Li's response to my own question.

One woman told me that, in the past, her husband's relatives had been concerned because she had two daughters, but no sons. They wondered who would carry on the family name. The psychic's interpretation of her painting was as follows: "Keep doing what you are doing; don't listen to others. Soon something good will happen." The advice turned out to be appropriate, she stated. She later gave birth to a son.

Another woman told of mentally asking about her parents' apprehension regarding her boyfriend, whose social status was low. The painting's interpretation was remarkably to the point: "Don't be prideful; the gentleman is suitable." The woman married her boyfriend, and the relationship has been very satisfactory. Later she came back to Dr. Li. Her in-laws placed too much pressure on her (a common problem in Chinese society). The painting's interpretation advised her to have patience, that the problem would go away. Now, seven years later, she

Figure 13. Dr. Li paints while in trance (photo by J. McClenon).

has developed a relaxed and warm relationship with her parents-in-law.

One young man told me that during a period of turbulence in his life, the calligraphy on the side of his painting stated, "The future is a burden: stand on a rock." His painting showed a Chinese landscape with a large rock prominently featured. From this point, he practiced his religious beliefs even more seriously, meditated on the painting, and found this a great consolation. "This psychic phenomenon is mysterious, but our belief in it is not superstitious. We base our belief on experience," he told me.

One woman mentally asked why she had such severe physical problems every four years. Her answer: She must change her mental attitude. Her painting contained a red fruit symbolizing the negative aspects she needed to change.

Another woman was concerned that her son's favorite teacher was transferring to another school. "Should he change schools?" she had asked mentally. Her painting showed an old man in a gray robe holding a lantern very low. The psychic's advice: "Do not follow this man. The lantern should be held higher."

One woman's painting contained six fruits. To her, these represented each member of her family. The fruits were grouped in a way that reflected a division in her family which was pertinent to her mental question, she explained.

One man told me that years ago he had silently asked that Dr. Li paint a picture of his grandfather, who had died when he was ten years old. Neither he nor Dr. Li had ever seen the grandfather and there were no known photographs of him. In 1978, fifty-two years after the grandfather's death, Dr. Li painted the grandfather's portrait while in trance. The man took the picture to some relatives who had known his grandfather. They stated that it was an exact representation. The man felt certain that Dr. Li had no contact with anyone who had known his grandfather since his relatives lived far away.

An American told me that he had visited the center alone a few years earlier to ask mentally if he should marry his Chinese girlfriend. "Do we match, even though our cultures are so different?" he asked mentally. Dr. Li's painting showed two birds sitting on a branch with the Buddha's hand underneath them. Beside this painting the words were written, "Their destinies will be tied together by the Buddha's hand." The interpreter advised a relationship based on universal ethical values. "I was amazed," he told me. "Usually women ask about marriage and families and men ask about their work. His painting seemed directly applicable to my question." The man and his wife are presently happily married and living in Taipei.

The answers were not always positive. An older woman mentally asked about buying a house, offered at a very good price. The psychic interpreted her painting to say: Do not act; everything has a spirit. He said that sometimes the spirit is good but sometimes not. The woman concluded that the house was haunted, which would have explained its low price.

One woman mentally asked about problems in her marriage. Her painting contained many references to struggle. After she left, the psychic interpreter remarked, "I think she will get divorced." Another woman had an unusually colored fruit in her painting. She was advised to see a doctor immediately. She had silently wondered about her future health. "I am afraid she has cancer," the psychic interpreter stated.

I silently asked for a painting that would be related to my finding a new job. My watercolor was of the branches of a cassia tree with bright blossoms. Although unaware of my question, the interpreter stated, "Tsi Gong will give you a kind of work where you must give of yourself to others, a job, perhaps, in teaching. Don't expect much in return. The cassia tree has fragrant fall blossoms but bears no fruit. If you expect little money in return for satisfying work, the situation will be perfect. This is the method of those people who are of quality." His response was appropriate. College professors should not expect great wealth.

Although social psychological theories may explain why people found their readings satisfactory, an experiential element also exists. Answers appeared to be correlated with questions. I hypothesized that blind judges could match Dr. Li's answers to clients' questions since they seemed to correspond. As one client noted, "We base our belief on experience."

I devised an experiment to test the correspondence between secret questions and Dr. Li's responses. I had four people record questions that were not revealed to other participants at Dr. Li's session. Afterward, outside judges (volunteers who did not come into contact with either Dr. Li or the four clients) attempted to match the clients' mental questions with the corresponding psychic paintings and readings. The results revealed little statistical correlation. We cannot conclude that Dr. Li's paintings corresponded to the questions. Although three of the four clients were highly satisfied with Dr. Li's output, the judges were unable to match questions to responses to a statistically significant degree.

From my vantage point, there did not appear to be very much correspondence between answers and questions within the experiment. Because of the small number of trials, it would be difficult to achieve statistical significance in this experiment. It also could be that the answers were more meaningful to the clients than the judges could ascertain. Outside the experimental protocol, most of Dr. Li's clients continued to feel that Dr. Li's responses matched their mental questions.

To a degree, clients socially construct the wondrous events they experience. "Good stories" are created through social interaction. By framing Dr. Li's process within the context of a statistically evaluated experiment, the wonderment within it was reduced and a "bad" story regarding failure resulted.

Dr. Li's method is comparable to many other fortune-telling devices. Clients often perceive that a particular psychic practitioner or method is effective. Sometimes tests themselves lead to belief. For example, Lin Jorgensen, D. Jorgensen's wife, recorded the process that led to her belief in the tarot:

I decided to attempt an experiment with this influx of new "clients," most of whom I did not know well: I asked each querente to write out a specific question for the Tarot to answer, without allowing me to see it. The results were frequently rather astounding to me: e.g., the cards for the querentes who asked about their love life showed a majority in the suit of cups [the suit associated with love]; students requesting information about their studies had a majority of cards in the suit of swords [the suit pertinent to intellectual matters]. (D. Jorgensen, 1992: 127)

As with Dr. Li's performance, tarot readings could be tested statistically by comparing the clients' questions to the percentage of pertinent cards. My observations suggest that success is more likely on an experiential level than within the realm of statistics.

D. Jorgensen (1992) evaluated verbal interactions between tarot card readers and their clients. He portrays the process in which "reader and querente interactionally negotiate meaning by way of the movement between general and particular expressions" (p. 224). To put it another way, there is "magic" in human interaction that occult practitioners harness when they provide counseling. Hyman (1977) depicts this process in a more negative light. He refers to "cold readings," where a practitioner picks up sensory cues and shapes statements in light of the client's response. In either case, the magic of human interaction sometimes allows wonder to evolve from these performances.

It would be incorrect to say that Dr. Li's magic failed, even though my experiment did not verify its anomalous qualities. Three out of four of my experimental subjects found his work to be valuable. In this context, experiential confirmation is more important than quantitative disconfirmation.

T. Shizuko

In 1983, I interviewed T. Shizuko, the middle-aged Okinawan founder of the Sei-tenkoh-shin-mei-gu (life-heaven-light-gods-bright) Shrine. A sign on her gate explained that she is concerned with "the ways of the old gods in the Rhukus and the origin of the light of the world." About a hundred people were participating in her religious ceremonies.

After the formal program was over, T. described her role as leader. She is not possessed by God, she explained. She was chosen to be God. She is "god" of all nature, the "god" of all the universe. (I use a lower-case "g" because her notion of God differs from that accepted by many Western readers. She is concerned with the Okinawan "old gods" or shamanic spirits.) She is permanently imbued with god, she argued; consequently, everything that she says is god-spoken. At the age of nineteen, the voice of god, her voice, stated that the Rhukus Islands, which include Okinawa, were to be destroyed if her teachings were not propagated. Prior to this event, she had numerous telepathic experiences. She began worshipping three rocks, one of which was an asteroid.

"Why were the Rhukus to be destroyed?" I wondered.

"The Rhukus are directly based in the magma of the earth's core," she explained. "They were originally even more completely connected than is the case at present. Today the union is metaphorical and its present lessened connection signifies the dissolution of spirit which must be corrected. We must spread the message. Your visit is part of the miracle. First, I set up the original shrine with its three rocks. Then I worshipped there. Gradually people were attracted to me. They were healed miraculously and experienced other paranormal events. Things seemed to fit together. The gods of each country of the world assembled at my shrine to launch my endeavor. I could see all of them." T. did not lack social skills. She merely felt certain that she was a god.

The sect members included many middle-class families who lived in the neighborhood. One man owned a health food store. Another ran a private school. One had a sea salt production company.

The salt producer described the basis for his belief. At one time, his business had been failing. Since joining the group, however, he had prospered and had had various telepathic experiences. He was certain that being a member of the group had been of great benefit to him. Other speakers echoed his sentiments. Being a group member brought financial prosperity, marital success, and psychological well-being.

This small, alternative religious group is one of many that have sprung up in Japan since World War II. When belief in Shintoism, whose doctrines were aligned with Japanese nationalism, declined, many small, alternative religious groups arose. Today, some of these organizations have many members. The history of modern Japanese religious movements supports Stark and Bainbridge's (1985) model of secularization and the spiritual marketplace.

Although T.'s recruitment of group members can be interpreted using "deprivation-ideological appeal" and "social network" theories, an experiential explanation is also appropriate. T. created anomalous experiences. She became the local shaman, explaining people's wondrous experiences and performing spiritual healings. People were attracted to her because of their wondrous perceptions.

Dr. U.

During my meeting with the Okinawan Dr. U., he wore a white laboratory jacket and chain-smoked cigarettes in his luxurious urban office. From the beginning, he was highly suspicious of me. He asked about my birthday and looked over his calculations based on it, seeking signs regarding my character. He struggled to decide if he would grant me an interview. Eventually, he began explaining his theoretical orientation.

He claimed that his theory was based on "unified science." Einstein had sought this realization but had failed. Dr. U. had figured it out. All material consists of gasses, liquids, or solids. You can control these elements through mind. He spent over an hour lecturing on how his doctrines explained the elements of psychology, Einstein's theories, mathematics, parapsychology, and the definition of time (time equals God, yet it has three elements: waves, light, and sound). He drew diagrams to illustrate the nature of miracles and the psychology of music. His thoughts were often unconnected. I felt that Dr. U. was mentally unbalanced.

I coaxed him to talk about his life. Although he had wished to study physics, his parents demanded that he become a medical doctor. He became a heart specialist but soon realized that medical science was flawed. His theories were the result of an intense struggle to understand "true reality."

He revealed his methods through a convoluted process of evasive answers. His office was not open to the public. His work needed to be kept secret since it was in an experimental stage. He treated selected people with mental disorders and skin problems by directing psychic energy into them. Sometimes he had Shinto priests assist him by exorcising his clients' demonic spirits. A photographer recorded these treatments. Dr. U. showed me many photographs of heavy black clouds dispersing above his clients. These indicated that evil spirits were leaving the afflicted person. Other pictures depicted strange lights radiating from a Shinto priest. Photographs of a statue of the Buddha also showed radiant light effects. My translator and I were warned not to touch the photographs. The images were dangerous, he explained.

His methods, as he explained them, were suitable for psychosomatic treatment. Clients were exposed to Dr. U.'s complex (if incoherent) explanation of reality. They then would experience magical ceremonies while photographs were taken within the context of a scientific experiment. Later, clients would view the photographs, which provided evidence that the treatments had been effective. (I assume that this process occurred, since Dr. U. did not allow me to observe any treatments.)

Although the authenticity of U.'s effects is not at issue, his photographic images are similar to those published by Eisenbud (1967, 1977), whose research is reviewed briefly in Chapter 10. Dr. U.'s clients would have every reason to believe that the photographs proved their treatments had been effective.

U.'s case illustrates an unorthodox example of behavioral medicine. Perhaps because he selects people who have problems that respond to psychological treatment, he finds that he can cure a high percentage of them. He is aware that he would be stigmatized by his peers if they learned of his therapeutic strategies. His clients, meanwhile, prefer to be treated by a licensed medical doctor rather than by a shaman, and they are willing to submit to his protocol. They believe in both science and spiritual forces.

C. Toshihiko

C. Toshihiko, whose parents were Japanese, was born in China in 1941. His parents brought him to Bolivia, where they farmed for thirty years. He immigrated to Okinawa in 1982, and in 1984 opened a psychical healing center.

C. claims to project healing energy from his hands and to perform psychic "eye operations," a skill he learned during a weeklong visit to the Philippines. He has studied the occult in Brazil, claims to go into trance with ease, and frequently receives messages from God and outer space. He considers himself more spiritually advanced than Okinawan shamans. He claims to require food only once every two weeks but still eats one meal a day. He has eighteen followers. Approximately twenty clients sought healing on the day of my interview. This steady flow allows him to maintain a middle-class lifestyle.

C. presents an ideology that he feels unifies all the great world religions. Like Dr. U., he believes that mental forces are the key to understanding the universe. He perceives his own mental capacities as highly advanced. C. visualizes a day when he will become a famous, internationally recognized healer. He views himself as equivalent to Jesus, Buddha, and Muhammad.

Although he made many astonishing claims in my interview with him, I found C. boring and self-involved. I hypothesize that C. will not attract international attention. My translator, Takamiyagi, however, was impressed by C.'s ability to attract clients and make money. He visited C.'s office a few weeks later. One of C's disciples gave him a free healing treatment, but it had no effect.

Although C.'s style did not appeal to me, I argue that he fulfills a need in Okinawan society. Although the traditional village shamanic system was destroyed by the disruption of World War II and its aftermath, perhaps half of all modern Okinawans still consult shamanic-type practitioners. Those who desire a more "modern," cosmopolitan approach are apparently attracted to C. His clients must be telling "good stories" of his successful treatments or else he would be unable to support himself.

The Reverend N.

Takamiyagi, my friend and translator, learned of an amazing new spiritual healer. "He is associated with a new religion," he told me. "They claim to do psychic healings." To my surprise, Takamiyagi brought me to a Christian fundamentalist-style church.

After the service, the Protestant minister N. explained his doctrines to Takamiyagi, who was unfamiliar with Christian beliefs. Our interaction with C. had whetted his appetite for knowledge about world religions. Takamiyagi became enthralled with the notion that God is love. He listened with extreme attentiveness. "Look how bright and intelligent these people are here," he remarked to me. Yet as the discussion continued, his critical faculties returned. "I have heard that Christians hate the Soka Gakkai [Nichiren Buddhism, a large Japanese group]," Takamiyagi remarked. The Reverend N. responded by describing the demonic forces that prevented Okinawans from perceiving Christianity as the only valid religion.

Takamiyagi argued that saying "God is love" was incompatible with the idea that only one religion is valid. "If God is love, then God loves the Soka Gakkai," he reasoned. N. was unable to convince him that the Soka Gakkai had rejected God's love and that this would cause them to be punished eventually.

The Reverend N.'s approach did not "work" for Takamiyagi. No one system is effective for all cases. N.'s Christianity benefits only a select group, those wishing a clear demarcation between good and evil.[4]

I asked N. to describe the process by which he, an Okinawan, became an evangelical Protestant minister. Although his parents practiced ancestor veneration, he visited a Christian service while in college, in Kyoto, Japan. He was impressed with how "bright" the church members appeared. He joined in order to participate in their pleasant social atmosphere. This is a common motivation among Japanese people who convert. He tried to act like his fellow members in order to gain the "brightness" they had. Yet after he returned to Okinawa, he realized that he had no real faith in Jesus and did not join any religions organization.

Then a series of problems began to plague him. He initiated a sexual relationship with a woman whom he later married. When she confessed she was not a virgin, he was intensely angered. He developed stomach ulcers, and the doctors were unable to help him. He was forced to quit his job, and it appeared that he would die.

N. began reading the Bible intensely. He realized that Jesus demanded that he forgive his wife, yet he had no inner Christian faith. He placed a paper on his wall that stated, "God, if you exist, mark this paper with blood." No mark appeared. He continued to read the Bible and prayed that his life would end. Eventually, after going through a convoluted and traumatic crisis, he placed his full trust in God and forgave his wife. His medical problems were resolved. God had healed him, he explained.

After this emotional experience, N. talked six others into converting to Christianity. A typhoon arrived on the day scheduled for their baptism. People were warned not to travel outdoors. Yet N. saw this as a test of their faith and assured his terrified flock that they could reach the bridge where the baptism was to take place. They made the arduous journey of only a few miles, and no one was injured. The wind whipped the water into a white froth. Yet as they entered the water, the sun burst forth and the winds died down. They took a photograph to help them remember this miracle. N. completed the ceremony, and the typhoon resumed its devastating activity.[5]

This baptism established a core group of converts whose faith never faltered. They too found they could heal by laying their hands on those in need. Although N. claimed to have had no previous experience dealing with demonic forces, he found that they were prevalent in Okinawa. The narrative that follows describes his first confrontation with these forces and exemplifies how experience can shape belief within a performance setting.

A twenty-two-year-old woman came to his service for healing. She had had many precognitive experiences and found that the spirit inside her made predictions that always came true. Now the spirit predicted that she would die within a few months. She had visited an Okinawan shaman, seeking help. The female shaman told her that she must become an shaman herself in order to survive.[6] She became desperate (shamans are stigmatized and she wished to avoid becoming one). When N. touched her, she shrieked in pain and fell unconscious to the floor. He perceived psychically the demonic forces inside her. Suddenly, she began speaking in a man's voice, saying, "You can't do it. You can't make me leave!"

N. responded, "I know I can't; I have no power, myself. But I believe in Jesus Christ and He has the power to make you leave!"

Finally, early in the morning, after hours of commanding the spirit to leave, the woman returned to her senses. N. claimed that, during the night, she had levitated above her bed (the Devil was demonstrating his power, he argued); now she was a normal woman, devoid of paranormal abilities. She became a Christian and a regular church attender.

N.'s story illustrates elements that are universal to possession accounts (Goodman, 1988). During the medieval era, church authorities viewed levitation and precognitive ability as indications of demonic activity. Western therapists have found similar demonic "entities" and have encountered paranormal features in multiple personality cases. N.'s account reveals how features related to the human capacity to dissociate and to experience wondrous events can lead to commonalities in beliefs about angelic and demonic forces. Using the Bible as a guide, he replicated medieval European findings regarding demonic forces.

Piyadasa K.

Piyadasa K. was a school teacher living in a small village in Sri Lanka. After his wife died in 1968, he read numerous Western books about psychic phenomena and spirit communication. After practicing "blank mind meditation," he found that vague information seemed to be coming from his wife. Later, his teenage daughter and son found that they could talk in trance, using the voice of a guiding spirit. The guiding spirit also gave them "X-ray eyes," that is, the ability to see through a blindfold. This ability was also gained by a medium who presently lives with the family (K. desired that his daughter and son devote their time to their school work rather than to mediumship).

K. feels he proceeded logically in investigating this phenomena. He took his daughter and the medium to various doctors who tested their X-ray vision, and special boards of examiners verified their psychic abilities. For example, the medium performed before a group that included the president of Sri Lanka, an event described in the January 2, 1982, issue of a Sri Lankan newspaper. On this occasion, the spirit of a suicide victim provided distinctive information about his death. Later, a coroner confirmed the spirit's statements as correct.

In 1978 K. began using his medium to conduct treatment sessions for the crowds of people who came to his house on weekends. The guiding spirits helped alleviate psychosomatic disorders, family disputes, alcoholism, and drug addictions. The spirits often aided clients by communication with whatever earthbound spirits were creating the difficulty.

At the time of my visit in August 1983, approximately seventy people arrived at K.'s house each weekend. He lectured them regarding the medium's X-ray ability and capacity to communicate with spirits. He showed them photographs and newspaper articles regarding events that have occurred in the past. He told his clients about people who have been helped. He then had the participants fill out questionnaires, requiring them to explain their problems (drinking, physical problems, mental instability, family problems, etc.) He then had his medium demonstrate her X-ray vision by reading the questionnaires while blindfolded. The guiding spirit, speaking through the blindfolded medium, was able to give specific advice to many of the individuals present. K. then attempted to put the entire audience into trance, using relaxation induction techniques. Afterward, using his medium to communicate with earthbound spirits, he conducted individual sessions to deal with specific problems. Based on the guiding spirit's advice, information provided by earthbound spirits, and K.'s counseling skills, clients were often able to decide upon logical courses of action.

K. has passed out and received more than ten thousand followup questionnaires from people who have participated in his weekend sessions between 1979 and 1983. He requests that individuals come for two consecutive weekends and then return for a "checkup" after about eleven weeks. He demands no payment but accepts donations (which average less than twenty rupees, or one U.S. dollar per person).

Many of K.'s clients are alcoholics who seek to stop drinking. He attempts to put them into a "positive mind" and to stimulate the proper "mind chemicals." He believes that only those who can go into trance are thereby benefited. Apparently, a large percentage of alcoholics respond to his treatments since the volume of testimonials he has received regarding cures is astonishing.

K. enjoys reading Western books about the occult and has a large library of New Age publications. He believes in pyramid power and has constructed a large pyramid (approximately fifteen by fifteen feet) next to his house. He uses this structure for treating those who request his aid and also sleeps in it himself. He believes in astrology, the lost city of Atlantis, and much of the information he has read in Western books on the occult.

After observing the medium's X-ray vision performance, I expressed my doubts to K. regarding its authenticity. It appeared that she used a standard magician's trick of looking down the side of her nose through a crack created by flexing her face (Gardner, 1966). I had K. blindfold me, and I duplicated her feats.

"In the beginning, I had my doubts but we have taken her to eye specialists!" he stated sincerely.

I remained skeptical. I do not consider the specialists' conclusions to be definitive since I cannot be certain that they are aware of the standard blindfold trick. Although K. later mailed me photographs of his medium performing with a box over her head, it seems to me that this test does not preclude fraud.

K. showed me numerous photographs of individuals who suffered possession-type mental disorders. I visited one former patient, a forty-four-year-old woman who described many psychotic episodes. She had suffered from severe headaches and periods of insanity during which she wandered in the jungle. K.'s medium determined that she was possessed by her father-in-law's spirit and the spirit then gave a long, detailed description of his anger. Eventually, the spirit was convinced to seek a higher mental plane. Now, with the aid of the spirit, the woman can heal other people. Her husband's business, which had been failing, has improved remarkably. The husband confirmed her story, noting that he had paid a huge amount of money to medical psychiatrists before turning to K.

K. has read a great deal about psychosomatic disorders and believes his methods are based on suggestion and hypnotism. He feels that he cannot help people with physical problems like cancer, though some of those diagnosed as having cancer have been cured through his program. He believes these cures involve incorrect diagnoses by medical doctors.

Although K.'s belief in spirits seemingly clashes with his assumption that he performs psychosomatic treatments, he perceives no conflict. He does not carefully distinguish between spiritual and mental problems. Neither he nor the spirits he communicates with claim to heal people physically, although they do attempt to resolve witchcraft problems that can contribute to medical disorders. K. perceives of himself as a negotiator between his clients and the spiritual entities that he summons. He believes that such communications are a form of psychosomatic treatment since, in the end, clients must heal themselves.

K. stages a kind of psychodrama in which paranormal forces are thought to be actors. The participants in these dramas provide information that seemingly aids clients in resolving their issues. K. has developed an ecumenical "New Age" ideology that fits the needs of Sri

Lankan society. His program joins miraculous performance with hypnotic suggestion, treating a large volume of clients at a low cost.

Observations

Chapters 5, 6, and 7 present narratives regarding twenty-one psychic practitioners. The accounts reveal a common theme: wondrous performances have an impact on observers' beliefs which contribute to tertiary wondrous experiences.

Variations in methodology allow practitioners to occupy a variety of niches within their societies. Some practitioners are capable of treating large audiences (Jesus, Alex Orbito, Olga Worrall, Mrs. Kim, Josephine Escandor-Sisson, Dr. Li, and Piyadasa K.). Small group leaders such as the Reverend N., T. Shizuko, K. Higa, and C. Toshihiko serve clients individually. Although the Thai chemist Chakara C., the "slow practitioner" A., and Dr. U. have no method for serving large numbers, they are seemingly effective with those they treat. Some psychic healers may also use deceptive methods (for example, Piyadasa K., Alex Orbito, and Josephine Escandor-Sisson).

As in many other domains, spiritual healing practices are shaped by supply and demand. Practitioners' methods tend to coincide with their audiences' expectations. When many within a society do not believe in spirits, secular healers are more prevalent (for example, Dean Kraft, Alex Tanous, and K. Higa). Westerners are less dependent on trance states than are Asians. Many practitioners use spirits to aid clients (Eleuterio Terte, Wilasinee W., Alex Orbito, Josephine Escandor-Sisson, David O., Dr. Li, and Piyadasa K.). Areas with large populations who are concerned with sorcery or demons require witchcraft cures and exorcists. Jesus, David O., Dr. U., and Reverend N. are examples of practitioners skilled at casting out demons. All of the Filipino practitioners, Piyadasa K., Reverend N., and Wilasinee W. claimed expertise in removing witchcraft and sorcery curses.

My observations do not call for the rejection of current theories pertaining to small, alternative religious groups but rather for an extension of them. The deprivation-ideological appeal and social network orientations explain why people choose specific psychic practitioners. Potential clients hear stories from friends, neighbors, or relatives. They tend to visit practitioners whose ideologies coincide with their own.

Wondrous experiences also play a role within this process. Successful practitioners generate good stories, and these stories attract new clients. The aesthetic qualities embodied in these accounts are critical for their transmission. Without "good" stories, ideologies and networks are useless. Spiritual practitioners compete within a religious marketplace, seeking to produce wondrous accounts superior to those of their competitors.

We can better understand Christian history by considering the role of wondrous performance in religious recruitment. Christianity developed within a spiritual marketplace. Audience needs undoubtedly shaped the practice of Jesus of Nazareth. In his world, devils were believed to be the source of sickness as well as sin, an orientation which probably originated from the Iranian influence on Judaism in the fifth and fourth centuries B.C. (Vermes, 1986: 61). Jesus conducted many exorcisms and trained his followers to perform similar services. The Gospel writers even include Jesus' discussions of relapses (Matthew 12:43–45; Luke 11:24–26). Some of those exorcised were repossessed, an occurrence that alludes to the transitory nature of many psychosomatic cures.

The aesthetic qualities that are demonstrated in spiritual practitioners' life stories affect the success of their movements. The stories generated by Jesus' life can be compared to those of his contemporary, Apollonius. Apollonius, a Greek neo-Pythagorian philosopher, was born in Tyana, in Asia Minor, and educated at Tarsus. He was described as performing 107 miracles, compared to the two hundred incidents described in the Gospels (Smith, 1978: 109). Both Jesus and Apollonius demonstrated extrasensory abilities. Both healed the sick and raised the dead.

Each had followers who provided the structure necessary for religious movements. Both were put on trial. Rather than allow himself to be convicted, however, Apollonius magically vanished and continued his ministry for many years (Smith, 1978). This variation creates a critical difference. Both Jesus and Apollonius were reported to ascend into heaven at the conclusion of their ministries.

Christians used the Gospel narratives to induce further wondrous events, particularly healings. Apollonius's followers had similar tales with the exception of the Resurrection story. Although many other factors were at play, the powerful Resurrection narrative seems to have been critical for the Christian movement's success; its narrative qualities, the stuff of "good" aesthetic performances, have contributed to the story's longevity, attracting large audiences over the centuries.

The practitioner stories illustrate the universal pool of extraordinary feats available to psychic performers. Yet wondrous performances by themselves cannot compel belief. Other factors such as trance logic, showmanship, deception, and aesthetic qualities within performance scripts are important factors within religious recruitment.

As a consequence, wondrous events may affect religious ideology but have little impact on scientific opinion. In future chapters, I will elaborate more fully on the influences of wondrous experience on scientific and religious ideologies. Religions lacking magical practices, such as early Buddhism, have a natural tendency to devise occult doctrines since magical performances are a valuable means for spreading religious beliefs.

Chapter 8
Wondrous Events and Religious History in Medieval Asia and Europe

The universal features that mark wondrous experience and performance contributed to parallel developments in medieval Buddhist and Christian ideologies. In both Asia and Europe, monks performed miracles in order to convert nonbelievers. Reports of these exploits fit the patterns of performance described in Chapters 5–7. Buddhism and Christianity were successful, in part, because their proponents were able to outperform their rivals.

An analysis of Buddhist and Christian medieval histories indicates the following: (1) Various medieval Asian wondrous accounts resemble modern anomalous reports (evidence in support of the experiential source theory). (2) Buddhism flourished in China and Japan partly due to its ability to use wondrous events within the performance model discussed in Chapter 7. (3) Reports of miracles in Asia stimulated skeptical rebuttals, illustrating the tendency for folk philosophers to encourage logical evaluations of anomalous claims. Particularly within more complex societies, wondrous accounts tend to incite skeptical reaction. (4) Wondrous performances contributed, in a parallel fashion, to the success of Christianity in Europe. Although medieval European attitudes toward the miraculous differed markedly from Asian beliefs, common features may be found in the wondrous accounts from both areas. (5) Although wondrous events are part of a symbiotic process in which culture shapes narrative accounts and these accounts, in turn, affect experiential reports, the thematic elements common within wondrous accounts have had an impact on religious ideologies, contributing to cross-cultural convergences in Christian and Buddhist folk belief. These common features include the belief in spirits, souls, heavens, hells, miraculous performances conducted by special individuals, the power of intermediary spiritual agencies, and the spiritual potency of relics, specific locales, and other elements associated with miraculous episodes.

I do not argue that wondrous events determined the success of medieval religious movements. Other factors were generally more important. However, the evidence suggests that wondrous experiences played a significant enough role to have had detectable and similar impacts on both Christian and Buddhist ideologies.

Wondrous Events in Medieval Asian Literature

Medieval Asian reports of apparitions, precognitive dreams, out-of-body experiences, contacts with the dead, and reincarnation memories reveal elements that are identical to those in modern narratives. These elements are apparent even though the stories have been culturally shaped through oral transmission and later transcription.

Chinese *chih-kuai* (records of anomalies) or *ch'uan-ch'i* (accounts of the extraordinary) during the Six Dynasties (317–589) and T'ang eras (618–906) furnish the narratives to be used for analysis. At least forty and perhaps as many as sixty *chih-kuai* collections were produced before and during the Six Dynasties, and about three thousand items of various length have been preserved (Kao, 1985: 48). *Chih-kuai* manuscripts were considered records of observable natural phenomena, even though they were based on hearsay. The writers who first assembled these stories hoped they could gain greater understanding of the natural processes behind experiential accounts by collecting and analyzing many cases.

Some *chih-kuai* narratives coincide exactly with modern extrasensory and precognitive accounts. For example, Pai Hsing-chien (618–589) marveled over unusual dreams in which a dreamer is seen as an apparition by a waking person, two people have the same dream, or a dreamer views the future. He wonders: "Are they just coincidental, or are they caused by some law of predetermination? That is something I cannot answer. I have written these down in detail so as to keep them as a record" (Kao, 1985).

The Chinese account of Lady Nijo (a court lady whose autobiography has survived from the thirteenth century) also describes apparitions, precognitive and clairvoyant dreams, as well as an incident of two people having the same dream (Braxell, 1973). Lady Nijo's accounts are equivalent to modern narratives. She accepts her experiences as valid and wonders about their meaning. Like many Asians, she regards them as unusual aspects of the natural order.

Many *chih-kuai* narratives also fit the patterns of modern apparitional cases presented in Chapter 4 and in the psychical research literature. In one example, a ghost during the Six Dynasties era (317–589) identifies its murderer (Kao, 1985: 89). Another Six Dynasties narrator describes some boaters who meet a seemingly real, but unknown, girl in a boat. She suddenly disappears, leaving a turtle in her place (Kao, 1985: 107).

The latter story is similar to the present-day "vanishing hitchhiker" theme (*Motif-Index*: E332.3.3.1 and also E332.3.2, "Ghost rides in carriage, disappears suddenly at certain spot"). In modern versions of this form, a motorist picks up a hitchhiker (typically female) who subsequently vanishes (Brunvand, 1981). Brunvand argues that these accounts evolved from earlier European stories and cites a prototype from the New Testament (Wolkomir, 1992). While driving his chariot, the treasurer of Ethiopia picked up the apostle Philip, who told him of the Gospel, baptized him, and then disappeared (Acts 8:26–39). Although Brunvand suggests that such accounts are cultural fabrications that migrate geographically over time, my data dispute his assumption. I have collected firsthand vanishing hitchhiker stories in North Carolina, the Philippines, Okinawa, and Taiwan. I argue that the Chinese Six Dynasties account, and many subsequent stories, probably originated with experiences rather than with the New Testament narrative.

Other narratives fit the patterns of modern haunting and poltergeist cases (Gauld and Cornell, 1979). In the medieval Tung-ko Buddhist Monastery (today Ts'in-hgan in Kansuh) "ill-boding and strange things" occurred:

Pot-shards were thrown down from the air, and dust was whirled, so that nobody dared to stand upright, and the resident monks found no rest at night. A Taoist doctor attempted to exorcise the temple but the poltergeistry caused various pieces of his clothing to fly off or disappear, disrupting his ceremony. Various officials were humiliated. (De Groot, 1967/1892: 472)

In two Six Dynasties poltergeist cases, residents heard a goblin chopping at their roof beam only to find the roof undamaged in the morning (Kao, 1985: 99, 176–177). In modern cases, people often hear destructive noises yet later find no damage (the Baltimore and Alexandria accounts in Chapter 4 include *Motif-Index* F473.5, "Poltergeist makes noises," and E402.1.6, "Crash as of breaking glass, though no glass is found broken").

An apparition (termed a *lai*) was perceived between 1119 and 1126 in the royal harem, fitting the incubus motif (F471.2) commonly reported in the West:

Sometimes the spectre lay down in the bed of a lady of the harem, which was then felt to be warm; and at daybreak it rolled out of the bed and disappeared, nobody knowing where it had gone. And when the ladies of the harem dreamed that they were sleeping with somebody, that somebody was the lai. (De Groot, 1967/1892: 473)

Some Chinese haunting incidents became collective social problems. In A.D. 564, whole towns and countries south of the Loh River saw apparitions that later appeared in the north (De Groot, 1967/1892: 476). Similar cases occurred in 781 in regions of the Yang-tze and the Hwai. In 1378, Chu Liang-tsu, the feudal ruler of Yung-kia, prepared sacrifices to ward off spectral visitors. Nineteen years later, the Emperor Kao took similar precautions. In 1544, in Kwangsi Province, people were plagued by specters for several months. Likewise, De Groot noted that a particularly malicious psychic phenomenon was said to have occurred in the 1870s and that people still remembered incidents at Amoy in 1886. "Indefinable spectres are frequently mentioned in books as invisible openers of doors and windows, as makers of mysterious noises, as throwers of tiles and various missiles, and as beings responsible for naughty tricks and mischief not assigned to human agency" (De Groot, 1967/1892: 785).

Some Chinese medieval accounts coincide with modern out-of-body narratives. T'ao Ts'ien (365–427) collected reports that included various tales of out-of-body souls producing apparitional experiences (De Groot, 1967/1892: 103). One of De Groot's tales is peripherally related to OBEs, one in which a particular monk had the reputation of causing those who visited him to journey through the Buddhist heavens. I witnessed an equivalent Taiwanese shamanic performance in 1986. After hypnotic induction (embedded within the ceremony), audience members felt they visited heavens and hells.

Some Chinese accounts are comparable to those collected by the modern researcher Ian Stevenson (1987), who has assembled cases wherein children seem to remember previous lives.

[A learned man of the Tsin dynasty,] Pao Tsing by name, when five years old, said to his parents that he had been the child of a certain Li family in Khuh-yang, and that he had perished there in a well at the age of nine. His parents then searched for that family and discovering it, their inquiries confirmed the matter. (De Groot, 1967/1892: 143)

The Thai chemist Chakara C. also described a reincarnation memory (see Chapter 5), and I have collected similar accounts from respondents in China. De Groot (1967/1892: 144) notes, "There are also cases recorded of previous lives detected by certain spots or marks on the body," a finding that Stevenson (1977, 1987) documents in modern cases.

Although the majority of the Six Dynasties (317–589) *chih-kuai* narratives do not coincide in content with the modern anomalous experiences described in Chapters 2 and 3, enough parallels exist to support the argument that primary features exist cross-culturally within specific types of experience. Other motifs in *chih-kuai* collections include sexual unions with animals taking human form (particularly foxes); sex with deities; and supernatural transformations of humans into animals and vice-versa. *Chih-kuai* narratives can be considered literary explorations of the forms of supernatural belief that existed in Chinese society at the time of their collection, a bridge between fiction and nonfiction literary forms (Yu, 1987). Medieval Chinese society appears to have granted internal "reality" a higher status than do modern psychologists.

Medieval Japanese documents also support the argument that universal features exist among some types of anomalous experience. The narratives of the *Nihon Ryoiki*, gathered by the ninth-century Japanese monk Kyokai, demonstrate that Japanese anomalous reports were equivalent to those from China (Nakamura, 1973). Kyokai's collection, written in Chinese, was the first of many Japanese anthologies to indicate that some forms of wondrous events contain features that transcend culture and era. The *Sambo-e*, completed in 984, was the first such collection written in Japanese (Matsubayashi, 1970). Later documents also record miraculous circumstances surrounding the founding of various temples. Japanese reports of apparitions, precognitive dreams, miracle cures, meditational visions, contacts with the dead, and near-death experiences (described in more detail in the next chapter) contain many of the narrative elements found in modern accounts (Anderson, 1969; Blacker, 1975; Mills, 1970; Ury, 1970, 1979).

Korean collections of anomalous accounts also contain universal features. Korean narratives, gathered in the 1600s, include stories of ghosts, ESP, near-death experiences, visions, and performances by psychic practitioners (Im and Yi, 1962).

Psychic Performance in Pre-Buddhist China

Chinese anomalous performances predate the arrival of Buddhism from India (approximately first century A.D.). Biographies of *fang-shih*, or Chinese magicians, during the later Han Dynasty (25–220) indicate that many elements of these psychic performances were similar to those of modern accounts. *Fang-shih* predicted the results of floods, military campaigns, fires, harvests, political intrigues, and their own deaths. Practical applications of psychic abilities, particularly predicting military events and rainmaking, were highly valued and frequently exhibited (De Woskin, 1983).

Many *fang-shih* performance stories contain elements that modern magicians could duplicate through deception. Examples include vanishing into thin air, summoning ghosts, pulling objects from empty basins, and supplying wine to hundreds from a single cup (a story similar to that of Jesus' miraculous transformation of water into wine: John 2:1–11). As with modern accounts, some of these exploits seemingly exceeded the domain of sleight-of-hand magic. *Fang-shih* ascended to heaven like Jesus did (Mark 16:19; Luke 24:51), changed from a woman to a man, and restored a baby to life (like Jesus' raising of the dead: Matthew 9:23–25; Mark 5:38–42; John 11:17–44). As with modern episodes, oral transmissions allow the embellishment of "normal" magical performances.

The Records of the Three Kingdoms (A.D. 220–265) contain lengthy accounts of three specific *fang-shih*. Kuan Lu (d. A.D. 256) made numerous predictions that later came true (for example, he uncovered a criminal act, predicted a woman's death, divined the robbery of a deer and how it would be returned, and specified the end of a drought). He was particularly skillful at playing a traditional game in which he guessed the names of thirteen hidden objects. His biography, transcribed soon after his death, stressed that his guesses were not always accurate. He achieved twelve out of thirteen correct on one occasion and frequently demonstrated high scores. His turtle-shell crack divinations were also less than perfect (interpreting turtle-shell cracks was an ancient Chinese means of gaining information paranormally). Kuan Lu might guess the names of seven or eight hidden objects out of ten. Although he taught his techniques (based on the *I Ching*) to his disciples, they were unable to duplicate his feats (De Woskin, 1983).

Accounts of Kuan Lu's performances are much like those of modern psychics. For example, Duke University professor J. B. Rhine's (1934) subjects were incapable of achieving perfect ESP card scores regularly, although they nonetheless convinced him that they had demonstrated statistically significant results.

Marvelous deeds were attributed to Chu Chien-p'ing (d. circa A.D. 220–226), whose predictions regarding specific people often came true. This type of performance—precognition of future events—is part of the repertoire of all fortune-tellers (M302, "Means of learning the future"). Accounts of Chu Chien-p'ing are notable in that his abilities were investigated and documented.

Chou Hsuan (d. circa A.D. 226–239) correctly predicted the capture of bandits as well as violence in the royal palace. He also interpreted dreams, accurately predicting future events in the life of the dreamer. Apparently he was tested rather thoroughly by several skeptics; although they described dreams that never happened, his predictions, based on their verbalizations, came true. His biographer notes that he, like other magicians, was not always correct.

Hua t'o, who was a medical practitioner rather than a *fang-shih*, aborted stillborn fetuses and performed surgery using anesthesia. He was credited with many marvelous cures using drugs and moxibustion (the stimulation of an acupuncture point by burning herbal material on the skin's surface). Hua t'o apparently combined psychosomatic and occult medicine with his surgical practice, using traditional Asian medical techniques as an organizing principal. Paranormal healings (as they might be deemed by Western interpretation) and precognition were thought to be within his capabilities.

These ancient practitioners were said to cause wonderment, even among the skeptics within their audiences. They were thought to reveal aspects of a hidden spiritual reality that could be explained within Taoist folk belief. Buddhist missionaries, in competition with this tradition, were forced to match these performances.

The Role of Wondrous Events in Early Chinese Buddhist History

As conceived by Gautama Siddhartha (563–483 B.C.), Buddhist ideology had little affiliation with the occult. Indeed, he specifically prohibited public demonstrations of magic: "You must not show the miracles of the *iddhi* [psychic powers] to the laity, O *bhikku* [monk], miracles that surpass the power of the common man. He who behaves in such fashion will make himself guilty of an evil deed" (Vinaya, II, 212, and Vinaya Texts, III, 81, quoted by Eliade, 1969: 174, 175).

Yet Buddhist monks arriving in China, especially in the north, became known as miracle workers. They converted nonbelievers, in part, through wondrous performances and cures. An analysis of Buddhist history suggests that one reason for this religion's success was its capacity to adapt to the performance model required for converting Asian audiences.

A legend of Buddhism's arrival in China tells of the Han Dynasty Emperor Ming (A.D. 58–75) who had a dream of a golden deity flying in front of his palace. He was informed of an Indian sage of golden hue who could fly. The delegation sent to fetch this man returned with the first Buddhist monks. Although the eminent historian Ch'en (1964) reviews historical evidence discrediting this story, he documents numerous other wondrous events that contributed to the acceptance of Buddhism in China. "Discounting these embellishments [surrounding

Emperor Ming], one is still inclined to believe that Buddhist monks like Fo-t'u-teng and Dharmakshema were able to perform magical feats which assisted them in the task of winning converts" (Ch'en, 1964: 79).

Fo-t'u-teng arrived in North China in about 310 seeking to establish a Buddhist center in Lo-yang. Because a war raged in China at that time, he could not attain this goal. Yet before his death in 348, he became an advisor to a prominent military commander and established Buddhism as a religion in northern China. By 528, Ts'ui Hung had written the *Shih-liu-kuo ch'un-ch'iu*, which describes Fo-t'u-teng's exploits. The *Liang Kao-seng chuan*, a biography of Fo-t'u-teng by Hui-chiao, was written between 519 and 554. The century and a half between the death of Fo-t'u-teng and the transcription of stories about him allowed sufficient time for a considerable legend to develop (Wright, 1948). Ch'en (1964: 79) writes,

By his display of magic, such as using spirits as his messengers, producing a lotus out of a bowl of water, and drawing water from dried-up wells with toothpicks, he gained the confidence of Shih Lo of the later Chao Dynasty and served him for more than two decades as imperial advisor. . . . His ability to produce rain was a boon to the agricultural people of the north, and his power of prognostication was extremely useful in military strategy and tactics.

Still, many descriptions of his actions do not exceed those of modern psychic performers, if we consider the embellishment that occurs over time:

He was proficient at intoning magic spells and could make the spirits his servants. When he took sesame oil, mixed it with rouge, and smeared it on his palm, events more than 1000 li distant were perfectly revealed in his palm as if he were face to face with them. He could also make those who kept the Buddhist regimen see [events as reflected in his palm]. Moreover, when he heard the sound of bells, he would foretell events there from, and [these prophecies were never once unfulfilled]. (Wright, 1948: 377, 378)

Miracle-working monks attracted broad followings, enabling Buddhism to secure a foothold in China. Gernet (1956) argues that between the fifth and tenth centuries Buddhism supplied a better means of doing what folk religion attempts to do: produce wonders associated with folk healing practices. The monk Srimitra (d. circa A.D. 335–342) practiced magical arts with brilliant results, contributing to the spread of Buddhism. She-kung (d. A.D. 380), a monk from central Asia, attained the ruler Fu Chien's favor because he could summon dragons and make rain. This is one of the earliest accounts in which a Buddhist monk in China prayed for rain, a skill highly valued by rulers (Chou, 1944–45).

The development of Buddhist folk healing practices illustrates how wondrous performances shaped Buddhist religious ideology. As mentioned above, Gautama Siddhartha clearly prohibited his monks from practicing medicine or demonstrating the miraculous abilities they attained through meditation. They were allowed to give medicines to each other or emergency care if no medical experts were available, but even these practices were to be done covertly. Early Buddhists did not deny that wondrous experiences occurred, but they restricted wondrous performances in deference to more important goals (Demieville, 1985).

Yet some of the first Buddhist monks to enter China did perform healings. An Shih-kao, the earliest Chinese translator of Buddhist texts (during the latter half of the second century A.D.), was thought to have medical abilities (Demieville, 1985). Jivaka, who arrived at Lo-yang in about A.D. 300, worked many miraculous cures. In one instance, he sprinkled pure water on a civil servant and, by reciting incantations, healed the man's twisted and paralyzed legs. Fo-t'u-teng, mentioned previously, was believed to have stopped an epidemic. During the fourth century, Yu Fa-k'ai practiced acupuncture and the examination of pulses,[1] and he reportedly spread Buddhist doctrines using his medical skills. The monk Ch'ang-on effectively combatted an epidemic in 720 (Demieville, 1985).

It is logical to hypothesize that those medieval Chinese monks who had high capacities for dissociative experience were influenced to do healings in the same way that practitioners become healers today. All monks were encouraged to meditate. Those with dissociative ability increased their chances of perceiving wondrous events, and their resulting experiences probably prompted some to become spiritual healers. Their success, and the conversions that resulted, contributed to changes in Buddhist attitudes toward spiritual healing.

Buddhist performances also included the oral presentations of previously enacted wondrous events. Buddhist chroniclers collected rhetorically powerful accounts to bolster faith and support ideological arguments. Some collections seem designed specifically for preaching (see Mills, 1970: 34). Kao (1985: 166) notes, "In general, Buddhist tales from the *Ming-hsiang chi* [a Buddhist collection] are more extended and less erratic in style than other [secular *chih-kuai*] stories, possibly due to their circulation as sermon pieces." Popular services in China and Japan had a carnival atmosphere with many means employed to sway the minds of audiences, including musical performances, plays, and other entertainments. Stories of wondrous events were performed to convert nonbelievers and to increase the faith of novices.

The use of wondrous accounts within preaching also contributed to ideological innovations. The notion developed that *bodhisattvas*, individuals with special saintly capacities, could use their merit to benefit others. Various patriarchs, producers of wondrous events, were recognized as bodhisattvas after their deaths. Buddhism thus changed from a set of canons that ignored wondrous events to a system wherein intermediaries, and ritual performances associated with them, brought magical benefits to supplicants. These new doctrines coincided with the universal features that characterize wondrous performances.

A more complete analysis than that presented here would review the many other factors contributing to Buddhism's success in Asia. I do not advocate a monocausal theory of this religious evolution. Buddhist ideology was transformed by the cultures it encountered, and economic and social factors were highly significant. Yet wondrous experience played an important role in Buddhism's introduction to Asian countries, particularly in northern China. After the establishment of Buddhism in China, wondrous performance became less important and esoteric Buddhism's power weakened (Chou, 1944–45: 246).

Skepticism in Medieval Asian Literature

Psychic practitioners throughout the ages have been caught engaging in fraud. Additionally, people's interpretations of wondrous events vary significantly, some being more skeptical than others. Because of these factors, wondrous performances stimulate skepticism in some observers, particularly in more complex societies where bureaucratic religious organizations attempt to shape people's interpretation of atypical perceptions and where competing ideologies struggle for dominance.

Medieval Chinese skeptics tended to focus on the interpretation of anomalous episodes, since all experiences were regarded as part of the natural order. Confucius (557–479 B.C.) is often quoted regarding his refusal to talk of prodigies and spirits (Analects 7/20), but he is also credited with the injunction "Respect the ghost and spirits, but keep them at a distance" (Analects 6/20; Yu, 1987: 403). Skeptics, too, sought to distinguish the true meaning of anomalous narratives from their religious interpretations, mirroring the Confucian ambiguity.

By the Han era (A.D. 25–220), skepticism about divination made magical practitioners' work more difficult, requiring debating and persuasion skills (De Woskin, 1983: 10). An early manual of fortune-telling strategies, the *Liu-t'ao*, warned that "such practices delude the masses, who would otherwise follow a virtuous path" and recommended that deception be prohibited (De Woskin, 1983: 14). Straightforward communication with ghosts and spirits declined by the middle of the Han, especially among court *fang-shih*.

One medieval story depicts the tension between occult believers and skeptics. Liu ken, a psychic practitioner, was arrested for deluding the people. At his trial, he summoned the ancestors of the local prosecutor. The spirits humbled and embarrassed the official, warning him not to trifle with such a powerful individual as Liu ken (De Woskin, 1983: 15).

Other practitioners were not as fortunate. Tso Tz'u performed magic that was "revealed to be conjury, and criminal at that" (De Woskin, 1983: 35). The term *fang-shih* came to be used in a disparaging manner, especially by officials whose arts and technologies competed with these magician's skills. For example, Ku Yung described himself as a conservative practitioner of prognostication who revered the five Chinese classical texts. Ku Yung cataloged *fang-shih* failures, beginning with examples from the Chou dynasty and continuing to his own time. He argued,

> If one listens to what they [the *fang-shih*] say, it fills the ears to overflowing. But should one seek to take hold of what might actually be found, in the end one will have gained nothing, for it is an evasive thing akin to binding the wind or clutching a shadow. Thus the enlightened king refused to be persuaded by such talk, and Confucius himself desisted from speaking of these matters. (De Woskin, 1983: 38)

Perhaps the most famous Chinese skeptic was Wang Ch'ung (27–91), who accepted the existence of nonhuman entities but remained skeptical of reports regarding their actions. In his work *Lun heng* ("Carefully Weighted Arguments"), he wondered why ghosts whose earthly murders are being investigated do not frequently appear in court. He concluded that the dead cannot speak since they have no throats. Wang Ch'ung also discussed the man who, "finding himself in some solitary place, perceives spectres merely because of his anxiety and fright" since many experiences are due to "natural sound produced by the autumn" (De Groot, 1967/1892: 415).

Yu (1987) notes that two nephews of the celebrated poet Juan Chi (210–263), Juan Hsiu and Juan Chan, were famous for their disbelief in ghosts. Their opposition caused writers of anomalous accounts during this era to include supportive information such as locations, dates, names of witnesses, and investigating authorities.

In this atmosphere of disbelief, Buddhist missionaries participated in contests pitting their magical skills against those of Taoist practitioners. Buddhist accounts invariably portrayed the monks as victorious. For example, during the Sui dynasty (591–608) Buddhist monks climbed a seventy-two-knife "ladder" in their competition with Taoist shamans (Covell, 1983: 49).

Skepticism was often justified. Religious practitioners could not always resist the temptation to use deception to create wondrous effects.

Various medieval writers expressed concern regarding the corruption that existed among monks. In one example, a manuscript attributed to T'ang Yin (1470–1523) contains many tales of Buddhist deception and sexual malfeasance (Yang and Levy, 1971).[2] In one account, childless women regularly spent the night at a temple, a site famous for miraculously aiding the infertile. Buddhist monks, hiding in hollow pillars, presented themselves as apparitional sex partners (K1315.1, "Seduction by posing as a god"). As might be expected, "miracle" pregnancies resulted. A magistrate eventually learned of this chicanery and had the temple destroyed (Yang and Levy, 1971: 79). Other anti-Buddhist stories from this period have similar themes, causing the collection to constitute a form of anti-Buddhist pornography.

Japanese anomaly collections also portray skepticism that reflects their society. The *Uji Shui Monogatari*, compiled in the early thirteenth century, contains various accounts of fraudulent behavior which caution against trusting miraculous claims (Mills, 1970). "Wondrous" monks were proved to be dishonest. Individuals who derided superstition were praised as wise. Impostors were exposed and credulous believers were ridiculed. In these accounts, skeptics do not mock religious beliefs; they merely reveal the true nature of spurious anomalous claims. In one example, a hunter, accompanied by a monk, sees an apparition of a Buddhist saint. Although the monk accepts the vision as real, the hunter shoots an arrow into it to test its authenticity. This causes the image to change into a badger and the hunter remarks:

It's all very well for you to see a vision like that, Your Reverence . . . but since a hardened sinner like myself could see it, I felt I'd better see whether it was genuine or not and took a shot at it. If it had been a real bodhisattva, the arrow would not have pierced it, so it is clearly something highly suspicious. (Mills, 1970: 298)

The narrator of this story draws conclusions and presents a moral:

For all his saintliness, the holy man was stupid and so had been tricked. The other man, though only a hunter, had had his wits about him, and so had killed the badger and shown up its trickery. (Mills, 1970: 298)

All complex societies have individuals who, like the hunter, cannot resist shooting, either figuratively or literally, at apparitional images and the beliefs associated with them. Such skepticism affected Buddhist ideology. Because of the existence of doubters, Chinese psychic practitioners were subjected to scrutiny. Their explanations were considered in light of alternate interpretations. Deceased miracle-working bodhisattvas were immune to debunking, however, and provided a focus for beliefs that, in turn, generated tertiary wondrous perceptions. Legends of their deeds provided a foundation for folk beliefs in human intermediaries.

The Role of Wondrous Events in Christian History

Unlike Gautama Siddhartha, Jesus used miraculous performance to recruit followers. His performances fell within the tradition of miracle workers of his era (Crossan, 1991; Smith, 1978). The Gospels contain twelve specific healing narratives, many other wondrous demonstrations, and the Resurrection, which constituted a special wondrous proof. Stories and dramatizations of the Resurrection became an important Christian performance.

After Jesus' departure, the early Church patriarchs continued his tradition by performing miraculous feats in order to attract converts. Christian saints used incantations both to heal potential converts and to harm their opponents. Their magic proved more powerful than that of their competitors (see Acts 13:9–11; 19:18–19, for examples).

As in Asia, stories of wondrous events in the West stimulated further wondrous experiences and conversions. Common features related to wondrous experience were prevalent on both continents. For example, relics from the bodies of holy persons were enshrined in both Asia and Europe. Even as early as the fourth century, Christian authorities attempted to forbid traffic in relics, since this aspect of folk religion was growing at an alarming rate (Hillgarth, 1986: 19). Their efforts proved futile, however, and belief in such artifacts became established within folk cultures. Thompson's (1966) *Motif-Index* includes: D1381.20, "Sacred relics protect against attack"; D2158.1.3.1, "Saint's relics control fires"; E64.12, "Resuscitation by sacred relics"; V221.0.1, "Relics of saint cure disease."

In both Asia and Europe, miracles resulted from encountering holy people or objects. Stories of these wondrous events became oral performances which stimulated further wondrous experiences. Authorities in Europe, as in Asia, contributed to this process by collecting and preserving miraculous tales. For example, Augustine (A.D. 354–430) explained his carefully recorded accounts of local miracles:

I have been concerned that such accounts should be published because I saw that signs of divine power like these of older times were not often occurring and I felt that they should not pass into oblivion, unnoticed by the people in general. (Ward, 1982: 30)

Not only were common people persuaded by these accounts, but political and military leaders were also swayed. Clovis, king of the Frands, was so impressed by the miraculous powers demonstrated by

Saint Martin of Tours and other saints that he converted to Christianity around A.D. 496. According to Gregory (History, IX, 15), the Visigothic Recared was converted, in part, due to his admiration for Catholic miracles. Saints such as Amand (d. circa A.D. 675) attracted converts through their miracles as well as their preaching (Hillgarth, 1986). Cuthbert, a seventh-century monk, reportedly "went through the pagan villages of Northumbria preaching and demonstrating the benefit of the miracles of the saints in opposition to popular magic" (Hillgarth, 1986: 10). Christian magic, however, could not always provide protection; Thompson's (1966) *Motif-Index* includes D1402.13, "Druid's spells kill Christian king."

The Virgin Mary was the greatest focus of anomalous claims in Europe (D2161.5.2.2, "Cure by relics of Virgin Mary"; D1586.2, "Prayer to Virgin protects against plague"). Feminine nurturance has universal appeal within folk religion; Mary's role was equivalent to that of Quan Yin, the Buddhist Goddess of Mercy (mentioned in Chapter 7 as one of Dr. Li's guiding spirits). Thomas Becket, Archbishop of Canterbury, became the second most frequent focus for European miraculous experience after he was murdered in his cathedral in 1170 (Ward, 1982).

In the Middle Ages, miracles were not merely bizarre sidelights of the period; they reflected a basic dimension of European life. Twenty-nine percent of the biographical descriptions in *Butler's Lives of the Saints* (Thurston and Attwater, 1956), include miraculous accounts (White, 1982). Virtually all towns had shrines and someone able to record the miracles that might happen there. "People believed that they had experienced or witnessed certain events, and they recorded what they thought had happened" (Ward, 1982: 215).

As in Asia, miraculous claims also stimulated skepticism. Even Jesus was exposed to skeptical attacks. He refused to comply with the demand for miraculous proofs (Matthew 12:38,39; Mark 8:11–12; Luke 11:16–29; John 6:30) and was unable to perform well around skeptics (Matthew 13:58; Mark 6:5; Luke 4:23–27). The Gospel writer Matthew (28:11–15) even notes skeptical explanations for the Resurrection, indicating a tradition of opposition to Christian claims (Smith, 1978).

As in Asia, skeptics often had grounds for their disbelief. Geoffrey Chaucer (1340–1400) noted the efficacy of false relics in his *Canterbury Tales*, and Thompson's *Motif-Index* includes K1976, "False miraculous relic"; V142.1, "Sham relics perform miracles if faith is great."

As was the case for Buddhist traditions, Christian skepticism formed the boundaries of belief; believers' explanations for wondrous events could be evaluated against alternate claims. Psychic performers were sometimes expected to compete against other magicians or to provide proof of their authenticity.

Comparison of Attitudes, Performances, and Social Effects

Medieval Asians' concept of the occult differed from that of Europeans. Asians believed that atypical effects were produced by their ancestors, ghosts, and other spiritual forces, but that these phenomena were all part of the natural order. They had no concept of the supernatural. Medieval Christians accepted the existence of ghosts but also believed that God produced miraculous events to reward the faithful or to punish the faithless. Some Europeans argued that wondrous phenomena helped people recognize the miraculous quality of all creation. These theologians classified relatively mundane events as miraculous since God was the original cause of everything. The modern notion of God intervening to create miracles did not develop before the sixteenth century at the earliest (Ward, 1982: 214). As the concept of "natural" scientific laws developed, Europeans came to believe that miraculous events required the direct intervention of God, who countermanded these laws in order that miracles might occur (Ward, 1982: 32).

Social factors determined the degree of dissemination of European and Asian wondrous accounts. Christian religious authorities attempted to ensure that only those miraculous reports supporting virtue were granted credence. For example, Pope Alexander III (in office 1159–1181) condemned the miracles alleged to occur after the death of a man killed in a drunken brawl (Ward, 1982: 186). Buddhists made similar efforts to use wondrous perceptions for religious purposes. Chroniclers focused on specific topics, such as believers' near-death experiences (which are discussed in the following chapter) or events supporting belief in a specific shrine.

In both Asia and Europe, many other factors besides wondrous events contributed to the success or failure of religious endeavors. Organizational ability, political power, and geographical location were merely some of the variables affecting a group's ability to attract new members. With reference to Europe, Ward (1982: 131) notes:

[M]iracles were not at any time the decisive factor in the survival of a cult. They were a vital ingredient in most cases and were seen as the primary power for spreading the fame of a shrine, especially at its beginning. But the survival or immediate failure of a shrine owed its chances to influences other than the presence or absence of miracles.

Accounts of miracles reflected the society in which they were transcribed. In Europe, earlier medieval stories more frequently portrayed supernatural acts of protection and vengeance; later miracles tended to depict mercy and cures, as society deemed these traits more appropriate (Ward, 1982). Written accounts of apparitions (Finucane, 1984) and Spanish visions of the Virgin Mary (Christian, 1981) both varied over time, reflecting the changing needs of the eras in which they were recorded. In Asia, some types of miraculous narrative also mirrored the needs of the time. Early near-death accounts presented clear images of heavens and hells; later recorded narratives lacked these features, perhaps because, by that time, audiences already accepted standard portrayals of these cosmic regions.

A number of factors explain the thematic variations within medieval wondrous accounts. First, although universal features are apparent within both Asian and European wondrous accounts, culture probably affected the frequency and content of individual wondrous perceptions (see Chapter 3). Second, the medieval accounts that are available for modern analysis undoubtedly were shaped during transcription. Third, narratives whose content did not coincide with social needs probably were not preserved.

Although medieval Europeans and Asians held different attitudes toward the miraculous and shaped their accounts using diverse perspectives, recurring features within their wondrous performances contributed to uniformities in folk belief. In both Asia and Europe, monks converted audiences by producing wondrous effects (D2161.5.1, "Cure by holy man"; V331.1, "Conversion to Christianity through miracle"). These monks were in competition with rival magicians and were forced to out-perform them (D1719.1, "Contest in magic"; V351.3, "Magician overpowered in contest with a saint"; V331.1.3, "Conversion to Christianity because heathen gods prove to be less powerful"). Audiences also found that special rituals, relics, and locations stimulated further wondrous events, particularly healings (V221.0.1, "Relics of saint cure disease"; V113.0.1, "Miracles at shrine"). As a result, both Christians and Buddhists came to believe that special individuals could intercede on behalf of supplicants. The demand for magical performances led to deviance, skepticism, and deception (K1970, "Sham miracles"; K1315.1, "Seduction by posing as a god"; K1976, "False miraculous relic"; V142.1, "Sham relics perform miracles if faith is great").

In all likelihood, Buddhist and Christian monastic practices tended to attract the types of dissociation-prone people who most frequently experience and produce wondrous events. Buddhist and Christian ideologies were successful, in part, because they were able to harness the abilities of these wondrous performers within their respective missionary programs.

Summary

Wondrous experience narratives in medieval Asian literature contain features that are equivalent to those in modern reports. Accounts of apparitions, contacts with the dead, precognitive dreams, and out-of-body and near-death experiences reveal universal elements. This evidence supports the argument that such episodes provide a foundation for folk belief in spirits, souls, life after death, and psychic abilities.

In all societies, certain people have high capacities for anomalous experience. Some of these individuals feel motivated to learn or devise wondrous performances. Buddhist and Christian movements trained and exploited such people. Asian and European miracle workers spread their beliefs by using wondrous performances to convert their audiences. The events they produced affected both Buddhist and Christian faiths, resulting in a convergent belief that special intermediaries could benefit those who requested their assistance. Christian saints, who had demonstrated the ability to perform miraculous events, became the focus of prayers. Buddhist bodhisattvas, who also had engaged in wondrous performances, fulfilled an equivalent role in Asian societies. In both cultures, supplicants experienced wondrous benefits and skeptics sought to counter the inflated claims of fantasy-prone believers. In both cultures, skepticism shaped the nature of belief. Lacking certainty, some people were motivated to seek further anomalous performances.

Some forms of wondrous experience were more important than others in shaping religious belief. Religious histories place a special emphasis on spiritual healing, but near-death experiences, discussed in the following chapter, also played a role in medieval European and Asian theological development.

Chapter 9
Near-Death Experiences in Medieval Europe, China, and Japan

In the general pattern of the near-death experience (NDE), individuals come close to death but later revive and are able to describe their experiences of other worlds. By comparing NDE reports from medieval China, Japan, and Europe to modern accounts, we can evaluate the possibility that these narratives contributed to ideological uniformities within folk belief. The present chapter, inspired by Becker's (1981, 1984) analysis of Pure Land Buddhism, applies the experience-centered approach to medieval European NDE accounts (Zaleski, 1987) and to medieval Chinese and Japanese "anomalous event literature" (in Chinese: *chih-kuai*, records of anomalies, or *ch'uan-ch'i*, accounts of the extraordinary). This strategy allows me to test two central hypotheses.

The cultural source theory suggests that NDEs are products of the society within which they occur and that cross-cultural similarities are due to either cultural diffusion or equivalencies among cultures. The experiential source theory suggests that some medieval Chinese and Japanese folklore reports are derived from *universal* features that are intrinsic to NDEs. Similarities between modern Western and medieval Asian conceptions of heaven and hell can be explained, in part, as a result of these common elements.

The existence of *universal* features among accounts from different cultures and eras supports the experiential source theory. Various researchers argue that NDEs occur in all societies and that they share universal features (Greyson and Flynn, 1985; Lundahl, 1982; Osis and Haraldsson, 1977; Sabom 1982). The incidence of NDEs also seems to be independent of religious belief. Ring (1980) found that the contents of NDEs did not closely correspond to the respondent's religious orientation or religiosity. Irwin's (1985a) review of studies of out-of-body experiences noted that religiosity is not closely related to the incidence

of these episodes. My evidence explores the effects of NDEs on religious ideology. My findings support the experiential source theory
but also suggest that social and structural equivalencies also contributed to the commonalities within Buddhist and Christian images of the
afterlife.

The Modern NDE

Modern researchers have found that NDEs occur with surprising frequency. Gallup (1982), for example, found that 15 percent of a randomly selected sample of the U.S. population has had a close brush
with death and that 34 percent of this group remembered events
during these episodes. Modern NDE literature indicates that recurring
patterns exist among these accounts. Ring (1980) hypothesizes five
NDE stages: experiencing "a feeling of peace," the sensation of "body
separation," "entering the darkness," "seeing the light," and "entering
the light." Moody (1975) describes parallel phases: "ineffability" (an
inability to describe one's perceptions in words), "hearing the news" (of
one's own death), "feelings of peace and quiet," hearing "the noise,"
passing through "the dark tunnel," being "out of the body," "meeting
others," encountering "the being of light," undergoing "the review" of
one's life, reaching "the border" between life and death, and "coming
back" to life. He also discusses the post-NDE events of "telling others"
and "corroboration." Most experiencers return to their bodies before
reaching the advanced stages, which involve contact with the "being of
light." Among Sabom's (1982) sample of nonsurgical cases, 28 percent
reported encountering "the light."

Moody's (1975: 21–22) model can be paraphrased as follows: A
dying person hears him- or herself pronounced dead, feels "out of" his
or her physical body, and, from that perspective, views attempts at
resuscitation or other events related to the physical plane. The person
then moves through a dark tunnel or transition area, is met by spirits,
relatives, or friends who have already died, and encounters a being of
light who questions the experiencer nonverbally regarding his or her
life. At some point, a form of barrier causes the experiencer to return
to the physical body. Sometimes, it is a decision on the part of the
experiencer that leads to the return to the body. Experiencers often
evaluate their NDEs as "more real" than normal reality.

Although most modern reports are associated with feelings of joy,
love, and peace, a small percentage of respondents describe experiencing barren, isolated domains filled with restless souls; they may feel
alienated and despondent, a condition they evaluate as a form of hell.
(Sabom [1982] found that 23 percent of his respondents described a

dark or void region.) In Ring's (1980: 249) view, hellish states within NDEs are transitional phases that some individuals pass through on their way to more pleasant realms, unless they return to their bodies beforehand.

Those describing NDEs sometimes report physical details, such as the medical personnel's identity, clothing, procedures, and conversation, information that theoretically should be unavailable to unconscious individuals (Moody [1975] reviews "corroboration"). Some NDEs have a "life-transforming" quality in that, following the event, experiencers report greater interest in spiritual matters and more compassion for fellow humans, but sometimes a lack of concern for traditional religious rituals and structures (Ring, 1984).

Medieval European NDEs

Zaleski (1987) compares medieval reports of "otherworldly" visits to modern NDEs, providing a framework for a cross-cultural analysis of the NDE folklore. Although fundamental divergences exist, medieval visionary experiences reveal the basic elements described in modern NDE reports. For example, the monk Bede, in his *Ecclesiastical History of the English People*, completed in 731 (Colgrave and Mynors, 1969: 488), describes the experience of a man named Drythelm. Drythelm "died" of a severe illness one evening in A.D. 696, yet revived in the morning to report meeting a man "of shining countenance and bright apparel" who led him through an enormous valley. One side of the valley was filled with flames while the other side had hail and snow. As Drythelm observed tortured souls being thrown from side to side, his guide explained that this was a temporary situation, that these individuals could be released through masses, prayers, alms, and fasts performed by the living on their behalf. Later Drythelm saw hell, a bottomless, stinking pit. When demons threatened him, his guide reappeared as a bright star. Together, they traveled to a realm of clear light, saw a vast wall, and suddenly were on top of it. Beyond was a bright, flowery meadow filled with happy people. Drythelm thought he was in heaven but was informed that this was a holding area for the slightly imperfect. The actual kingdom of heaven was filled with far greater fragrance and light. After his return to his body, Drythelm distributed his property, retired to a monastery, and began a life of devotion, austerity, fasting, and frequent cold baths.

As with many medieval and modern NDEs, Drythelm's experience did not conform to the image of the afterworld that was commonly accepted during his era. In the later seventh century, the notion of Purgatory was not theologically acceptable, and the word "purgatory" had not come into usage. Zaleski (1987: 33) notes that later narratives, mainly from the twelfth and thirteenth centuries, followed the Drythelm pattern:

Among them are the visions of Adamnan, Alberic, the Boy William, Tundal, and the Knight Owen (St. Patrick's Purgatory). Although they depend on sources shared by all medieval otherworld journey narratives (the Bible, apocalypses, legends of martyrs and desert saints, Gregory's Dialogues, and classical works such as Vergil's Aeneid and Plutarch's Moralis), the narratives in this group display a remarkable similarity in their choice of which set phrases and images to borrow. Typically the visionary is told, after viewing purgatorial torments and mistaking them for the punishments of the damned, that there are far worse sights to come (Drythelm, Tundal, Owen); he sees souls tossed between fire and ice (Thespesius, Drythelm, Tundal) and rising like sparks from the pit of hell (Drythelm, Alberic, the Boy William, Tundal); he is temporarily deserted by his guide (Thespesius, Drythelm, the Boy William, Tundal); he finds paradise surrounded by or on top of a wall, which he surmounts without knowing how (Drythelm, Adamnan, Alberic, the Boy William, Tundal, Owen); at the end, after a brief taste of heavenly joys, he is compelled against his will to return to life (Drythelm, Tundal); and after he revives, his newly austere mode of life testifies to the authenticity of his vision (Drythelm, Alberic, and Tundal borrow Gregory's phrasing for this). In addition, the test-bridge [walking across a dangerous structure functions as a form of judgement] . . . recurs with many similarities in the visions of Adamnan, Alberic, Tundal, and Owen.

Wetti (824), Charles the Fat (circa 885), Thurkill (1149), and Edmund of Eynsham (1196) saw specific individuals in purgatory. Stories of these visions were particularly well-suited for encouraging performance of rituals for the dead (*Motif-Index*: E341.3, "Dead grateful for prayers").

Although Zaleski (1987) notes fundamental similarities between medieval and modern visions, her analysis also discloses many differences. While medieval accounts focus on Hell and a "bad" death, modern accounts point to a "good" death associated with relaxation, peace, and love. Medieval guides and deities are parallel to hierarchical, feudal authorities, whereas modern otherworldly figures symbolize parental acceptance. Medieval accounts reveal a prominence of judgmental obstacles, tests, and purificatory torments; the modern "life review," in which the individual evaluates his or her own life, is regarded as an educational experience. Medieval NDEs consolidated Catholic teachings on Purgatory and retained vestiges of older conceptions of planetary schemes as places of punishment and interrogation. Modern narratives are vague regarding cosmic topographies and are shaped by optimistic, democratic, "healthy-minded" principles reflecting contemporary ideologies and sentiments. In medieval accounts, the returner generally promotes a particular penitential and monastic institution.

Modern NDEs tend to advocate service and humanistic ideals coupled with a change of life-style toward renunciation of worries and fears (Zaleski, 1987: 188–190).

Zaleski (1987: 153) argues that many NDE stories appear to be "formed in an inner dialogue between the visionary and his culture" which "develops in the telling and retelling until it finally comes into the hands of an author who shapes it further for dialectic, polemic or literary use." She argues that "the otherworld journey is a work of the narrative imagination. As such, it is shaped not only by the universal laws of symbolic experience, but also by the local and transitory statutes of a given culture" (Zaleski, 1987: 7).

Zaleski's data do not demonstrate that NDE accounts are *entirely* a product of the imagination. Her "universal laws of symbolic experience" are anomalous. Differences between medieval and modern accounts can be attributed to variations in cultural shaping after the original experiences. Why are medieval NDEs so similar to those of modern ones?

Cultural source theorists might point to cultural commonalities as an explanation. For example, the New Testament book of Acts (7:55–60) describes the vision of Saint Stephen who, prior to his death, reported seeing Jesus standing to the right of God. Before dying, Stephen asks his Lord to forgive those who stone him, an event witnessed by Saul, the future Saint Paul. Since Western medieval and modern experiencers share this Christian heritage, cultural diffusion could explain the prevalence of the "perceiving a deity" theme within NDEs.

Yet the "universal laws of symbolic experience" are also apparent in medieval Chinese and Japanese NDE narratives. Recurring motifs among these stories duplicate, in a general manner, the differences Zaleski found between Western modern and medieval otherworldly visits. Zaleski's concept of "universal laws" runs parallel to Hufford's (1982a) notion of "primary features." Although European NDEs reveal the effects of cultural shaping, Zaleski's data support the experiential source hypothesis because the same universal elements found in modern NDE accounts are present in both medieval Christian and Asian NDE folklore.

Medieval Chinese NDEs

The NDE motif existed in Chinese folklore prior to the introduction of Buddhism to China. Since ancestral worship was a major component of their religious practice, Chinese people were particularly curious regarding the nature of the afterlife. This interest probably lent NDE narratives special rhetorical power for shaping religious ideologies.

Pre-Buddhist NDE accounts contain the common features found in modern NDEs: guides, deity figures, and divine structures. De Groot (1967, 113–114) relates two Taoist NDEs within one narrative: The ruler Kien-tsze of Chao, while ill, lost consciousness for five days in 498 B.C.; his physician diagnosed his condition as equivalent to that of the ruler Muh of Ts'in (658–620 B.C.), who, while in a similar state, experienced being taken to the residence of the Emperor of Heaven. There, Muh had learned information about future political events which later proved valid. Basing his advice on this precedent, the physician counseled patience and, after two-and-a-half days, Kien-tsze awoke and described his NDE. He had met the Emperor of Heaven, heard beautiful music, saw ten thousand dances, and participated in a symbolic dream that eventually produced prophetic information.

Sanskrit scriptures containing NDE elements were translated into Chinese as early as the second century. One such text, although peripheral to Indian Buddhist ideologies, was eventually to become one of the fundamental scriptures of the Pure Land School of Buddhism, later becoming the major Buddhist faith in China and Japan. In the text, Dharmakara bodhisattva (Amitabha) made forty-eight vows, affirming that he would meet believers at the moment of death and transport them to a wonderful "Pure Land" heaven (Takakusu, 1947). Another text, the Bhaisajya-guru sutra, or *Yao-shih liu-li-kuang ju-lai pen-yuan kung-te ching* ("Sutra on the Merits of the Fundamental Vows of the Master of Healing, the Lapis Lazuli Radiance Tathagata"), was first translated into Chinese early in the fourth century A.D. It narrates the dying person's experiences even more clearly:

> Then, while his body lies in its original position, he is seized by the messengers of Yama who led his spirit consciousness before that King of the Law. The inborn spirits attached to all sentient beings, who record whether each being's conduct is good or bad, will then hand down these records in their entirety to Yama, King of the Law. Then, the King will interrogate this person, and he will sum up the person's deeds. According to the positive and negative factors, he shall judge him. . . . [If the proper scripture is recited] that person's consciousness may be returned to his body [immediately]. He will clearly remember what he has experienced, as if it were a dream. (Birnbaum, 1979: 165)

NDE folklore can be categorized by the visionary's destination. Narratives that focus on Yama's judgment, as outlined in the Bhaisajya-guru sutra, are equivalent to European visions of Purgatory. Other Asian reports portray Amitabha's Pure Land and are similar to modern heavenly NDEs. Some tales synthesize these traditions by describing visits to both heavens and hells.

Chih-kuai (records of anomalies) from the Six Dynasties era (A.D. 317–589) provide near-death visions of hell that fit the Bhaisajya-guru sutra pattern (Kao, 1985). In an important early story, Chao T'ai, a native of Pei-ch'iu in Ch'ing-ho (modern Hupeh, bordering on Shantung), died at the age of thirty-five some time during the Chin Dynasty (265–420). Ten days later, he revived and told of being carried to the east by two horsemen. He then arrived at a large city wall, passed through the city gate, and was presented to the magistrate. He was ordered to describe his sins before a scarlet-clothed individual who then directed that he take the role of inspector of the internal waterworks. This allowed him to view the harsh punishments in the different hells and to note the efficacy of rituals performed by the living for the dead. He followed a group that was released as a result of these rituals. He also saw a godly person with a beautiful countenance (assumed to be the Buddha).

After completing his waterworks inspection, Chao T'ai asked an overseer how one might avoid the hellish tortures. The overseer informed him that embracing Buddhist doctrines ("serving the Dharma") wipes out even those sins committed before acceptance of them. It was then discovered that Chao T'ai had been prematurely called to hell due to a bureaucratic error. He was returned to life and directed to inform people of what he had learned. Upon his return, he convened a great mass on behalf of his deceased relatives and ordered his sons and grandsons to mend their ways and to honor the Dharma (Buddhist doctrines). Chao T'ai's story included the names of an imperial officer and a marquis, who were among ten visitors who came to his house inquiring about what he had seen. "Every one of them was dreadfully frightened by what he heard, and thereupon decided to honor the Dharma" (Kao, 1985: 166–171).

A later tale sheds light on the degree to which Chao T'ai's narrative circulated. Ch'eng Tao-hui, a Taoist from Wu-ch'ang (in modern Hupeh), reportedly died in A.D. 391, but revived after several days. He described being bound, but later released, by ten or more people who took him along a road with dense brambles on both sides. Sinners were being driven through the brush as a form of punishment. Ch'eng was taken to an audience hall in a large city and was told that he had been treated kindly because he had been a devout Buddhist in a previous life. A magistrate listened to arguments regarding Ch'eng's past deeds. His past-life virtues were considered sufficient, and he was sent on a tour of the hells so that he might inform the living of the nature of Buddhist Dharma. (The tale refers to Chao T'ai's report, described above, indicating that "what Ch'eng Tao'hui saw was more or less the same" [Kao, 1985: 173–174]. Apparently, Chao T'ai's story had circulated widely since the narrator assumes the audience's familiarity with it.)

As Ch'eng's soul returned to his house, he observed familiar people visiting his neighborhood. After he revived and described his observations, these people corroborated his account. This "corroborative" element, also present in the Taoist tale, corresponds to features in some of Moody's (1975) NDE narratives.

Both Hindus (as specified by the *Bhagavad Gita*) and early Buddhists believed that a person's condition in the afterworld was determined by his or her state of mind at the moment of death. This belief gave NDEs special importance since they indicated the soul's destination. Through meditation, chanting, and special practices, one could increase the probability of focusing one's mind on a heavenly destination at the moment of death.

Accepting this doctrine, Tao-an, in A.D. 379, assembled seven of his pupils who collectively vowed to seek rebirth in the heaven of Maitreya, a Buddhist bodhisattva. Legend tells us that "when [Tao-an] died in A.D. 385, a strange priest appeared and pointed to the North-west, where the clouds opened and a beautiful heaven became visible to his dying eyes" (de Visser, 1935: 318).

Tao-an's leading disciple, Hui-yuan, attracted more than one hundred devotees and scholars to his famous monastery at Lu-shan Mountain. They vowed devotion to Amida (Sanskrit: Amitabha, the Buddha of the Western Pure Land) in A.D. 402 and engaged in austere meditative practices. Their NDE-type visions were regarded as precursors to what one could expect at death. One disciple, Liu Ch'eng-chin (354–410), claimed to see the Buddha and the Pure Land on many occasions. Not long before his death, another disciple, Seng-chi, who was afflicted with a grave disease, had a form of NDE in which he "saw himself proceed through the void" where "he beheld the Buddha Amitabha." The following night he suddenly stood, as if to see something. He then lay down, and stated, with a joyful expression on his face, "I must go," after which he died (Zurcher, 1959: 221–222).

In A.D. 414, another disciple, Hui-yung, also appeared to see something from his deathbed. When attending monks asked what he saw, he replied, immediately before dying, "The Buddha is coming!" (Zurcher, 1959: 222).

The Pure Land Buddhist patriarch T'an-luan was recruited to Buddhism in part as a result of an NDE. T'an-luan (476–542), a Taoist scholar from northern China, recovered from a serious illness after he suddenly saw a golden gate open before him. The experience led him to search for everlasting life. After gathering many Taoist texts, he met the Buddhist monk Bodhiruci, who revealed to him the Pure Land doctrines (circa 530). T'an-luan discarded his Taoist scriptures, which he had gone to great effort to obtain, and devoted his life to spreading the Pure Land religion (Ch'en, 1964: 344). His NDE led him to focus his attention on the specific Buddhist scriptures that depicted the imagery of a deity coming to meet the believer at death (Becker, 1981). T'an-luan popularized Pure Land doctrines since he advocated repetitive chanting, a method suitable for lay people.

Tao-ch'o (562–645), a Pure Land Buddhist monk who attracted a large following, was also affected by an NDE episode:

At the age of sixty-five, aged and sick, he felt himself to be on his deathbed, and summoned his disciples and many followers to recite the sutras. Thereupon T'an-luan appeared to him, and in a voice heard by all present, commanded that Tao-ch'o must continue to teach people for many years. It is said that flowers fell from heaven, which were carefully preserved by his followers. From that day on, Tao-ch'o became progressively healthier, even regaining another set of teeth, and continued to teach for almost two decades, living to the rare age of eighty-three. (Becker, 1981: 166)

Shan-tao (in Japanese, Zendo; A.D. 613–681), one of Tao-ch'o's followers, developed a strict regimen: he ate only small amounts of rice and vegetables, controlled his thoughts through meditation, repeated tens of thousands of mantras, went without sleep for seven days at a time, and accepted the objective reality of his visionary experiences. He and later Pure Land Buddhists devised methods that produced experiences to support their faith. By engaging in ascetic meditation techniques, they increased the probability of having a heavenly NDE; some succeeded in catching glimpses of the Pure Land before their deaths.

Shan-tao directed his monks to record the deathbed visions of Pure Land Buddhists, a task that generated a body of written "evidence" regarding the afterworld. The *Ching-t'u-lun*, a document compiled shortly after Tao-ch'o's era, contains twenty NDE accounts, half from monks and half from lay people.

In at least one case, (that of Dharma-master Chu-Hung) not only the dying person but all present were said to have seen the body of the Buddha coming from the Pure Land to welcome the dying monk. . . . In other cases, devout laywomen and laymen described visions of heavenly hosts on their deathbeds. In yet another, a butcher first had a vision of hell, where upon he was terrified into chanting the name of Amida; he then had a vision of Amida offering him the lotus seat, and passed peacefully away. (Becker, 1984: 60)

NDEs not only shaped the Buddhist concept of heaven, they also played a role in generating and clarifying doctrines regarding hells. The hells described in the Pali Canon, the original Indian Buddhist texts, lacked systematization. Paintings by Chinese artists who visited hell while near death contributed to an eventual formalization of images, leading to standardized iconography (Teiser, 1988b). For example, Chang Hsiao-shih (circa late seventh to early eighth centuries) painted hells "thought to have been inspired by the wanderings of his spirit while his body lay near death" (Teiser, 1988b: 440). These paintings were judged to be qualitatively better than versions based solely on hearsay. Such images were widely copied and, by the tenth century, Chinese hells were consistently associated with ten kings, each of whom had particular iconography (Teiser, 1988a).

The development of a well-known image of the bodhisattva Ti-tsang is also related to an NDE tale. In the Tunhuang manuscript "Huan-hun chi" ("The Record of a Returned Soul"), probably copied in the ninth century, the monk Tao-ming is summoned to purgatory by mistake, then instructed by Ti-tsang to paint his image correctly, as well as to chant his name. The deity vows to save those who hear his name, see his statue, or meet him personally in hell. Tao-ming was returned to life and produced what became a standardized image of the bodhisattva. By the twelfth century, Tao-ming became, in folk belief, a compassionate guide for spirits arriving at the netherworld.

The seventeenth-century *Yu-li* (Jade Register) presents examples of post-medieval Chinese NDEs (Clarke, 1893–94). In one story occurring between 1662 and 1723, Mr. Mo, a medical practitioner, died but then returned to consciousness. He reported that the judge in hell rebuked him for medical malpractice and sentenced him to become an ass. A recording clerk argued for leniency, citing Mo's benevolent motivations. When Mo awoke, he found a piece of ass's skin on his back (Clarke, 1893–94: 279). In another story, Mr. Yang, a hunter, died in 1774, lay unconscious for several days, and then awoke. He described his stay in hell, where birds continually pecked at his back. After being beaten by the ruler, he was set free so that he could exhort people not to kill birds (Clarke, 1893–94: 336–337).

As in Zaleski's (1987) findings, the Chinese narratives reveal common features (transition phases, guides, authority figures, life reviews, barriers, corroboration, and change of life-style following the episode). Some features are culturally specific, coinciding with the social, didactic needs of the experiencer's era. Although the documentary data (names, locations, witnesses, dates, times, etc.) suggest that these accounts originated with actual incidents, many narratives appear to have been shaped by prescriptive requirements, since they stress specific doctrines. The Taoist stories describe heavenly visits, while early Buddhist accounts present detailed descriptions of hells, which were useful for proselytizing. Pure Land patriarchs focused attention on specific sutras that coincided with NDE imagery, which were useful for inducing favorable NDEs. Later NDE accounts from the *Jade Register*, for example, show less concern with hellish topography (visitors are not allowed to take tours); by this time the imagery of the Chinese hells had been systematized so that descriptions of them were unnecessary. Although medieval Chinese otherworldly visits portray "primary" NDE features, they also reflect cultural needs.

Japanese NDEs

Japanese Buddhism was also affected by the spontaneous incidence of NDEs. The *Nihon Ryoiki* ("Japanese Miraculous Stories"), compiled in the ninth century by the monk Kyokai, provides the first written Japanese accounts of NDEs (Nakamura, 1973). Although some *Nihon Ryoiki* narratives provide specific names, dates (down to the day and hour), locations, and other information favoring their historicity, many harbor a fantastic quality, following Chinese patterns. At the time of Kyokai's compilation, the idea of a Pure Land heaven had not gained popular support in Japan. Kyokai borrowed a number of stories from earlier texts. (For example, stories in Volume 2 of the *Nihon Ryoiki*, nos. 10 and 19, reviewed below, were taken from the *Myohoki* ["Record of Invisible Work of Karmic Retribution"].)

Although six narratives in the *Nihon Ryoiki* describe "hellish" aspects related to NDEs, the earliest account in this collection is of a heavenly visit. Lord Otomo no Yasunoko no muraji revived after being presumed dead for three days. After his return to life, he described walking on a roadway of colored clouds to a golden mountain where he met the late Prince Regent Shotoku and a saintly monk. His vision expressed a fusion of Taoist and Buddhist symbols, a motif that was valuable for early Buddhist proselytizing (Nakamura, 1973: 111–115 [*Nihon Ryoiki*, Vol. 1, no. 5, a tale from the era of Empress Suiko, A.D. 593–628]).

The *Nihon Ryoiki* also includes the narrative of Kashiwade no omi Hirokuni, who died in 705 but came back to life four days later. He described two messengers who took him across a golden bridge to a golden palace. There he saw his deceased wife and his father being tortured. He was allowed to return to life because of his past good deeds. To aid his father, he created images of the Buddha, copied scripture, and made offerings (Nakamura, 1973: 143–146 [*Nihon Ryoiki*, Vol. 1, no. 30]).

In another account, a youth who ate bird eggs had a vision of a strange soldier who led him through a field. He perceived the field to be aflame and ran about shouting, "It's hot, it's hot." A villager who saw no flames caught the boy and pulled him from the area. The youth was severely burned and died the next day. The compiler Kyokai comments, "Now we are sure of the existence of hell in this world" (Nakamura, 1973: 174–175 [*Nihon Ryoiki*, Vol. 2, no. 10, a tale attributed to the year A.D. 754]). His statement indicates confusion regarding Chinese Buddhist ideology, which does not grant hell an earthly existence.

In another story, Aya no kimi's wife rectified a situation in which her husband had neglected to help some old people. Following his death, his spirit asked, through a diviner, that his corpse not be cremated for seven days. Later, he returned to life and described seeing a golden palace where his virtuous wife would be reborn. Because of his sins, he had been forced to suffer grievous hunger and thirst; due to specific virtuous deeds, however, he was allowed to return to the world of the living (Nakamura, 1973: 182–183 [*Nihon Ryoiki*, Vol. 2, no. 16, a tale attributed to the reign of Shomu, A.D. 724–749]).

Tokari no ubai, an extremely virtuous woman from Kawachi province, died in her sleep but returned to life after three days. King Yama, ruler of the netherworld, had summoned her merely to listen to her recitation of scriptures. She was told that, in three days, she would meet her three guides again. This prediction was fulfilled symbolically. Three days after she returned to life, she recovered three books of scriptures which had previously been stolen from her (Nakamura, 1973: 186–187 [*Nihon Ryoiki*, Vol. 2, no. 19, a tale attributed to the reign of Shomu, A.D. 724–749]).

Fujiwara no asomi Hirotari, who lived in a mountain temple in Yamato Province, died but returned to life three days later. Upon his return, he told of being led by men over a deep river to a many-storied, shining pavilion. There he met a king and learned that his wife, who had died in childbirth, was in purgatory. He agreed to copy, expound, and recite sutras to end her torture. As he departed he learned that King Yama and the bodhisattva Jizo (the being who saves people from hell) were one and the same (Nakamura, 1973: 233–235 [*Nihon Ryoiki*, Vol. 3, no. 9, a tale attributed to the year A.D. 768]).

Tanaka no mahito Hiromushime, a governor's wife who collected debts by force, died in 776. On her deathbed, she told of a visionary dream in which King Yama had admonished her. After seven days she was restored to life, but her body above the waist had turned into an ox. This creature lived on for five days, embarrassing the family and astonishing other witnesses (Nakamura, 1973: 257–259 [*Nihon Ryoiki*, Vol. 3, no. 26]).

Except for the first story, which fuses Buddhist and Taoist symbols, the *Nihon Ryoiki* stresses karmic retribution and Buddhist values. Hellish NDEs consistently include transition phases, guides, authority figures, and judgment.

Genshin's *Ojo Yoshu*, completed in 984, presents a summary of Buddhist sutras regarding heaven, hell, and the process for attaining rebirth in the Pure Land of Amida (Sanskrit: Amitabha) (Reischauer, 1930). The *Ojo Yoshu* clearly describes Yama's hells and its tortures, as well as Amida's golden palaces, bejeweled halls, and green groves. Amida is expected to arrive at the deathbed of believers to transport them to the Pure Land. Even before Genshin's work began to disseminate Pure Land doctrines, Buddhist artists portrayed images that were used as meditative tools for eliciting visions. The famous tapestry at the Taima-dera, probably imported from China in the eighth century, shows Amida arriving at a believer's deathbed and transporting him away (Okazaki, 1977).

Honen (1133–1212), credited as the founder of the Jodo (Pure Land) School of Buddhism in Japan, chanted the name Amida more than seventy thousand times a day and carefully recorded his visions between 1198 and 1206. He described heavens and hells, as well as Amida, the merciful individual whose function it was is to guide those who seek him. For example, in 1198,

while he was engaged in a special practice of the Nembutsu [chanting], a bright light appeared to him, then a body of clear water and finally some blue emerald ground. In the second month of the same year, he saw the so-called jewel-ground, the jewel-pond and the jewel-palace. From that time forward he was continually having visions of the most wonderful things. (Coates and Ishizuka, 1930: 207)

Believers regarded Honen's visions as equivalent to NDEs since he provided detailed descriptions of heavenly components: jewelled trees, jewelled ground, voices of many birds of variegated plumage, as well as harp and flute music. (These images correspond to the Christian iconography of heavenly streets of gold where angels play harps.)

It became the custom for Pure Land Buddhists to attempt to stimulate NDEs by setting a statue of Amida by the bed of a dying believer and placing cords attached to the effigy in the patient's hands.

[During Honen's last hours] his disciples brought him an image of Amida three feet high, and, as they put it on the right side of his bed, asked him if he could see it. With his finger pointing to the sky, he said, "There is another Buddha here besides this one. Do you not see him?" Then he went on to say, "As a result of the merit of repeating the sacred name, I have, for over ten years past, continually been gazing upon the glory of the Pure Land, and the very forms of the Buddhas and Bodhisattvas, but I have kept it secret and said nothing about it. Now however, as I draw near the end, I disclose it to you." (Coates and Ishizuka, 1930: 636)

The *Konjaku Monogatari Shu* (Ury, 1979), compiled in 1120 in Japan, contains two Chinese tales that have NDE forms. The monk Ting-sheng strongly desired to go to the Lotus-Matrix heaven but did not keep the precepts. After death, he was sent to the Red Lotus hell, which he mistook for the Lotus-Matrix world. Rapt in contemplation, he exclaimed, "Homage to the Lotus-Matrix world," a statement which miraculously caused the hell to be transformed into a heaven. Ting-sheng returned to life and recounted what he had observed (Ury, 1979: 60–61). This story is notable in that it fails to include some common NDE features, such as guides, authority figures, or judgment. Yet, like Pure Land visions, the narrative stresses grace attained through faith. In a second tale, Sun Hsuan-te, from Ii-an District, made a vow to copy the Wreath Sutra. While hunting, he fell from his horse and died. After one day, he returned to life and tearfully repented his sins. He described three officials of the land of the dead who had brought him to a great castle where King Yama chastised him for killing animals. He was allowed to return to life so that he might fulfill his vow of copying the sutra, an action that allowed him to be reborn upon his death in the Tusita heaven (where bodhisattva Maitreya waits to be born).

The *Uji Shui Monogatari*, compiled in the early thirteenth century, contains various Japanese accounts of NDEs. In one story (Mills, 1970: 204–205), a minor priest at a temple in Inaba Province took responsibility for, and attempted to complete, a wooden statue of Jizo. Unfortunately, he fell ill and died, but was restored to life after six days. He described being carried off by two demons, who later released him by order of the bodhisattva Jizo. The priest was allowed to return to life so that he could complete the statue. The *Uji Shui Monogatari* also contains a slightly variant version of the *Nihon Ryoiki* narrative that supports the equivalency of Yama and Jizo.

The *Genko Shakusho*, completed in 1322, also recounts NDE narratives, generally in concise form. In A.D. 941, monk Nichizo of Kyoto had an NDE in which he saw both heaven and hells (Ury, 1970: 279–282). In 916, the monk Chiko had an NDE in which he visited hell and was warned regarding his envy of another monk (Ury, 1970: 304–305). Other stories include that of the nun Nyozo, who was returned to life by Jizo, and of the daughter of the governor of Kaga Province, who was instructed in the netherworld to read two sutras in addition to the Lotus Sutra (Ury, 1970: 327–328). The Monk Myotatsu was cautioned by informants in the netherworld about the sinfulness of the monks, nuns, and lay people in his society (Ury, 1970: 334). Monk Genson gained the ability to recite the entire Lotus Sutra as a result of his NDE. Monks Josho and Ajo were separately saved by Jizo in different NDEs (p. 335). The monk Enno died and came back to life, only to find that he could not speak for three years. When he regained his faculties, he described the Pure Land, Maitreya's Palace, Yama's hells, and his rescue by six images of Jizo (Ury, 1970: 335–336).

Experiential Reports and Religious Ideology

Although medieval Chinese and Japanese NDE narratives reveal signs of cultural shaping, they also include basic features that are congruent to modern NDEs. Guides, bridges, paths, or other transitions, various barriers, deity figures or judges, great structures or beautiful terrains, and judgmental past-life reviews are often present. These similarities support the experiential source hypothesis as applied to NDEs; they suggest that some oral traditions originated with actual experiences.

Differences in NDE accounts may reveal cultural selection and shaping. "Heavenly" and "hellish" NDEs probably occur in all societies. Visions of Yama's court coincide, to a degree, with medieval European accounts of Purgatory, and Pure Land visions parallel modern NDE reports. Asian visits to hell generally entail more "out-of-body" time than travel to the Pure Land; the Pure Land journey is equivalent to a modern NDE. Chinese and Japanese hell narratives probably were shaped by retelling to a greater degree than were Pure Land vision stories. Many Pure Land narratives were transcribed immediately by a literate monk who attended the sick or dying experiencer. As with modern NDEs, Pure Land visits tend to include less activity and change of scene than do hellish accounts.

The history of the Pure Land movement suggests that religious doctrines evolved in harmony with, and benefited from the existence of, the primary features of NDEs. The patriarch T'an-luan's NDE was instrumental in determining the specific sutras granted importance in future Pure Land doctrines. Throughout the history of Pure Land doctrinal development, NDEs provided rhetorical tools for ideological innovation. Concepts supported by NDEs included the notion of karma, the superiority of Buddhism over Taoism, the prohibition against killing animals, the value of chanting, statue making, and sutra copying, rituals for the dead, as well as the equivalency of Yama and Jizo (supporting the Pure Land notion of salvation through grace). NDEs aided in systematizing doctrines regarding both specific personalities and images of heavenly and hellish domains. Individuals separated by great distances and hundreds of years reported proceeding through a transition stage after death, being greeted at death by a being of light assumed to be Yama, Jizo, or Amida, and seeing similar images of Yama's hells or Amida's Pure Land. Pure Land proponents felt these accounts validated their faith (Becker, 1984).

Explaining Similarities in the Images of Heaven and Hell

Previous scholars have noticed the striking similarity between Chinese conceptions of heavens and hells and those which evolved within Christian and Muslim cultures (Asin, 1926; Duyuendak, 1952). Duyuendak suggests that a common cultural foundation affected the development of Muslim, Christian, and Buddhist concepts of hell, thereby accounting for the various commonalities. Other cultural diffusion hypotheses include the theory that Pure Land Buddhism was a Chinese distortion of Indian Christianity (Takakusu, 1947: 166), or that is was borrowed from Zoroastrianism or Manichaeism (Reischauer, 1917: 69). These cultural source hypotheses do not clearly specify when or exactly how medieval near-death narratives were influenced by foreign doctrines.

Although cultural diffusion presumably played a role in the development of parallel Chinese and Japanese images of the afterworld (for example, pictorial tapestries were transported from China to Japan), universal features within NDE accounts probably increased the degree of similarity within divergent religious traditions. NDEs consistently supported belief in life immediately after death, in guides who carry the experiencers through a transition area, in a deity who administers a life review, and in an otherworldly hierarchy.

Zaleski (1987: 34) notes that if one were to arrange European accounts of otherworldly visits in chronological order, no natural progression, sequence of literary transmission, or causal mechanism would be revealed. This finding does not support the cultural source diffusionists.

Chinese and Japanese narratives provide vague patterns of transmission and progression. Early Taoist NDEs were heavenly visits, as was the earliest narrative in the Japanese *Nihon Ryoiki*. Early Chinese Buddhist accounts established clear images of heaven and hell. These stories served to teach the Buddhist doctrine of karma and to bolster the practice of special rituals for the dead. Later, Pure Land NDEs supported a belief in grace and in special meditative techniques. Subsequent NDE accounts from the Chinese *Jade Register* (Clarke, 1893–94) or the Japanese *Genko Shakusho*, for example, seem to more closely resemble modern NDE narratives in terms of their general brevity and simple messages. Detailed portrayals of hellish topography were by this time no longer necessary. Although the Asian medieval narrative collection supports the experiential source theory, many accounts appear to have been shaped by cultural needs.

Social factors probably resulted in the selective survival of NDE tales. In medieval China and Japan, NDE accounts that fit the needs of Buddhist preachers undoubtedly outlasted tales that were not useful for didactic purposes. A variety of NDE events probably occurred during all eras and in all societies. Social selection determined which reports survived.

Some of the common features of NDE accounts may reflect the equivalently structured hierarchies of Asian and European societies (*Motif-Index*: E755.1.1, "Heavenly hierarchy"). Yet many motifs seem surprisingly universal (E177," Resuscitated man relates visions of beyond"; E374, "Dead returns to life and tells of journey to land of dead"; E367, "Return from dead to preach repentance"; E722.2.9, "Dead friends come for dying man's soul"; E722.2.10, "Soul taken away by God or angel"). Comparison of folklore accounts cannot verify that actual experiences were the sources of NDE motifs, but the present study provides support for that hypothesis.

Summary

The prevalence of similar elements in Asian and European NDE accounts suggests that this form of experience has primary features that shaped religious ideologies in a common direction. The data support the experiential source hypothesis. NDEs provided a rhetorical tool useful for some, but not all, ideologies. This contributed to the diffusion of those religious doctrines that coincided with NDE primary features. This argument should be qualified by three points: (1) Because early Christian and Buddhist scriptures portrayed primary NDE features, we cannot preclude cultural diffusion as an explanation for some commonalities among later accounts. (2) European and Asian accounts served the didactic needs of the eras in which they were transcribed and reveal traits associated with narrative imagination. (3) Parallel hierarchical social structures may have contributed to equivalently structured images of heaven and hell in medieval European and Asian societies.

Modern NDEs continue to have an impact on popular culture, although they have little effect on scientific ideology. This differential influence reflects both the nature of modern science and the central qualities of NDEs. We can predict that future societies will also be influenced by such incidents. NDEs will provide support for persistent beliefs in life after death, afterlife evaluations, and powerful deities.

Chapter 10
The Scientific Investigation
of Wondrous Events

Although wondrous events have affected religious beliefs, they have had little impact on scientific theory. Miracles are more important to theologians than to scientists. Yet scientific efforts to investigate psychic phenomena, like the phenomena themselves, reveal recurrent patterns. Scientific investigations most often focus on wondrous *performances*, or demonstrations of psi, a term that includes extrasensory perception and psychokinesis. The psychical research literature suggests that psi (1) manifests sporadically in laboratory environments with nearly undetectable effects; (2) occurs more frequently during altered states of consciousness; (3) has universal features yet also appears in culturally specific forms; (4) has contagious qualities associated with social movements; (5) has elusive, obscure, or hidden features. Psychical researchers often encounter fraud and unusual social situations associated with it (dissociated personalities, confessions of fraud, and retractions of confessions). Investigators who claim to have verified the existence of psi are frequently labeled as incompetent.

Parapsychological textbooks provide a body of cases suitable for social scientific analysis (Broughton, 1991; Douglas, 1977; Edge et al., 1986; Nash, 1978). Although the assertion that psi exists is speculative, the argument that investigators tend to believe that it has certain features is open to empirical testing within the social scientific domain.

The literature suggests that psi occurs sporadically, perhaps more frequently in uncontrolled situations and during altered states of consciousness. Psi seems to resist long-term practical application under controlled conditions. The inability of wondrous events to have a major impact on scientific ideology does not preclude their having social effects. Mesmerism, Spiritualism, and psychical research were shaped by anomalous reports. Each of these social movements involved wondrous performances that revealed both universal and culturally specific features.

The stigma associated with paranormal claims has contributed to the difficulty of parapsychological research. One basis for this stigma is the fact that various psychic performers have engaged in fraud. One result is that established scientists tend to label those claiming to have demonstrated psychic effects as incompetent (McClenon, 1984).

Wondrous Events and Scientistic Ideology

Scientism is the collection of assumptions that justify the scientific approach. Scientism reduces the potential of wondrous events to affect scientific theory. Scientistic ideologies are generally unarticulated, having developed along with scientific advances.

Early scientists sought to exclude nonmeasurable parameters from scientific discourse. For example, Galileo distinguished between primary qualities that were thought to be genuinely inherent within objects and secondary qualities that were "no more than mere names . . . [having] their habitation only in the sensorium" (Galilei, 1960/1623: 311). This distinction, refined by Locke, Descartes, Boyle, Newton, and others, became a part of the metaphysical foundation of science.

Newton's publication of his *Principia* in 1684 allowed scientists to portray the universe as being like a clock that was governed by immutable, physical laws. The ongoing success of the scientific endeavor seemed to verify this model, and scientists gave spiritual forces no role in scientific explanations. For example, when Napoleon asked the French astronomer Laplace about the place of God in his system, Laplace replied, "I have no need of that hypothesis" (Durant and Durant, 1965: 548). Mystical or religious experiences stimulated little research since scientists assumed such events were caused by the peripheral aspects of the brain's function.

Overall, scientific logic advocates skepticism toward the occult. This orientation is based on Occam's razor, which holds that theories requiring excessive formulations should be replaced by equivalent, simpler ones. If a "normal" explanation is available to explain an anomalous perception, scientists will prefer the normal explanation to the paranormal one. Hume's (1967/1748) argument regarding miracles, and variations of it, extend this logic. Because a miracle is a violation of the laws of nature, which experience has established, no testimony is sufficient to confirm a miracle, unless it would be even more miraculous for that testimony to be false. Exceptional claims require exceptional proof.

Using these philosophical grounds, skeptics need not actually resolve the conflicts regarding paranormal claims; skeptical explanations are granted overwhelming weight because these philosophical assumptions are part of the foundation of science. The burden of proof is always on the claimant, creating a virtually insurmountable barrier for advocates of the paranormal.

These philosophical formulations create a paradox for scientists investigating wondrous events. Although sociologically real, wondrous performances lack the qualities that would permit them to have impact on the physical sciences. Parapsychology is therefore rejected, categorized as a deviant science (McClenon, 1984). Yet social scientists can predict some of the characteristics of future inquiries by parapsychologists based on recurring patterns within psychical research.

Review of Cases

Even ancient studies into the occult involved empirical methodologies. For example, King Croesus of Lydia (circa 550 B.C.) tested the seven best oracles of his era by having them describe his actions on a specific day. Only the Delphic oracle was exactly correct, asserting that Croesus was making a lamb and tortoise stew in a bronze kettle. Because the seer's statement was valid, Croesus asked whether he should go to Persia to attack his enemy. The oracle responded, "When Croesus has the Halys crossed, a mighty Empire will be lost." Trusting his own interpretation of the oracle's reply, Croesus attacked his rival and lost his *own* empire (Broughton, 1991: 50, 51). This narrative illustrates the tendency for research to inspire belief, yet it also portrays psi's limited practical value.

Prospero Lambertini (later elected Pope Benedict XIV in 1740) was assigned to investigate miracles and psychic experiences. He concluded that such events were not unique to saints and that they often occurred in symbolic form within dreams. He argued that such phenomena should not be attributed to divine or demonic forces but rather to human consciousness (Haynes, 1970). Many modern researchers agree.

These cases illustrate early attempts to evaluate paranormal claims. In theory, modern science should be able to resolve the issues surrounding the occult, but the ideological foundations of the scientific endeavor, or perhaps the complex nature of wondrous events themselves, have thwarted this objective.

It was not until the era of Franz Anton Mesmer (1734–1815) that the scientific community achieved sufficient authority to replace religion as the prime investigator of paranormal claims. Mesmer used hypnosis-like procedures to induce therapeutic, contagious convulsions in his patients. Excitement spread from client to client as Mesmer circulated about the room, waving his iron wand or motioning with his hands. Mesmer and his supporters argued that the unusual effects, and the cures resulting from his treatments, demonstrated the existence of "animal magnetism."

Mesmer seemed to brush aside the medical knowledge of his era, an attitude that encouraged scientific hostility. French government investigative commissions, which included some of the most distinguished scientists of his day, found no evidence for the existence of animal magnetism or any other unknown forces. They concluded that Mesmer's successful cures were the result of suggestion. These findings signaled the beginning of Mesmer's fall from grace and his eventual forced retreat from active practice (Fuller, 1982).

One of Mesmer's pupils, the Marquis de Puységur (1751–1825), found that "mesmerized" subjects could also demonstrate clairvoyance. Although de Puységur published his findings in his *Mémoiers* in 1784, mesmerism had been associated with the old regime in France and these claims did not attract widespread attention until after the Restoration in 1815. Later researchers replicated du Puységur's claims, and many regarded clairvoyance as a characteristic of the mesmeric state. Experiments with mesmerism and telepathy were described by Dr. Alexandre Berthrand in his *Traité du Somnam-bulisme*, published in 1823. In 1825, Baron du Potet claimed to induce somnambulism from a distance. In 1826, a committee of the French Royal Academy of Medicine began investigating this assertion, and Dr. M. Husson, chief of staff at the Hôtel Dieu, later presented a favorable report. Yet other academy members disagreed and refused to let these findings be published (Podmore, 1964).

Du Potet visited London in 1837 and met the British surgeon John Elliotson, founder of University College Hospital and the first to use the stethoscope in England. Elliotson eventually became satisfied that mesmerized individuals could sometimes experience sensations felt by the mesmerizer even when there was no direct contact between them. His research stimulated intense scientific opposition. The council of University College Hospital passed a resolution forbidding the use of mesmerism, and Elliotson resigned from his post. James Braid, the first to use the word *hypnotism*, was denied the opportunity to present a paper before the medical section of the British Association for the Advancement of Science in 1842. In 1843, W. S. Ward, a London surgeon, read a paper before the Royal Medical and Chirurgical Society describing his use of mesmerism to amputate a patient's leg, but the society rejected his claims and removed Ward's paper from its minutes. Victorian medical journals were filled with denouncements of mesmeric practices (Douglas, 1977; Podmore, 1964).

The reaction to early hypnosis research illustrates the process involved in the labeling of scientific deviance. The Victorian discovery of a relationship between mesmerism and clairvoyance (Podmore, 1964) parallels the finding by modern parapsychologists that hypnosis increases the capacity for ESP (Schechter, 1984). In both cases, researchers observed astonishing phenomena and encountered intense skepticism. In both cases, scientists were unable to stimulate major investigative programs because they were stigmatized as deviant (McClenon, 1984).

Science is based on a rhetorical and political process, one incapable of resolving some issues. It is rhetorical because the quality of a scientific argument affects its acceptance. Science is political because more powerful groups often restrict the dissemination of unusual claims. Investigators who found that mesmerism (hypnosis) was associated with clairvoyance (ESP) could not force skeptics to accept their arguments; their experimental findings could not be replicated by all colleagues, a situation making their arguments rhetorically weak and allowing rejection by more powerful groups. Only researchers willing to accept sporadic results were convinced of paranormal relationships.

Yet Mesmer established a significant social movement and provided a foundation for future innovative therapies. Mesmeric remedies were often effective, and the treatments had a contagious quality. People who witnessed a performance could later replicate the magical cures. Mesmerism spread to America, where it provided the ideological groundwork for Spiritualism and, eventually, parapsychology.

The Spiritualist movement began with the poltergeist rapping that occurred in 1848 at the Fox family home in Hydesville, New York. The Fox children, Kate and Margaretta, developed a code for communicating with the raps and concluded that a spirit was seeking contact. Neighbors came to listen, and before long, special committees were set up to investigate the phenomena. In 1849 and 1850, the two sisters gave rapping performances in major towns in the northeastern United States. Horace Greeley, editor of the New York *Tribune*, estimated that "of those who have enjoyed proper opportunities for a full investigation, we believe that fully three fourths are convinced, as we are, that these singular sounds and seeming manifestations are not produced by Mrs. Fox and her daughters, nor by any human being connected with them" (Gauld, 1968: 13).

The Fox sisters had hoped to retire from the public limelight, but the crowds gathered at their house prevented this option. Gauld (1968: 14) notes, "[T]he rapping spread by a kind of contagion, those who came to witness the phenomena afterwards suffering comparable disturbances in their own homes. Indeed people who simply heard of the phenomena were liable to find themselves or their wives and daughters similarly visited." The town of Rochester had between fifty to a hundred individuals who could contact spirits by the summer of 1850. By 1853, there were perhaps thirty thousand such people in the United States (Gauld, 1968). "Table tipping" was added to the Spiritualist repertoire: Groups placed their hands on a table and found that it would rock and sway, sometimes spelling out messages thought to be from spirits.

Although the Fox sisters technically were never detected engaging in fraud, controversy surrounded their performances. A relative of the Fox family by marriage, Mrs. Norman Culver, claimed that Margaretta had confessed to her that the raps were produced by movements of the knee joints, a hypothesis offered by three professors from the University of Buffalo (Podmore, 1902/1963, Volume 1: 184). Years later, in 1888, Margaretta confessed that she had used this method. Because numerous scientific committees had ruled out this possibility and many other spirit rappers were active, the Spiritualist movement's strength did not diminish. Not long afterward, Kate denied Margaretta's claims, and Margaretta herself retracted them (Broughton, 1991: 59).

Believers suggested that Margaretta, an alcoholic, needed the $1,500 payment she received in exchange for her confession. They point to events that ostensibly established the authenticity of the phenomena. For example, on one occasion, E. W. Capron took a handful of small shells from a basket, without counting, and twice the raps indicated the number correctly (Gauld, 1968: 8). The Fox family narrative illustrates a pattern in many paranormal cases. Accusations of fraud, presentations of evidence supporting those accusations, confessions, refutations, and retractions of confessions often follow psychic performances, making scientific evaluation difficult.

By 1860, some mediums had added slate writing to their repertoire of paranormal performance. Participants would hold a slate board under a table and hear spirits scraping out a message (while the medium was theoretically in trance). Afterward, the medium would reveal that writing had appeared on the board. "Dr." Henry Slade became the most famous of these practitioners, deeply impressing early investigators, such as J. C. F. Zollner. Although Slade's abilities exceeded those of most magicians of his day, he was unable to pass stringent tests by later investigators, such as the Seybert Commission in Philadelphia. In October 1876, he was tried and convicted on a charge of obtaining money under false pretense.

These cases illustrate the evolution of phenomena over time and the tendency for astonishing claims to be followed by accusations of fraud. Mesmeric trance became mediumistic trance. Spirit rapping lead to table tipping and slate writing. Although some investigations inspired belief, there were many indications of deception. Most modern parapsychologists evaluate the evidence regarding the Fox sisters, Slade, and the many other mediums of this era, as too ambiguous to draw conclusions.

The most evidential investigations during the Spiritualist era were of Daniel Dunglas Home (1833–1886). He demonstrated an incredible quantity and variety of anomalous effects: fireballs wandered about the room and through solid objects, spirits appeared as apparitional images, flowers fell from the ceiling, spirit hands appeared and touched sitters, furniture moved about as though weightless, and Home himself could float like a balloon (Medhurst et al., 1972). Home also reportedly handled fire, elongated his body anomalously, and played an accordion without touching the keys, ostensibly through paranormal means. His demonstrations generally took place in adequate light. He sat among his observers and allowed scientific investigators to control his movements.

Although most historical reviews of Home's life state that he was never observed cheating, skeptical writers emphasize a variety of suspicious incidents that suggest Home performed his feats through deception (Christopher, 1970). They also focus attention on a domestic court case he lost which revealed his unorthodox personal life.

Yet many investigations of Home appear to have been conducted under highly controlled conditions. Sir William Crookes, one of the most famous scientists of his era, made particular efforts to verify Home's paranormal abilities. He constructed special devices for precluding the possibility of fraud. Skeptics prevented Crookes from addressing scientific audiences, and he eventually gave up psychical research. (He later discovered thallium, invented the radiometer and Crookes tube, and was knighted in 1897.) Although Crookes remained convinced that psychic phenomena were real, modern skeptics argue that his experimental accounts are incomplete.

Richard Hodgson and S. John Davey conducted experiments that justified the skeptical approach. Davey duplicated the slate-writing demonstrations of the 1880s by using conjuring techniques. Supported by Richard Hodgson, Davey gave several performances, after which participants were asked to describe what they had observed. All misreported commonplace incidents, and many described events that never happened. Witnesses failed to note the most crucial movements of the slates, even though the action took place only three feet from their eyes (Hodgson, 1892).

The early members of the British Society for Psychical Research, established in 1882, found that virtually none of the mediums they investigated could produce paranormal effects under controlled conditions. Gauld (1968: 208–209) notes that "certainly there does not seem to be the slightest reason for supposing that the vast majority of the spectacular physical phenomena reported in the eighteen-seventies and eighteen-eighties were anything other than fraudulent."

Yet later investigations proved more fruitful. Patterns within these possibly authentic cases suggest that some mediumistic performances harbor basic characteristics intrinsic to wondrous phenomena. Phenomena were of the same types as occurred in haunting cases. Investigators noted that raps frequently accompanied table tipping but that raps and table tipping would decline when the medium entered a trance. The medium's trance utterances had a standard quality, seemingly associated with the medium's dissociated state. The messages sometimes supplied information that was apparently not from the medium's mind but shaped, to a degree, by the medium's subconscious. (These features are evident in a modern investigation described in Chapter 11.)

The case of William Stainton Moses (1839–1892) illustrates some of the characteristic features of Spiritualist performance: Moses's phenomena were:

very striking and bore a marked resemblance to those which occurred in Home's presence. They included raps, sometimes conveying "evidential" messages, independent movements of objects; levitation of the medium; "materialized" hands and figures, strange luminous effects of various kinds; mysterious musical sounds, direct writing; and the drenching of the medium and sitters with various liquid scents. (Gauld, 1968: 217)

Moses's book *Spirit Teachings*, which was based on spirit messages, provided an ideological framework for the Spiritualist movement. The messages stated that good spirits sought to aid people in raising their spiritual levels and that false spirits sometimes produced the appearance of fraud. Many people found these doctrines to be consistent with their observations of the mediums of the time.

Due in part to their inability to verify claims of psychokinetic effects, the early psychical researchers turned their attention to what they termed "mental" phenomena (i.e., extrasensory perception). Eventually, they gathered evidence which indicated to them that some mediums were authentic.

Mrs. Leonora E. Piper, whose mediumship began in 1884, was the most investigated medium of her day. She allowed the American Society for Psychical Research to monitor her readings for fifteen years.

These observations provided an astonishingly large amount of evidence that supported belief in her paranormal ability. On some days, Mrs. Piper ostensibly obtained knowledge about subjects which could not have been gained through normal means. Correspondences were so close that they could not be explained as guesses. Yet many of her trance utterances were patently absurd. Her early "control" (a spirit who acted as a kind of master of ceremonies) claimed to be French but was unable to speak or comprehend that language. Often the information she gave was false.

The British Society for Psychical Research arranged for her to travel to England, a country she had never visited. There, she was followed by detectives, and the selection of her subjects was done completely under the supervision of the society. Nevertheless, she supplied subjects with information about deceased relatives, convincing them that they were indeed in communication with the dead.

Although Mrs. Piper was never caught cheating, skeptics focused on the inanity and inaccuracy of many of her trance statements. As with other seances, her performances often had an absurd quality that left her open to mockery.

The medium Eusapia Palladino (1854–1918) was also frequently investigated. While she was in trance, objects would move about her seance room, apparitional figures would appear, and participants would experience a wide variety of anomalous sensations. Born to an extremely poor family in Naples, Palladino had a vulgar, earthy, and sometimes sexual quality that clashed with the proper upper-class gentlemen who attempted to hold her feet and hands in the dimly lit seance rooms.

On various occasions, researchers documented anomalous effects during well-controlled sessions with Palladino. For example, in 1894 Charles Richet (who later won the 1913 Nobel Prize in physiology and medicine) invited F. W. H. Myers and Oliver Lodge to join him on an island off the southern coast of France where they held a series of sittings with her. Tables moved inexplicably, participants felt phantom hands, objects moved about, an accordion and music box played without being touched, and phantom shapes were observed, all while Palladino's hands and feet were being held by the researchers (Feilding, 1963).

When investigated at Cambridge, England, in 1895, Palladino's performance was somewhat restrained. When the skeptical Richard Hodgson arrived, he relaxed the restrictions he normally imposed in order to gain a better understanding of the methods she used to cheat. (She had admitted to using deception whenever given the opportunity.) One of her methods was to lead two participants to think that each was holding one of her two hands while, in fact, they both held the same hand. With one hand free, she was able to create seemingly paranormal effects. Hodgson convinced those present that all the previous phenomena they had witnessed could have been fraudulent.

Palladino's career did not end with this exposé since she had never denied that she sometimes used deception. In America in 1910, she was asked if she had ever been caught cheating:

> Many times I have been told so. You see, it is like this. Some people are at the table who expect tricks—in fact, they want them. I am in a trance. Nothing happens. They get impatient. They think of the tricks—nothing but tricks. They put their mind on the tricks, and—I—and I automatically respond. But it is not often. They merely will me to do them. That is all. (Doyle, 1926: 8)

Although the British Society for Psychical Research, led by Henry Sidgwick, discouraged investigation of mediums caught cheating, Palladino was later tested by Dr. Paolo Visani-Scozzi in 1895 and by Carmille Flammarion in 1897. These individuals became convinced of the authenticity of some of her effects. Another researcher, Guillaume de Fontenay, successfully photographed unidentified white material that rested briefly on Palladino's head during a 1908 performance.

The persistent claims concerning Palladino led the Society for Psychical Research to conduct new tests. The most capable team of spiritualistic investigators ever assembled—including Hereward Carrington, W. W. Baggally, and Everard Feilding—was sent to test her in Naples in 1908. Their report indicated that they could not find normal explanations for the many anomalous phenomena they witnessed under the controlled conditions they had devised (Feilding, Baggally, and Carrington, 1909: 357).

Beloff (1985) has challenged modern skeptics to explain the evidence gathered by the these Victorian investigators.[1] Since no equivalent mediums are currently practicing, the skeptics have no way of evaluating such claims to their satisfaction. Although reports of paranormal phenomena from the past can provide data for philosophical analysis, these events have had little impact on modern scientific theory (Braude, 1986).

After the deaths of the major early leaders of the Society for Psychical Research (Henry Sidgwick died in 1900; Myers in 1901), an unusual series of events transpired. Between 1902 and 1930, several mediums in various geographical locations received "spirit" messages, often through automatic writing, ostensibly from Myers and other deceased society members. Even Mrs. Piper received communications. Some mediums received fragments of Greek expressions even though they had no knowledge of the language. When pieced together, these words clearly referred to classical phrases that would have been familiar to Myers. It appeared that Myers, who had spent his life attempting to demonstrate that the human personality survived death, was making a final, ingenious attempt. It was logical to assume that Myers's mind, rather than those of the mediums, produced the obscure references since the mediums had no knowledge of Greek literature. The argument that the individual practitioners generated the information using their telepathic powers, or that the phrases were produced at random, seemed highly improbable. The alternative hypothesis was that Myers's personality had survived his bodily death (Saltmarsh, 1938/1975).

Gladys Osborne Leonard was another medium who generated evidence supporting belief in life after death. While in trance, she revealed information about departed relatives. During the World War I era, the Society for Psychical Research reserved part of her time each day for the use of selected, anonymous subjects so that her performances might be monitored. Her demonstrations often defied normal explanation. For example, in response to a question, Mrs. Leonard might suggest that the subject go to a certain bookcase in his or her house and select a particular book from a specific location and read a certain line from a particular page. Eleanor Sidgwick (Henry's widow) analyzed 532 "book tests" and found that 36 percent were "approximately" successful. Since the rate of "approximate" success achieved by non-psychics making guesses was 4.7 percent, Mrs. Leonard's rate revealed a statistically significant difference. On various occasions, Mrs. Leonard foresaw the details in newspapers that had not yet been published (Smith, 1964). Skeptics suggest that such correspondences might be attributed to coincidence or nonverbal clues.

In St. Louis, Missouri, in 1913, Mrs. Pearl Curran began communicating with a disembodied entity who eventually identified herself as Patience Worth. Patience Worth spoke in what seemed an archaic English dialect and claimed to be an early English immigrant to the United States who had been killed by Indians. She dictated various historically based novels whose literary quality far exceeded what would be expected from the relatively uneducated and untraveled Mrs. Curran. The psychical researcher Walter Franklin Price, as well as other investigators, felt that this case revealed anomalous aspects. For example, while in trance Mrs. Curran demonstrated knowledge of many obsolete and archaic words, foreign lands, and historical facts, as well as unusual intellectual powers and dexterities. Yet an analysis of Patience Worth's words and syntax revealed that she used a mixture of archaic styles rather than the speech patterns of an immigrant of her era (Price, 1927).

Investigations of the Schneider brothers, Willi (born in 1903) and

Rudi (born in 1908), produced evidence that supports both belief and skepticism. Although Willi was caught cheating on several occasions, various scientists felt they had verified the authenticity of his anomalous powers. He produced materializations of spirit forms, moved objects by invisible means, and caused musical boxes to wind up, play, and stop, on command, all under highly controlled conditions.

His brother Rudi also demonstrated anomalous effects. Investigators used special equipment to verify the paranormal nature of his abilities. The tests involved four cameras which were specially designed to take pictures whenever an infrared beam, created by a special device, was broken by something blocking it. On two occasions the mechanism was triggered, but whatever had interrupted the beam was not visible in the photographs. Later, Rudi gained control of his capacity to interrupt the ray and would announce when the "force" would occur (Gregory, 1985).

In 1933, the psychical researcher Harry Price, apparently angered by Rudi's willingness to cooperate with other researchers, announced in the *Sunday Dispatch* that he had photographic evidence that Rudi had cheated. However, modern investigators believe this evidence was faked and that Price wished to destroy Rudi's credibility for personal reasons (Gregory, 1974, 1985).

The mediumship of Mrs. Mina Crandon of Boston, Massachusetts, began with table-tipping demonstrations but evolved into direct voice phenomena (spirit voices not attributed to a living human), psychokinesis, materializations, and other astonishing events. Believers felt that the phenomena were too robust to be regarded as fraudulent. On one occasion, the wing of the medium's special cabinet was torn off, apparently by a paranormal force. A *Scientific American* investigation was begun in 1924, but was not conclusive. One member of the team, the famous magician Houdini, had a special restraining cabinet built to control Mrs. Crandon's movements during seances. While she was confined inside the cabinet, a bell in the room rang, apparently paranormally. Houdini, however, refused to accept this evidence as conclusive. During a second session, Walter, the spirit of her deceased brother who spoke through Crandon, claimed that Houdini had planted a collapsible ruler in the cabinet in order to "frame" her. (The ruler, presumably, would have allowed Crandon to create physical effects which would appear to others to have been created paranormally.) Houdini solemnly swore that he had no knowledge of the ruler, arguing that it was undoubtedly a prop for creating fraudulent effects. Because of his suspicious movements prior to this incident, however, Houdini's sincerity is suspect.

On many occasions during Crandon's mediumship, Walter, speaking through her, claimed to leave his fingerprints in wax that had been expressly left out to provide physical proof of his "presence." Since the fingerprint detected in the wax after each seance did not match those of the participants, people marveled over this "proof." Later it was found that the wax fingerprints were those of Crandon's dentist, who had given her the idea of using dental wax and provided her a sample. Most observers assumed she used an instrument to transfer the finger-prints to the wax during her seances. Although various investigators remained convinced that some of her phenomena were paranormal, the evidence for fraud was overwhelming. A schism developed within the American Society for Psychical Research due to differences of opinion regarding this case (Tietze, 1973).

J. B. Rhine attended one of Mina Crandon's seances and was dis-gusted by what he perceived to be cheating. This experience contrib-uted to his eventual establishment of the basic research paradigm for modern parapsychology. While at Duke University, Rhine standard-ized the nomenclature and techniques of parapsychology by having subjects guess at symbols on a specially designed deck of cards. The results could be analyzed statistically, by comparing them against the probability of their occurrence through chance. Rhine found that approximately one in five individuals attained statistically significant scores using this procedure (Rhine, 1934).

Rhine's publication of *Extra-sensory Perception* in 1934, and his es-tablishment of the *Journal of Parapsychology* in 1937, launched para-psychology as a scientific field. Later, he verified to his satisfaction that some humans could mentally influence physical events, such as dice scores, a phenomenon termed psychokinesis. Rhine referred to all psychic phenomena using the Greek letter "psi." Psi includes both extrasensory perception (ESP) and psychokinesis (PK).

Although other researchers replicated Rhine's results, it became apparent that ESP and PK were not easy to elicit. Some investigators were successful; others were not. Results were sporadic and unstable. As Beloff (1977: 18, 19) notes: "these early successes were deceptive. Enthusiasts soon learned to their cost that the vast majority of ESP tests end, as they begin, by reaffirming the laws of chance. . . . [I]t soon became apparent that a good guessing subject is just as rare a com-modity as a good medium or a good clairvoyant."

Laboratory experiments fall within the same performance model as other demonstrations of wondrous events except that subjects are expected to produce paranormal effects for a scientific rather than a general audience. As within the larger society, some scientific observers are satisfied while others remain skeptical.

Rhine found patterns within his data which were equivalent to those discovered by previous investigators. Psi appeared to have a elusive quality; its incidence was dependent on the psychological atmosphere of the laboratory environment. As early as 1889, Charles Richet had found that some subjects could achieve success at a low, but statistically significant, rate, but that during long sessions, their ability declined. Richet's star subject, who had demonstrated skill at guessing concealed playing cards, was not successful before scientists at Cambridge. Rhine, too, found that his subjects failed when placed in skeptical environments.

As data accumulated from laboratory studies, Rhine noted patterns that he termed "signs of psi." After three decades of research, he concluded that psi (ESP and PK) were real phenomena, that certain internal statistical variations were associated with their occurrence (abnormal variance, the decline effect, and, at times, performance *below* chance level), and that certain attitudes and personality traits were related to their detection.

Although Rhine sought to legitimate the study of psychic effects, his experiments differed from normal psychological studies. Because parapsychology was subject to special criticisms involving sensory cues and fraud, parapsychologists were forced to create more restrictive environments, which some felt reduced the incidence of observed psychic phenomena. To Rhine's disappointment, parapsychology did not become integrated with mainstream psychology.

Many researchers came to believe that psi had a "hiding" quality that was moderated by human consciousness. Gertrude Schmeidler discovered what she termed the sheep/goat effect: those believing in ESP had a greater probability of achieving high guessing scores than did those who disbelieved. Literature reviews and meta-analyses of the many attempts to replicate this finding support belief in the effect (Palmer, 1978; Lawrence, 1993). Studies also indicate that researchers' treatment of their subjects influences experimental results (Honorton, Ramsey, and Cabibbo, 1975) and that experimenters themselves seemingly affect results paranormally (Kennedy and Taddonio, 1976; White, 1976). These findings place psychic researchers on the same level as mediums and psychics since the researcher's ability to elicit psi determines the experimental result.

As with mediumistic performances, the field of parapsychology does not lack researchers who have committed fraud. Major perpetrators who tampered with experimental data include W. J. Levy, who was to have replaced J. B. Rhine after his retirement from the Institute for Parapsychology (Rhine, 1974; Rogo, 1985); S. G. Soal, whose deception was uncovered years after his death (Markwick, 1978, 1985); and Harry Price, whose framing of Rudi Schneider has already been mentioned (Gregory, 1974, 1985). Other individuals dropped out of the field after being accused of deception.

The dilemma of researcher fraud in other disciplines is generally overcome through experiment replication, but critics of the field of parapsychology have been quick to point out that no such verifiable, standard parapsychological experiment has been developed. Although no procedure exists to ensure that psi can be produced on demand, some lines of inquiry, and some research centers, claim statistically significant results with relative frequency. Examples include Charles Honorton's Ganzfeld experiments, Helmut Schmidt's research with machine-recorded guesses at random targets, and experiments with certain talented people (Beloff, 1985; Honorton, 1985; Honorton et al., 1990; Honorton and Ferrari, 1989; Radin and Nelson, 1989).

A form of laboratory folklore has arisen regarding the nature of psi phenomena. Parapsychologists who are most successful in eliciting psi are thought to be more outgoing, dynamic, creative, fun-loving, and easy-going. It is believed that psi occurs more frequently in less structured, less controlled environments. Some researchers who have taken these factors into account claim anomalous effects on a frequent basis.

One line of research, known as the Ganzfeld method (named after the originator of this sensory deprivation technique), has been particularly successful in producing replicable results. Subjects listen to a relaxation tape while wearing goggles made from halved ping-pong balls over their eyes. This procedure is designed to reduce normal sensory input in order to increase the extrasensory faculty. Subjects then verbalize their thoughts which sometimes contain information pertaining to an image (the "target") they are attempting to perceive. Afterward, a group of judges rank order possible "targets" with regard to their similarity to the subjects' verbalizations. By statistically evaluating these rankings, the researcher can determine the probability of the result being due to chance. Richard Broughton (1991: 288), director of research at the Institute for Parapsychology, claims, "While it would be rash to say that anyone can run a successful ganzfeld experiment, there can be no doubt that *in the hands of a competent experimenter* the ganzfeld-ESP is a repeatable experiment."

Honorton and Schechter (1987) devised a profile of subjects most likely to be successful in Ganzfeld experiments. Factors include previous spontaneous psychic experiences, the practice of a mental discipline such as meditation, and a suitable personality profile (a form of extraversion is desirable). The Ganzfeld paradigm coincides with the yoga sutras of Patanjali, formulated in India perhaps as early as 3,500 years ago, which hold that normal perceptions obscure the reception of extrasensory information and that by stilling the mind, one can gain knowledge through nonsensory means (Prabhavananda and Isherwood, 1953). Like Honorton, the yogis found that people have varying capacities for extrasensory experience. These capacities can apparently be increased through mental disciplines such as meditation.

Ganzfeld research has led some psychology textbook authors to include discussions of parapsychological research (see, for example, Atkinson et al., 1990). Yet the field of parapsychology, unlike the rest of science, has not grown exponentially since the 1930s. During the 1970s, the number of researchers increased gradually, and the number of research centers remained stable. During the 1980s these numbers declined. In my 1984 study, I listed twenty-three "parapsychological research centers" (McClenon, 1984: 247–249). By 1993, eleven of those centers no longer conducted parapsychological research, and only two new centers had been established. The membership of the Parapsychological Association was 205 in 1970, 279 in 1980, 306 in 1983, 275 in 1986, 247 in 1991, and 246 in 1992 (McClenon, 1984; Palmer, 1992; *PA News and Annual Report*, 1993).

Although most modern parapsychologists devote their time to laboratory research, some study field cases. For example, in 1962, Dr. Jule Eisenbud began his investigation of Ted Serios, a man who seemed able to create paranormal images on photographic film. Eisenbud (1967, 1977) found that these anomalous images sometimes differed from realistic photographs in a manner that reflected Serios's consciousness (words were misspelled similarly, for example). Other photos seemingly would require a photographer to rent a hot air balloon, or to take simultaneous photographs from different angles, in order to produce the same effects through normal means.

To generate the images, Serios often looked through a small cardboard tube that he oriented toward the camera lens. His use of this device, which he called a "gizmo," introduced a means for sleight-of-hand deception. Photographers employed by the magazine *Popular Photography* used a similar device with a small lens to produce an equivalent image. Yet Eisenbud challenged anyone to duplicate Serios's effect under his experimental conditions (Douglas, 1977).

Investigations during the 1960s and 1970s of Oskar Estebany in Canada, Pavel Stepanek in Czechoslovakia, Nina Kulagina in the Soviet Union, and Uri Geller, an Israeli investigated in the United States, revealed similar social patterns of verification, skepticism, and contagion (Douglas, 1977; Broughton, 1991; Edge et al., 1986). As during the Spiritualist era, performers convinced their investigators of their authenticity but were unable to convert most skeptics. Modern cases also reveal the "contagious" quality observed among Spiritualists and mesmerists. Geller's spoon bending has triggered like feats, especially among children. Chinese children with "exceptional capacities" found they could cause matter to pass through matter immediately after seeing demonstrations of the feat by their peers. Yet these performances have been difficult to authenticate. Controlled tests of young metal benders have yet to verify anomalous effects (Broughton, 1991). A skeptical delegation sent to China from the United States in 1988 saw no proofs of paranormal capacities (Kurtz et al., 1988; but see Zha and McConnell, 1991).

Wondrous performances, and studies of these events, have features that reflect the eras within which they occur. Modern researchers do not photograph ectoplasm, as did investigators of Mina Crandon and Eusapia Palladino. More recent performers affect film (Serios) or bend metal (Geller). Modern experiencers receive telephone calls from the dead and see images of the deceased on their video terminals. Psychic claims, in other words, have kept pace with technological advances.

Some features, however, have remained constant. Throughout recorded cases, careful investigators have detected that: specific anomalous effects have recurring features,[2] the phenomena have a contagious quality, fraud is uncovered, performers confess, some retract their confessions, and unusual forms of dissociation abound. At the same time, the evidence supporting the anomalous claims is never adequate to convince most skeptics.

Some parapsychologists argue that psi has a special nature that thwarts its investigation (Beloff, 1994). Braud (1985: 157) suggests that "the verification, replication, and understanding of psi are systematically and, perhaps, actively, being obscured." This argument is supported by numerous anecdotal reports. Spontaneous cases are often associated with uncertainties, unknowns, and uncontrolled factors that defy confirmation. Ghosts and poltergeists, too, seem to avoid scientific verification. Seance room and sitter group phenomena (where people sit around a table, waiting for paranormal effects) occur more frequently under uncontrolled, darkened conditions rather than in controlled, well-lit settings. Experimental situations generally yield mild effects, at best. Analytical sophistication within an experiment seems to reduce paranormal results, whereas "loose" demonstrations yield psi more frequently. Psychic events seem to occur more frequently when laboratory equipment breaks down, or in situations with faulty protocols or procedural mistakes. Apparently, subjects who might regularly display psychic feats cannot perform under close scrutiny.

Broughton (1991: 163, 164) provides an example of this phenomenon. He attempted to videotape a twelve-year-old who claimed to bend spoons paranormally. Although she could not perform before the camera, she later bent a spoon, seemingly through paranormal means, before three witnesses, including one who was observing behind a one-way glass window.

Braud's (1985) observations regarding the quirkiness of psi coincide with those of previous psychic investigators. William James (1960/1909) speculated that psychic phenomena might remain eternally baffling, perhaps resistant to full corroboration. Randall (1978) and Bierman (1979) noted the "camera shy" nature of psi, and Brookes-Smith (1973; 1975) and Batcheldor (1966, 1979, 1984) sought empirical methods to circumvent this difficulty. Giesler (1984, 1985a) tried to surmount the phenomena's obscured quality through special field methods.

Some researchers have presented psychological explanations for the elusiveness of psychic events (Batcheldor, 1966, 1979, 1984; Tart, 1984, 1986; Tart and Labore, 1986). Eisenbud (1963, 1972, 1983) theorizes that psi is a kind of ordering principle in nature. He hypothesizes that psi actually *maintains* the laws of statistics; the violation of these laws constitutes a deviant train of events which is eventually rectified naturally. He suggests that attempts to devise a fully "replicable experiment" are doomed to failure. Beloff (1994: 7) proposes that psi phenomena "represent a local violation of the natural order and that nature may react to them in much the way our bodies react to an infection."

A roundtable at the 1985 meetings of the Parapsychological Association addressed the issue of "fear of psi." Fear of psi was attributed to its uncontrollability, dangerousness, and unnaturalness (Weiner and Radin, 1985: 149–155). Precognition of negative events, a common form of experience, contributes to this fear. One participant, Dr. Charles Tart, later suggested to me that infants may psychically perceive their parents' ambivalence toward them and, as a result, close down or reduce their psychic capacities.

Broughton (1991: 351) speculates that psi is elusive because of the way it developed within human evolution: "The most effective psi might be imperceptible psi, since if it became too obvious, one could get into trouble. . . . It could even be that psi has evolved to be deliberately self-obscuring because it works best when it is unhampered and unnoticed by the individual it is serving."

Broughton's suggestion that evolutionary selection has shaped human physiology to restrict wondrous perception can be expanded. Highly developed extrasensory capacities might place organisms at a disadvantage by interfering with normal perceptive or coping faculties. Advanced wondrous capacities might reduce the competitive drive. Many spiritual adepts seek ecstatic experiences rather than engage in mundane affairs (such as procreation). Full awareness of the actual nature of human consciousness might eliminate the fear of death and the motivation to survive. In addition, people may have natural mechanisms that prevent psi, since excessive belief in it is seemingly dysfunctional for groups. Psi's hiding, capricious qualities may be related to the fact that paranormal perceptions are often based on mental malfunctions, misperceptions, and deception. On the other hand, if strong forms of psi occur, their frequent use by individuals would also be socially disruptive.

Although neither psi, nor its hiding quality, has been proven to have a physiological basis, belief that psi "hides" is widespread among parapsychologists. Almost all of the American, British, Chinese, and Japanese psychical researchers I interviewed between 1978 and 1986 noted various elusive features.[3]

Personal observation of the Japanese metal bender Masuaki Kiyota helped me better understand other researchers' belief in psi's hiding quality. Although Kiyota claims to be able to bend metal paranormally, I never observed him perform under completely controlled conditions. Skeptical magicians are able to duplicate most metal-bending feats in which performers hold the test object in their hands. Normally, when Kiyota attempts a bend, observers closely scrutinize his movements (Figure 14 depicts what I observed on a typical occasion). After a time, observers relax their vigilance and a bend may occur (see Figure 15). When observers refuse to avert their gaze, the metal does not bend. Normal people cannot fix their attention on an object for extended periods of time, a situation that provides the opportunity for sleight-of-hand effects. When subjected to well-controlled experimental conditions (using videocameras from a variety of angles, for example), PK performers rarely (if ever) have produced anomalous effects. Naturally, skeptics find this situation suspicious.[4]

One method for investigating psychic claims involves special equipment and props. Some researchers have found that psychic performers can permanently affect the "memory" of nitinol wire (Byrd, 1976; Randall and Davis, 1982). Nitinol wire normally returns to its original shape when heated (Schetky, 1979). PK performers have been requested to bend nitinol wire since the permanent transformation of its memory seems to be a paranormal feat (but see Gardner [1977] for normal explanations of Byrd's [1976] experimental results).

I designed an experiment using nitinol wire which precluded the possibility of fraud, as suggested by Gardner (1977). I glued nitinol wire along the edge of a spoon and glued aluminum foil around the wire and spoon neck. Crimping of the wire, a fraudulent method for changing its "memory," would be revealed by deformations in the aluminum foil. I also prepared a number of "control" spoons and wires.

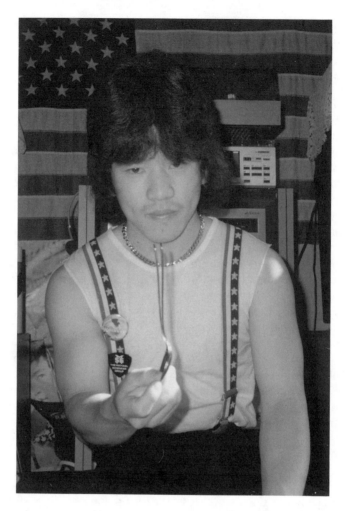

Figure 14. Kiyota is photographed holding two spoons (photo by J. McClenon).

Kiyota bent the spoon and wire, ostensibly through paranormal means. I noted that the aluminum foil and wire had not been crimped. I then placed the spoon and wire on a table, far away from Kiyota. As another observer and I watched, the spoon and wire slowly un-bent, becoming almost straight. Later, I found that its "memory" was unchanged. Although I observed usual effects, my experiment pro-duced no results convincing to those who suspect I was deceived. I describe this episode not to convince skeptics, but to illustrate the

Figure 15. One spoon "bends" after close scrutiny is relaxed (photo by J. McClenon).

types of experiences that lead investigators to believe psi has a hiding quality.[5]

Conclusions and Predictions

Recurring features within the history of psychical research allow predictions regarding future inquiries. The following summarizes observations from the historical data:

1. Many investigators have detected effects they believe to be anomalous. I reviewed about thirty cases above; thousands of published reports exist in the parapsychological literature.
2. Many fraudulent incidents have also been observed (I review five cases of subject fraud above).
3. Wondrous effects are often related to altered states of consciousness. Dissociative states may account for psychic performers' erratic behavior (confessing to fraud, retracting confessions, acting as if unaware of deception in the face of overwhelming evidence).
4. Researchers find that psi has an unreliable quality, producing belief, but inconsistent benefits.
5. Psychic phenomena have universal features. Haunting and poltergeist events have qualities similar to those produced within spiritualistic seances (percussive rapping sounds, for example). Laboratory effects involving ESP and PK appear to be weaker forms of these phenomena. The phenomena often have culturally specific features. Mediumship performances during the Spiritualist era, for example, differ from modern demonstrations of psi.
6. Wondrous events have a contagious quality. Seeing a performance can stimulate similar events (for example, mesmerism, the Fox sisters' rapping, Uri Geller's metal bending).
7. Scientists investigating wondrous performances are often labeled as deviant.
8. Many psychical researchers believe that psi has a hiding quality; they feel psi avoids skeptical scrutiny.

These characteristics allow predictions regarding future investigations of wondrous performances. Future recurrent wondrous phenomena will incite belief in many, but not all, investigators. Many investigators will come to believe that the phenomena have an elusive quality. There is a high probability that focal individuals will be accused of fraud or exposed as fraudulent. Some performers will acknowledge fraud, but their explanations may seem insufficient to account for previous reports. Accusations of fraud may reflect bias or scientific dishonesty. Even in cases where fraud is not a factor, the phenomena will appear absurd, silly, or scientifically unsuitable. Future investigations will generate belief and skepticism rather than consistent results.

Future psychic performers will create events that are "contagious"; some will even stimulate the formation of social movements. Phenomena associated with each movement will be culturally specific, yet will also include universal features. As time passes, the culturally specific phenomena will occur less frequently, and the social movement will decline.

Scientists will label colleagues investigating such effects as deviant, and researchers who feel they have verified paranormal effects will have difficulty publishing their findings in mainstream scientific journals. Although some researchers may successfully replicate anomalous effects, others' failures will reduce the significance of such experiments within the scientific community.

These arguments can be evaluated through further historical analysis and investigation of cases involving psychic phenomena. The following chapter presents results from one such investigation.

Chapter 11
Wondrous Events in a Small Group: A Field Study

The Society for Research on Rapport and Telekinesis (SORRAT) was founded by John G. Neihardt in 1961. This organization's emphasis on miraculous events exhibits a pattern common among various religious groups throughout history. My participant observation of SORRAT between 1981 and 1993 provides data for (1) testing hypotheses regarding recurrent features within scientific investigations of psi; (2) testing hypotheses pertaining to recruitment into small, alternative religious groups; and (3) developing a theory that can be applied to group perceptions of wondrous events.

My formulations are relevant to the sociology of religion and deviant science rather than to the fields of physics or parapsychology. Various readers have expressed concern that in my discussion believers' views are expressed without rebuttal. (I generally present people's statements in their own words.) Skeptics also have requested that I state that informants "thought" or "claimed" they experienced particular anomalous events. I do not comply because critical treatment of firsthand accounts clashes with the experience-centered approach. Participant observers cannot determine the authenticity of claimed paranormal incidents, but they can contribute to our understanding of the factors related to group wondrous perceptions. I provide narratives not to advocate belief in paranormal phenomena, but to facilitate the evaluation of hypotheses regarding the recurrent features of psychic experience, the formation of alternative religious groups, and group perceptions of wondrous events.

Recurrent features among scientific investigations of psychic phenomena allow for some clearly stated hypotheses. As I noted in Chapter 10, researchers often accept the authenticity of paranormal claims, encounter fraud and unusual behaviors associated with it, observe altered states of consciousness, and come to believe that the phenomena have a hiding quality. Those making paranormal claims tend to be labeled as deviants. I predict that future investigators will encounter similar features. My observation of SORRAT allows us to evaluate this argument.

The SORRAT study also allows us to analyze theories pertaining to recruitment processes within small, alternative religious groups. I consider SORRAT a form of religious group even though it does not have specific religious objectives. Group experiences in SORRAT have affected participants' religious beliefs, and religious topics are often discussed during meetings. SORRAT is relatively small. Its membership numbers between twenty-four and seventy-nine participants, depending on the criteria one uses for inclusion. Participants in SORRAT sessions report perceiving levitations, psychokinesis, ESP, and contacts with the dead.

Sociologists have devised various theories to explain the process of individuals' recruitment into unorthodox religions. The "deprivation-ideological appeal" model suggests that potential members have needs or deprivations that correspond to the movement's ideology (Glock and Stark, 1965). Based on this paradigm, we would predict that people attracted to an occult group have special needs that are fulfilled through accepting the paranormal beliefs within that group.

An alternate theory emphasizes the importance of social networks (Stark and Bainbridge, 1980): People are attracted to a group because of friendships, relatives, or other relationships. Later, they come to accept the group's ideology. Based on this theory, we would predict that people's alliances with occult groups result from, and are strengthened by, their affiliations with other believers.

"Structural availability" has also been recognized as a factor within these groups' recruitment processes (Snow et al. 1980). Novices must be free from conflicting ideological and temporal commitments. Those participating in an occult group, for example, must be unfettered by beliefs that reject paranormal claims.

I argue that wondrous experiences are also a factor in many alternative groups' methods of recruitment. I provide ethnographic narratives to capture the social environment that gives anomalous experiences their impact and have reduced the formal academic discourse which masks the persuasive elements within the drama of these experiences. These accounts portray only a small percentage of SORRAT claims.

Since SORRAT phenomena manifest as forms of an intelligent poltergeist, this case study contains various recurrent features noted in Chapter 4. As hypothesized by the experiential source theory, the firsthand accounts in this study coincide with folklore motifs. I provide citations from Thompson's (1966) *Motif-Index of Folk-Literature* to indicate these correspondences.

Part of my research entailed mailing these narratives to SORRAT participants and eliciting their comments. Selected responses and parapsychological observations are presented in the endnotes.

Narrative 1

William Edward Cox and I attended the Southeast Regional Parapsychological Association meeting in 1980. I presented a paper describing a haunting investigation (McClenon, 1981). Afterward, Cox showed me photocopies of segments of film from a case he was investigating in Rolla, Missouri. Cox had been an associate of the parapsychologist J. B. Rhine. Since then, he had retired and moved to Rolla to monitor developments there more closely.

"This is a copy of an eight-millimeter film," he said, flipping through a notebook full of photocopied pages. "Look, you can see each frame of the film. This is an inverted aquarium that has been secured with a lock and seal onto the board with these metal bands. We call it a mini-lab. If an object moves inside, it triggers a microswitch which activates the camera." Cox puffed on his pipe and watched my eyes to observe my reaction. "See the pencil standing up in this first frame? It triggered the camera. Now in the next frame, you can see that it's writing. And there—it's writing 'Rethink time.' And, now it falls back down to the bottom of the mini-lab in these final frames" (F1083, "Object rises into the air").

I was bewildered. "What caused the pencil to write?" I asked.

He shook his head. "I don't know. I guess the powers on high, or whatever, want us to rethink time." He pointed to the next page. "Now look at this. It should be impossible to link two leather rings without cutting one of them. Such a cut could be detected easily. Here the two leather rings are rising up in front of the mini-lab. Look! Now they link. They remain linked. And look, here they break apart; one falls to the table on the outside and the other hangs on the edge of the aquarium. I have carefully examined these rings. They have not been cut. How can you explain this? Isn't this the best case of matter passing through matter that you have ever seen?" he asked proudly.

I was puzzled. It was too bizarre to accept. "Well, for one thing, I have never seen a case of matter passing through matter; this is the *only* case I have ever seen, if it's authentic. I'm afraid that this is a bit beyond my depth. My haunting cases are baffling enough."

Cox became indignant. "How do you explain these images? You can see the untampered lock and seal in every frame."

"I don't know, Ed," I said lamely. "Maybe there is some kind of trick photography involved with this."

"I have scrutinized these films carefully. By using a locked and sealed mini-lab, we preclude the possibility of fraud."

As he grew more emphatic, I became more skeptical. I tried to figure out the psychological dynamics of what was going on between us. He had granted me entrance to a private, controversial aspect of his research and I was rejecting him. Since I had investigated a few hauntings, he had hoped that I might be sympathetic.

Our dialogue illustrates a typical pattern within scientific evaluations of the paranormal. Scientists judge the quality of anomalous claims on the basis of their previously conceived assumptions (Collins and Pinch, 1982; McClenon, 1984). I rejected Cox's evidence as too bizarre on a priori grounds. Because I presumed that fraud explained his findings, I concluded that his methodology must be flawed. This strategy allows scientists to avoid wasting time examining claims that seem totally implausible.

Cox later described the history of his case. The mini-lab was in the basement of a medium, Dr. John Thomas (Tom) Richards, an English professor in Missouri. Cox believed that Tom Richards's power allowed the pencil to stand up and write, the leather rings to link, and matter to pass through the glass front of the mini-lab. Richards did not attribute these feats to his own abilities. He believed that spirits caused the paranormal events to occur.[1]

Narrative 2

The following year, Cox presented his films at the Southeast Regional Parapsychological Association Conference. The audience saw his movie showing the pencil write "Rethink time." Leather rings appeared to link and unlink. Cards emerged from a sealed box and jerked themselves into order. They then popped back into their sealed box. One segment of the film showed a balloon spontaneously inflate and deflate, its securely tied neck clearly visible while inside the sealed and locked mini-lab. Objects moved in and out through the solid glass face. A toy car, pushed by some unknown energy, rolled around inside the mini-lab. A pinwheel turned as if blown by the wind, while a sheet of paper waved back and forth in the windless, sealed container. Pens lifted themselves up and wrote brief messages. Objects would disappear from one point and reappear instantaneously at another (F473.1, "Poltergeist throws objects"; F473.2, "Poltergeist causes objects to behave contrary to their nature").

The images on the film were of poor quality, and the camera work was amateurish.[2] The assembled parapsychologists were highly skeptical. Few were convinced that Cox's research was valid.[3]

Cox invited me to visit J. T. Richards in Missouri to evaluate the case. Since the study of deviant behavior is one of my specialty areas, I decided to conduct a sociological investigation of alleged recurrent psychokinesis.

Narrative 3

In April 1981, I drove to Rolla, Missouri, to investigate. Tom and Elaine Richards seemed sincere and friendly people. They invited me to stay at their house. As we talked in their living room, I felt somewhat awkward. I had accepted the hospitality of people whom I expected to reveal as frauds.

Then we heard some raps coming from the floor in the center of the living room. "Rap, rap, rap. Rap, rap, rap. Rap, rap, rap." They came in patterns of three. "Rap, rap, rap. Rap, rap, rap. Rap, rap, rap" (E402.1.5, "Invisible ghost makes rapping or knocking noise.")

Elaine had gone into the kitchen to begin supper. "There's Three-times-three," she called. "Ed Cox must be coming back soon."

"Three-times-three?" I asked. "What's that?"

"Three-times-three is an entity who is derived from Mr. Cox's subconscious," Tom told me. "The story that we have gathered from talking to the raps is that Mr. Cox's subconscious refuses to accept the fact that some psychokinetic phenomena come from disembodied spirits. As a result, a part of his subconscious has created the entity Three-times-three, whose sole purpose is to help Ed Cox do this research. He got his name from the signature he uses to identify himself."[4]

Three-times-three rapped out his signature again, "Rap, rap, rap. Rap, rap, rap. Rap, rap, rap." I looked at the area on the floor from where the raps seemed to be coming. Tom made no movement while the raps sounded, and I could see nothing that would indicate that he was responsible for producing them. "Rap, rap, rap. Rap, rap, rap. Rap, rap, rap." I felt faint vibrations on my feet at the point where the raps seemed to originate. I was amazed. This was the same phenomenon that had occurred among the Fox family in Hydesville, New York, launching the Spiritualist movement in 1848 (see Chapter 10, note 2).

Elaine was correct. Glancing out the window, I saw Cox arriving. Three-times-three's rapping grew louder, as if happy that Ed was returning.

Maybe it was just a coincidence that Cox arrived soon after Three-times-three began rapping, I mused. We knew that Ed had gone on a short errand. Perhaps some kind of rapping device was hidden in the floor. A typical magician's method for creating rapping sounds involves misdirection, a method that was not applicable in this instance since I could identify the exact point from which the percussions originated.[5]

As soon as Cox walked in the door, Elaine called out from the kitchen, "Mr. Cox, Three-times-three is here to talk to you."

"Oh, good," he exclaimed. "I have some questions for him I've been meaning to ask. Three-times-three, are you there?"

"Rap, rap, rap. Rap, rap, rap. Rap, rap, rap." Three-times-three gave his signature.

"Hello," Cox called happily. "Would you try to demonstrate your paranormal abilities to this gentleman here, Mr. Jim McClenon?"

"Rap." The raps followed a special code. One rap signified "yes." Two raps signified "no." Three raps meant "maybe."

"Why don't you ask Three-times-three a question?" Cox asked me.

I was struck speechless. I had never talked to a disembodied entity. I turned on my tape recorder and self-consciously fiddled with the microphone.

"I don't know. What can I say?" I tried to think of a question. "Three-times-three, how are you?"

The raps began spelling out letters, using a code system developed during the Spiritualist era. One rap stood for "A." Two raps stood for "B." Three raps signified "C," and so on. Listeners could distinguish this letter system from "yes, no, maybe" responses by evaluating the raps within the context of the conversation and by the raps' pacing.

"F-I-N-E," the raps laboriously spelled out. I laughed nervously.

"He might be able to rap directly on your microphone while you watch it," Cox stated. "This has happened before. I cannot imagine how that could be replicated through fraud. Three-times-three, will you rap right on Jim's microphone?"

The raps were becoming fainter. "Rap, rap, rap." Maybe.

"Will you please try?" Cox requested. The raps did not respond. "Maybe he can demonstrate his ability to rap wherever I direct him. I have had astonishing results within some of my field experiments. At times, they are capable of rapping at the exact point at which I direct them."

Cox made another request. "Three-times-three, will you please rap on the wall over there." He indicated the far wall.

The raps began faintly spelling out letters. Cox lay down on the floor and pressed his ear to the spot from which they seemed to be emanating.

We labored to keep track of the letters as they were spelled out: "O-N-T-H-E-W-."

"He's saying 'on the wall over there,'" Elaine ventured.

"Rap." Yes.

Cox was irritated. I was amused.[6] "Three-times-three," he exclaimed, "this is an important scientific test. Will you please make it seem as if your raps are coming from the far wall. This is very important. I am attempting to convince my colleague of your authenticity."

There was no sound of rapping from anywhere.

"Please, Three-times-three," Cox begged. "Demonstrate your ability to rap at a different location besides this point on the floor. My colleague might think that you don't really exist, that you are created by a hammer concealed in the floor."

The raps were virtually inaudible.

"I guess the energy's down," Tom remarked.

"You want him to prove that he is real. Do *you* believe that he is real, Mr. Cox?" Elaine asked sharply.

"I believe that vibrations occur paranormally in the floor," Cox said, "although I must admit that I cannot prove this in a manner acceptable to my scientific colleagues."

"But do you accept the entities as real? You are asking Three-times-three to prove that he is real, but I don't think that you really accept the entities yourself, Mr. Cox," she said.

"Scientifically, there is no proof of the survival-after-death hypothesis, if that is what you are getting at, Elaine," Cox responded. "As a scientist, I must suspend my judgment."

"I suppose everyone forms their opinions based on their own experiences," Tom said diplomatically. "I think that Three-times-three probably would make every attempt to help Ed since he is supposedly a derivation of Ed's mind."

It was a strange drama, an allegory. Cox symbolized soulless science attempting to direct what seemed a magical force. And, ironically, the force was believed to come directly from him. Now it would not, or perhaps could not, obey him. He was reduced to lying on the floor with his ear pressed against the point where the raps had last been located as he argued about survival after death. His absurd position weakened the forcefulness of his arguments.[7]

"Do they always come from the same points?" I asked. "Skeptics would suggest that there are hammer devices hidden in the floor."

"No, I have also heard and felt them outdoors. I have put my hand on the exact source of the energy. It's as if someone is under the ground with a hammer, trying to get out. I've heard and felt them coming out of solid concrete floors."[8] Cox looked at me seriously. He lifted his ear off the floor. "I've been interested in parapsychology since 1932," he stated. "I never have had experiences like these before I met the

Richardses. I've made every attempt to preclude the possibility of fraud, and you should realize that I am a knowledgeable magician. No normal explanation can explain satisfactorily the filmed effects that I have documented." (I provide this interaction to portray Cox's motivations. He was not attracted by SORRAT's ideology or social networks but by the anomalous events that he sought to investigate.)

Cox directed me down to the basement room where his mini-lab was set up. His apparatus was a Rube Goldberg-like invention with clothespins holding together electrical connections, an old eight-millimeter, spring-wound movie camera, and many wires and microswitches, all connected to an inverted aquarium that was attached to a heavy wooden board by metal bands padlocked together.

"This is the mini-lab," Cox exclaimed with pride. I puzzled at the contraption. Steve Calvin, a tall, thin, scholarly looking man in his midthirties, joined us. Calvin was responsible for the mini-lab's design and construction.

I looked at the mini-lab. It was filled with all manner of junk: leather rings, crayons, paper, balloons (one of which was inflated), toys, aluminum foil, pinwheels, plastic rings, sealed containers, and ESP cards. The edges were dusty; the glass sides had not been disturbed for many days. Dust covered the caulking. Cox secured the mini-lab with a padlock; he also inserted a special wax-like thread through the latch. He then melted the ends of the thread together with a match flame and then sealed them using his notary public stamp. The melted and sealed thread created a unique configuration, one difficult to duplicate.

"You have a golden opportunity to keep track of this mini-lab since you will be staying here at the Richardses' house," Cox said to me. "I hope you will call me immediately the minute that something happens within the lab."

I was disturbed by his suggestion. I did not want to become too closely associated with Cox, his mini-lab, or these strange people. I remembered the ridicule that his films had elicited among the parapsychologists. If I accepted his mini-lab research as valid, I knew my career as a social scientist would be damaged.

Narrative 4

In the evening, the Richardses, Ed Cox, Steve Calvin, and I conducted what they called an "ESP/PK experiment." They brought out a metal television tray and we sat around it with our hands touching the top. Although the lights had been turned off, the street lamps and moonlight outside allowed a high degree of visibility.

The table began vibrating rapidly. It seemed impossible for a person

Figure 16. Typical levitating table photograph (photo courtesy of J. T. Richards).

to duplicate the effect through normal means. I clearly saw that everyone's hands were on top of the table. Cox then laid on the floor. He wanted to maintain a position of complete vigilance and to locate the point of origin of the raps that had begun sounding.

"Rap, rap; rap, rap, rap. Rap, rap; rap, rap, rap."

"That's Black Elk," Elaine exclaimed. "That's Black Elk's signature."

"Rap, rap; rap, rap, rap." It sounded like the beat of a tom-tom.

Black Elk was the Sioux medicine man with whom John G. Neihardt, the founder of SORRAT, had been closely associated. Neihardt had become Black Elk's spiritual son and later described the medicine man's philosophy in the best-selling book, *Black Elk Speaks*. During his lifetime, Neihardt had been poet laureate of Nebraska, Plains States poet laureate, and an authority on the history and customs of the Plains Indians.

Cox scrambled around the floor to locate the exact point from which the raps seemed to be coming. I noticed that they came from different places than they had earlier in the afternoon.

Then the table began jumping around. It seemed to have a life of its own. Suddenly, it hopped about two feet up and seemed to hang for a few seconds. It then fell to one side as it dropped to the floor. How did this happen? Was it a sleight-of-hand trick? It then leaped up again but dropped almost immediately. Did someone lift it with his or her foot? The table continued to make small hops, but I could not detect the cause of these movements.

After the session, Elaine showed me many photographs of levitating objects which they had taken during past experiments (Figure 16). During my investigation, I found that various SORRAT members kept scrapbooks filled with such photographs. One goal was to get the table to levitate and then snap its picture. Tom and Elaine knew that such pictures could be faked. Their photographs constituted personal mementos of evenings during which were certain that psychokinesis had occurred (F1083.0.1, "Object floats in air").[9]

Narrative 5

In the morning, I joined Ed Cox while inspecting the mini-lab. The balloon which had been fully inflated was now only half-full of air. Some plastic rings in the mini-lab had been moved and were now resting on top of a sealed container. A message, "Hi, Jim," had been written in crayon on a paper inside.

It worried me that I could think of no good normal explanation for the writing or movement of the rings. The dust on the edges of the glass panels remained undisturbed. The lock remained closed; the melted thread was in its original position.

"You know, Ed," I said. "This seems like a magic trick. The raps, the table tipping, things moving around in the mini-lab. Although I can't explain it, I can't be certain that anything paranormal happened. After all, I have seen a magician pull a rabbit out of what seemed to be an empty hat, but I didn't conclude that psychic phenomena occurred."

"But what you don't realize is that the magician requires props," Ed replied. "*He* has control over what occurs. With these mini-lab experiments, *I* maintain a specific area over which I have complete control. The magician would be unable to pull a rabbit out of his hat if I were allowed to inspect it and to place it in a locked and sealed mini-lab. I know what magicians can and can't do; I am one."

Narrative 6

Steve Calvin provided me with written comments regarding the possibility of faking movements inside the mini-lab:[10]

"When sealed and locked, there are no cracks or holes exceeding 1/32 inch (actually the largest is less than that), and with the bottom board in, any entry would also require at least one 90 degree bend as well. Any postulated procedure for faking that would require opening and closing the box during filming (single frame), even without a lock, is untenable for several reasons. The metal straps are very springy and get in the way, usually causing major unintentional disturbances of the contents of the box. If any objects are touching the sides of the box, they are guaranteed to be disturbed. Another criteria that would rule out single frame operation while manipulating the contents of the box is a characteristic of the camera that I did not reveal to anyone until over half of the 29 reels of film had been exposed. When operated in the single frame mode (also for the first frame of a full speed run), the camera shutter speed is a nominal 1/28 second. Nominal shutter speed at 16 f.p.s. is 1/32 second. This is enough to produce a noticeably brighter image during single frame operation. With only one exception, this was not observed on sequences shot inside the box (the one exception being the moving die sequence). This was observed on some sequences outside the box, but is not particularly relevant for several reasons: 1) anything we (corporal beings) can do, the entities could also presumably do (though the converse is not true) and 2) events outside the box have been considered suggestive, but not evidential, by all parties concerned.

"Any procedure involving an open side of the box is quite preposterous.[11] All glass was in place on all occasions when I inspected the box. There was never any evidence that the glass had been removed and replaced, such as broken glass fragments, sloppy gluing or the acetic acid odor of curing silicone rubber glue, which lingers for several days after application. Considering the number of separate events observed and the frequency of checking of the box (often Mr. Cox or I would check the box on several successive days, with events occurring in between) postulating the removal and replacement of the glass as a mechanism for permitting animation is ridiculous.

"Substitution of film exposed at an identical setup elsewhere would be impossible for a number of reasons. The contents of the box often included unique objects that were unduplicable. The film sequences often included one or more of us doing something to show a setup or the results of an RSPK [recurrent spontaneous psychokinetic] event. Records of events filmed were kept by both Cox and Richards.

"I believe that either the padlock with seal or the melted string seal would be adequate to prevent undetected entry, and that both together would prevent multiple undetected entries. Mr. Cox did not have sufficient unobserved access time to permit faking of even a small fraction of the events, ignoring all the other constraints preventing anyone from faking events occurring within the locked and sealed mini-lab.

"Another constraint preventing faking events by single frame operation is blur as a result of movement during the finite open time of the shutter. A number of high speed events have occurred inside the locked and sealed mini-lab which showed an amount of blur consistent with the observed amount of movement. The best example that comes to mind is a sequence showing an uninflated balloon with string (loose). The string is rapidly tied around the neck of the balloon (several frames, with blurred string). The balloon then rapidly inflates. The balloon was examined later. No entrance for air other than the normal opening (now tied) was found.

"Summary: Using the available equipment, many of the events filmed inside the mini-lab could not be duplicated by any corporal being, including Mr. Cox and Dr. Richards, even if the locks and seals were not present. The addition of the locks and seals would seem to preclude multiple undetected entrances to the mini-lab by Richards or any other corporeal outside agent."

Narrative 7

Neihardt believed that rapport within the group was a primary factor in eliciting psychokinetic phenomena. While living in Columbia, Missouri, he organized SORRAT to test this theory. I asked Tom about the types of people who formed the original group.

"We were mostly college students at the university. I was the oldest, and since I had a car I was often instrumental in getting people to Dr. Neihardt's home," Tom told me.

"What happened at the meetings?"

"At first, nothing. We would sit around and talk. He had a forty-pound wooden table, and we would put our hands on top of it and try to get it to levitate. Although nothing happened for week after week, it was still fun. Dr. Neihardt was a very wise and warm man, and the group was building rapport so people still enjoyed themselves. I guess it was after about three months that we got the first raps. In the beginning, they were not very clear. I think it was Black Elk. As time passed, they got stronger, and Neihardt put a great deal of effort into investigating them. Once the raps came from the arm of a chair, and he had the chair disassembled to look for rapping devices. Another time they pulled up the floorboards looking for an explanation for the raps. Once he had everyone place their feet on pillows to prevent anyone from making rapping noises with their feet.

"Dr. Neihardt knew Black Elk very well and asked the raps many questions to which only Black Elk and he knew the answers. He eventually became satisfied that Black Elk was authentic.

"We also began to get vibrations from an extremely heavy table and later we even got it to levitate. Dr. Neihardt borrowed an infrared scope so an observer could see in the dark and attempt to spot fraud. After much effort in precluding the possibility of fraud, he corresponded with Dr. J. B. Rhine at Duke University and that is how they came to devise the concept of the mini-lab. In 1966, Rhine gave a lecture in Missouri, and Neihardt gave him some photographs of levitating tables. That attracted Mr. Cox's attention, since he was an associate of Rhine's at the Institute for Parapsychology in North Carolina. Mr. Cox first came out here in 1969."[12]

Tom went on to tell story after story of paranormal events the group had experienced. In the early days, the sessions attracted huge crowds. Officials at the University of Missouri learned of the sessions and harassed members of SORRAT, since they were engaging in what many considered occult activities. One woman was temporarily committed for psychiatric examination by her parents (apparently, they attempted to force her to deny that she had seen tables levitate.) A German student had to return to her country because a dean at the university blocked her visa renewal. Other members lost their scholarships because of university officials' disapproval of the group. One was disowned by his family after the university informed his parents of his SORRAT activities. Eventually, Neihardt and the core group decided that small, private meetings would be preferable.

Tom had notes from virtually all SORRAT meetings he had attended. He tape-recorded SORRAT table-tipping experiments for many years. I listened to more than thirty hours of his recordings of these sessions, a small segment of what he offered me. The group reported many astonishing events, such as tables levitating, objects appearing out of nowhere, and messages being obtained from the deceased; they also spent much time in mundane conversation. They described some of Neihardt's early sessions. Once, Neihardt tested the authenticity of the entities' ability to teleport objects by requesting that a specific book be paranormally transported from his library to another room. The entities complied.

Although many sittings produced few results, others were filled with astonishing perceptions. Tom had carefully labeled each taped session. For example, one tape, titled "The Night the Table Climbed the Tree," described an incident where the group followed the table outdoors and saw it ascend into a tree.

Although skeptics might assume that Neihardt created the "magic tricks" to attract group members, phenomena also occurred when he and any other member, such as Tom Richards, were absent. To explain all SORRAT phenomena as fraudulent, skeptics must hypothesize that SORRAT members engage in a group hoax, which they undertake merely for their own amusement.

The entities frequently counseled the group to love wisely and to show altruism to people who were worthy of it. Although universal love was a goal, the entities reasoned that this seemed to be beyond the grasp of the average person. They advocated the more realistic objective of loving friends and relatives as completely as possible. The messages also explained the nature of the "other side" (after death). They stated that on the "other side" a soul mentally creates whatever setting it desires.[13]

The early members were not attracted to SORRAT so much by the degree to which their deprivations coincided with the group ideology as by their attraction to a charismatic figure, Dr. Neihardt, and by their interest in wondrous phenomena. The group created an atmosphere conducive to anomalous experience but then reacted to social stigma by limiting invitations to meetings. Later participants, such as Ed Cox and Steve Calvin, were attracted almost completely by the anomalous events rather than by ideological factors. SORRAT history can be viewed as prototypical; groups generating anomalous effects must cope with emotional social reactions as well as stigma.

Although many aspects of mini-lab phenomena are culturally specific, many SORRAT perceptions are equivalent to those described in the anthropological and Spiritualist literature. For example, Black Elk's tribe members, the Oglala Sioux, ritually shut themselves inside a tent and summoned spirits to answer their questions. The sides of the tent would shake paranormally as a means of spirit communication. Tent shaking and percussive sounds have been observed within various Native American and Asian shamanic ceremonies. Barnouw (1942; 1975: 257–258), Hallowell (1934, 1942), Hultkrantz (1992: 37–39) and Landes (1968) describe similar psychokinetic effects among such groups.

Narrative 8

I attended two SORRAT meetings at John Neihardt's former residence. On the second occasion, little occurred, aside from anomalous
rapping. The first visit, however, was very impressive. The group
formed a circle of seventeen people. Raps sounded from many places
in the floor simultaneously, each rap claiming an individual personality. While the participants had their hands on a television tray, the
tray seemed to leap in the air. Later, the whole room started to shake, as
if an earthquake were occurring. This phenomenon occurred repeat-
edly (D2148, "Earth magically caused to quake"). Various members
went into trance and answered questions addressed to them by participants (D1810.13, "Magic knowledge from the dead"). During one
"earthquake," I felt waves of rapport sweeping through the room, a
sense of unity and love for all beings, and amazement at what I was
experiencing.

The entities rapped out a message, "E-M-B-R-A-C-E." Everyone put
their arms around each other in a large circle. One SORRAT member,
in trance, gave the entities' message: "All life, all entities, all the universe, are one. No matter how lonely you feel, you should know that we
are one with you. We are always with you. We will help you. Even in
death, you are not alone. All life is one." The entities' message coincides
with Huxley's (1945) "perennial philosophy," a doctrine that mystics
have advocated throughout the centuries. Such ideas are often presented in trance messages.

The sociologist Emile Durkheim (1965/1912) argued that religion
originated with group emotional excitement. He hypothesized that
primitive people falsely attributed this feeling to supernatural sources.
He believed that religious practices are a way of symbolically worshipping one's own society, an action that helps hold society together.
Durkheim's theory explains why a society's religion tends to reflect its
social structure.

The "feelings of community" that Durkheim believed were important for stimulating religious impulses may occur most forcefully during wondrous group experiences. Within prehistoric cultures, the raps
would be treated as "real," and this was also the sentiment within the
SORRAT group. The ideology presented by the sounds would shape
religious belief. Whether the rapping sounds are a product of group
consciousness (assuming that the human mind can produce psychokinetic events), a trickster, or even supernatural forces, SORRAT's
group perceptions provide insight into the forms of experience that
affect folk, and probably prehistoric, religious belief.

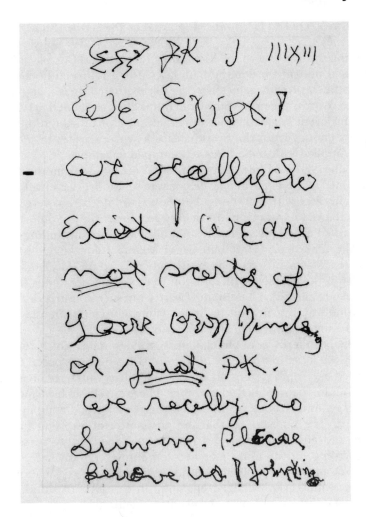

Figure 17. Early message from SORRAT spirits (photo courtesy of J. T. Richards).

Narrative 9

The SORRAT members believed that the spirits could create written messages. Figure 17 provides one such example. It contains symbols for four spirits: Native American Good Thunder (pictograph of clouds and lightning), sixteenth-century buccaneer John King (J.K.), Elaine's deceased infant brother Jay (J.), and Cox's mental projection "Three-times-three" (111X111). John King acted as the scribe (E557, "Dead man writes").

During my first visit to the Richardses' home, I had Cox place a self-addressed postcard inside the mini-lab. After I returned home, I received the card with a message, in Elizabethan English, signed by Patience Worth, a famous spirit from the 1920s (mentioned in Chapter 10). This event began a series of communications through the mail. Famous entities from the Spiritualist era sent messages to me after being supplied with self-addressed, stamped envelopes.[14]

As other SORRAT members learned of my letters from the spirits, they joined in this experiment. People sent self-addressed envelopes to the Richardses with questions they hoped would be answered. The replies found their way into the mail system (ostensibly paranormally), postmarked from places far from Rolla, Missouri, including Bethlehem, Connecticut; Columbus, Ohio; Atlanta, Georgia; and Middlesex-Essex, Massachusetts. The entities also placed uncanceled foreign stamps on the envelopes (in addition to the domestic stamps that we had already affixed). These stamps were from such countries as Portugal, Honduras, Brazil, French Guinea, Chile, Hungary, Yugoslavia, the United Kingdom, Mexico, and Germany.

A few postmarks were anomalous, signifying dates which followed the day the letter arrived. Yet on various occasions, the postal service returned envelopes (ostensibly sent by the spirits who have no earthly return address) to a SORRAT member. These envelopes have included written requests from a fictitious "postmark collector" living in Rolla, Missouri. The notes asked that the postmaster at a distant location cancel the enclosed envelopes (which contained entity messages). Handwriting on the notes matched the entities' typical style. When SORRAT members wrote the spirits, asking for an explanation, the entities readily acknowledged engaging in this type of fraud. They admitted simulating paranormal events by requesting postmarks from distant postmasters. They argued that this was a suitable means of stimulating belief in newer members (K1970, "Sham miracles"). Tom and Elaine Richards deny writing any of these messages.

The letter-writing phenomenon gave me the opportunity to monitor SORRAT postal activity. Writers were requested to send copies of their entity answers to me so that I might mail out an annual summary newsletter to all participants. Most people complied.

The number of letter-writing participants has varied. Between 1981 and 1993, more than one hundred people have received entity messages after writing letters to the spirits. Generally, only four or five people correspond regularly at any one time. Some writers have requested spiritual healing. The majority of these supplicants reported benefits and some claimed anomalous cures (D2161, "Magic healing power").

The behavior of the human letter writers revealed certain patterns. Many began by seeking proof of the entities' paranormal abilities. Since the spirits rarely supplied such evidence, most correspondents participated only briefly. Some long-term participants wished to discuss esoteric issues. Other writers patiently requested demonstrations of paranormal effects and sporadically received unusual artifacts (objects inside a light bulb or other sealed container, for example; E544 "Ghost leaves evidence of his appearance"). These objects always had ambiguous qualities such that they did not, in my opinion, provide compelling evidence for paranormal phenomena. No expert verified that a human trickster could not have inserted objects in the light bulb, for example.

The letter-writing component of SORRAT activities supports the social network theory. The spirits encouraged interaction among participants by misdirecting correspondence (answers to my inquiries were typically mailed to someone else). The entities claimed that this enhances member rapport, since respondents must communicate with each other when redirecting mail.

Table-tipping members tend to participate in SORRAT for longer periods than do letter writers. Table tippers generally have witnessed more anomalous events and have developed stronger bonds with other group members. They live, or have lived, geographically close to the Missouri members. The spirits urge letter writers to visit table-tipping sessions at Neihardt's former house.

Narrative 10

My investigation of SORRAT attracted the attention of George Hansen, who, in 1981, was a research fellow at the Institute for Parapsychology in Durham, North Carolina. George prepared a carefully sealed test deck of ESP cards and a "control" deck that could later be examined by skeptics (ESP cards have special symbols thought to be more suitable for extrasensory perception than normal cards). He sent one deck to Rolla with the request that the entities paranormally sort the cards without disturbing the seals. The package was mailed from Rolla to a SORRAT member (ostensibly by paranormal means), returned to the Institute for Parapsychology by the member, and remailed to Rolla. The entities then stated, in other letters and by rapping, that they had mailed it to another SORRAT member.

It eventually came to George by mail. It appeared to him that an address label had fallen off and, as a result, the package had been delivered to the institute's address. George and other parapsychologists carefully opened the deck and found evidence of fraud (they detected solvent near some of the glue). There was "spirit writing" in pencil on the heat-sensitive paper inside the package. George considered the "readdressing" to be an attempted coverup of the botched job of tampering with the package (Hansen, 1982; Hansen and Broughton, 1983, 1991). These findings caused most parapsychologists to believe that the Rolla case was fraudulent. Unlike the postmark situation, the entities did not admit to fraudulent behavior in this instance. Tom and Elaine Richards were furious at the inference that they were dishonest.

Hansen's failure to receive a proof through the mail was one of many such attempts. Numerous cases within the psychical research literature fit this pattern. "Outside" investigators detect fraud with ease, while those conducting more lengthy studies gather evidence convincing only to "insiders." Feilding, Baggally, and Carrington (1909) investigated Eusapia Palladino; Carrington investigated Mina Crandon; and Cox investigated SORRAT. Although outsiders remained skeptical, "inside" investigators were convinced that they had observed paranormal phenomena.

Some parapsychologists have suggested that Tom and Elaine Richards go into trance before engaging in fraud. Similar theories were presented to explain Mina Crandon's and Eusapia Palladino's cheating (fraudulent behavior is common while in shamanic trance). I have witnessed Tom slip into unplanned trances and speak using an alternate personality, but I have never observed him engage in any complex activity while in that state. In response to this paragraph, one SORRAT participant wrote to me stating, "There are many reports of somnambulistic people carrying out the most intricate of tasks while going about in a profound trance." His observation illustrates the diversity of opinion, and apparent open-mindedness, of some SORRAT participants. Many acknowledge that fraud may explain *some* but not *all* of their perceptions.

Ed Cox and I have collected data that indicate a close relationship between Tom Richards's consciousness and the content of many entity messages. Misspelled words in the entity messages were misspelled in the same manner by Richards when Cox quizzed him. The entity messages have contained unusual phrases and puns similar to those used by Richards in his conversation and correspondence. Still, Richards denies any role in writing entity messages.

Narrative 11

I sent this chapter of my manuscript to George Hansen, seeking his response. He comments: "I spent a total of five nights as a guest in the home of Dr. and Mrs. Richards. As Jim McClenon indicates, they were very warm and open people; they wanted to have the phenomena scientifically studied and were very cooperative in experiments.

"During my visits, I heard hundreds of raps which communicated in an intelligent fashion. At the beginning of a 'rap session,' the raps would frequently seem to be coming from directly below Dr. Richards's feet. As the session progressed, the raps seemed to move gradually some distance from him (usually up to two or three feet). Nearly all the raps occurred under very well lighted conditions. A number of times I sat on the floor near Dr. Richards (with my eyes within three feet of his feet). I never observed anything suspicious.

"In one session, hundreds of tiny raps emanated from a small metal snack tray around which five of us were seated with well lighted conditions. Everyone took their hands off the table and then I put mine back on. The raps continued for several more seconds but gradually died out. Everyone put their hands back on the table, and the tiny raps again started. We took our hands off and the raps died out.

"Others have reported observing trickery by Dr. Richards in producing the raps. Tony Cornell, in a workshop at the 1982 Parapsychological Association convention in Cambridge, reported observing Richards knocking on an object with his knuckles during a rap session. Cornell also reported hearing raps which he could not explain.[15]

"Clearly the raps occurring around Richards are anomalous. A satisfactory explanation has not yet been given. Perhaps the raps are a trick. Certainly I have been fooled by magicians on other occasions. Perhaps the raps are paranormal. Unfortunately, parapsychologists have not yet developed adequate tools to study the phenomenon. For those still interested in scientifically studying the SORRAT phenomena, the raps might be the best place to start."

Hansen's observations coincide with a recurring pattern within psychical research. He uncovered fraud,[16] yet also observed unexplained events. Duke and Hansen (1991) assembled a bibliography with ninety-six items regarding SORRAT. This literature provides many other examples of ambiguous/anomalous perceptions stimulating both belief and skepticism.

For example, Stillings (1991) provides photographs revealing what appears to be a phony SORRAT table levitation. Richards denies having engaged in fraud that evening but admits to using deception on a previous occasion. He argues that SORRAT need not resort to fraud, even though deception creates fertile grounds for authentic paranormal events (Richards, 1984). Stillings has come to believe that psi has a hiding quality.

Narrative 12

On various occasions in Missouri I observed extremely anomalous table vibrations. Once I was the only participant with my hands on the table while it vibrated. I searched for hidden wires but found none. Other investigators and SORRAT members have had similar experiences.

These events are merely some of the many that SORRAT participants have experienced. Other bizarre events include the linking of two continuous plywood rings, the linking of continuous special metallic alloy rings, objects entering into sealed containers, writing appearing in sealed containers during group meetings, Neihardt's signature appearing after his death,[17] and objects entering into light bulbs. All events could be reproduced through fraud, but each would require a special type of expertise. Many of these performances were highly persuasive to SORRAT members since they had a degree of control over their surroundings while the anomalous events occurred.

Narrative 13

I interviewed many SORRAT members as part of my study. John Hunt, for example, described the process by which he became involved with SORRAT: "In 1978, I heard raps in my apartment wall. The raps came three at a time, seemingly from a disembodied entity. I demanded that if they were 'real' that they come from the other wall in order to prove themselves. Then they rapped out two sets of three on the other wall!

"It was about this time that I ran into Steve Calvin. Steve invited Tom and Elaine [Richards] over to my apartment where they did the standard table-tipping experiment. They tried to make contact with the entity at my place. The raps came again! I didn't know what to make of it! It's hard to accept, but I'm into science fiction, so this was like a game for me.

"I decided to devise a test of the raps during an ESP/PK experiment with Tom and Elaine. I demanded that the raps tell me what I was thinking at that moment. I thought of the Rolling Stones album, 'Goat's Head Soup.' The raps spelled out 'goat.'"

Narrative 14

In 1981, I mailed out thirty-eight questionnaires to people who had participated in SORRAT meetings. Twenty-one (55 percent) were returned. I interviewed three other SORRAT members in person. Overall, I received information from 63 percent of my target population. Respondents described table-tipping sessions at various people's homes. During some sessions, the entire room shook. The respondents reported seeing tables vibrate, move, or levitate without anyone touching them. Some members reasoned that if it were possible to duplicate SORRAT phenomena through sleight-of-hand, then professional magicians would have good reason to perform such actions frequently because this would be a good show and would attract much money. One woman remarked that her children communicated with raps in the room where a table-tipping experiment had taken place the day before. The children were successful again the next day, but as the days passed they were less able to reproduce the effect.

Although the nature of respondents' beliefs varied, many claimed that their initial skepticism had been transformed by experience. For example, one respondent wrote:

Originally, the group consisted only of other faculty members who were essentially non-religious, intellectually curious people. All of us looked at the evening meetings with great skepticism, partially scientifically, and also for the purposes of entertainment . . . [The respondent went on to list various paranormal experiences:]

1. I witnessed a television tray "climb" the front of a fireplace.
2. I felt a whole room shake violently.
3. One Sunday, raps, with whom we engaged in conversation, followed us from a graveyard, to buildings in [name of city], Missouri, rapped in the floor of our car, in the corner of the living room when we came in the front door of our home, and in the kitchen floor and table as we had lunch. All of this was during the day.
4. One evening, we broke up into groups and among other things levitated an ordinary small sofa pillow. There was cold air underneath the pillow which was suspended above the floor several inches.
5. Another time, the center of a television tray began to pop rhythmically up and down. You could put the palms of your hands above and below the center and the metal would still pop back and forth.
6. One evening a large group of people (students, mainly) gathered (all novices to this phenomena) to witness exorcising a poltergeist. There were many, many raps from all over the room, ceiling, floor, walls. A large heavy wooden table levitated in spite of a man who stood on it trying to keep it on the ground.
7. During this year we met in many different houses, with personal friends that

I knew very well, and who were all very skeptical, yet the phenomena still occurred. There was no way that the houses or furniture could have been rigged.

Narrative 15

A variety of modern experimental groups have reported anomalous experiences. Batcheldor (1966, 1979, 1984), Brookes-Smith (1973, 1975), Brookes-Smith and Hunt (1970), and Owen and Sparrow (1976) published accounts of table-tipping experiments. I have collected similar narratives from other individuals.

Batcheldor (1966, 1979, 1984) sought to explain why some Spiritualist-type "sitter" groups experience anomalous events while others fail. Sitter groups, so called because their experiments are conducted with participants seated in a circle, seek to communicate with spirits. Batcheldor theorized that psychokinetic effects are the result of latent mental processes and that people tend to thwart such effects due to unconscious fears. He labeled one such unconscious process as "witness inhibition," the reaction of shock or fear associated with directly observing a PK event. An additional process preventing PK is "ownership resistance," the fear of being personally the source of PK phenomena. Although occult believers may claim they seek to produce wondrous effects, Batcheldor argues that most subconsciously fear the actual phenomena. Actual psychic events are often unrestrained and uncontrollable. They generally act symbolically, fulfilling unconscious, rather than conscious, needs. People are naturally fearful of such powerful subconscious projections. Only in unusual situations, where witness inhibition and ownership resistance are overcome, do psychokinetic events occur.

Batcheldor used the term "artifact effects" to label phenomena that seem paranormal but occur through normal means. Examples include creaking floors, subconscious muscular movements, and fraudulently produced events, all of which may be mistaken for psychokinetic phenomena. Artifacts help overcome ownership resistance since witnesses feel no responsibility for the perceived event. Witness inhibition is overcome through attenuation and attitudinal change. The absolute belief resulting from artifact effects permits actual paranormal events to follow.

Batcheldor hypothesized that groups sitting in darkness are more likely to experience paranormal events since they tend to evaluate artifact effects as authentic. Groups such as SORRAT may create artifact effects through subconscious muscular movements or fraud.

Brookes-Smith and Hunt (1970) sought to test Batcheldor's theory. Although these researchers experienced astonishing events, the phenomena avoided direct observation. Brookes-Smith (1973, 1975) constructed a specially equipped seance table that monitored pressure from all sides. He had sitters draw lots before the sitting. One person, the designated cheater, was to discreetly simulate paranormal effects by pushing the table sideways. Afterward, the recordings from the instrumented table distinguished the cheater's effects from ostensibly paranormal movements that followed. Brookes-Smith's (1973) findings supported the argument that artifact effects can stimulate authentic psychokinetic events.

Batcheldor tested his hypotheses within small group environments for many years. During my correspondence with him, he described many anomalous experiences, such as percussive sounds, table movements, and phantom figures. Visitors to his home also reported witnessing anomalous phenomena during sessions. Gissurarson (1992: 331) writes:

I had the opportunity to participate in one of Batcheldor's last sittings in 1987. On that occasion, in the presence of two other sitters besides Batcheldor and myself, I witnessed a 46-pound table rising completely off the floor and swinging from side to side in the air, small objects "flying" around, and I heard repeated rapid tappings, loud scratching, and heavy knocks on the furniture and raps in the air. The sitters said they felt gusts of wind, and whistling was purportedly heard. One of the more impressive happenings was the repeated apparent "materialization" of strangely shaped animated forms, such as fingers, a small head, and lifelike tentacles that could be touched.

Owen and Sparrow (1976) conducted experiments that further revealed the factors contributing to group experiences. They sought to induce wondrous perceptions by having the group devise a fictional story. The original goal was to perceive an apparition of a fictional entity in order to demonstrate that actual spirits are not required to experience psychic phenomena. The narrative they devised concerned an aristocratic Englishman, Philip, who lived in the middle 1600s. According to their story, he was married to a sexually frigid woman, the daughter of a neighboring nobleman. While riding on his estate, Philip encountered, and fell in love with, a beautiful gypsy woman. He brought her to live near his family estate. His wife discovered the affair and accused her rival of being a witch. Philip remained silent while his mistress was burned at the stake. Suffering severe guilt, he eventually committed suicide.

The group meditated together for a year but were unsuccessful in producing any paranormal effects. Batcheldor suggested that they "ease-up" a bit and try light-hearted conversation as a method to induce PK. When they followed his advice, they heard rapping sounds and experienced anomalous table movements, some of which they captured on video. The raps claimed to be Philip and elaborated on the Philip story. Acoustic analysis of the sounds indicated that the Philip raps died away more quickly than did normally produced raps. Because they had used a fictional narrative as the basis for these effects, the group interpreted their results as indicating that real spirits are not required to produce psychokinetic phenomena. As hypothesized by Batcheldor, group subconscious processes can create wondrous perceptions (Owen and Sparrow, 1976).

Analysis

I will discuss these narratives within the context of the scientific investigation of psychic phenomena, sociological theories of small, alternative religious group recruitment, and social-psychological processes related to wondrous experience.

Predictions Regarding Scientific Investigation

The SORRAT case provides data supporting the predictions outlined in Chapter 10. Psychical research involves recurring patterns. The SORRAT accounts had features similar to shamanic performances, revealing universal qualities (narratives 4, 7, 8, 12, 13, and 14). Major investigators (Cox and Calvin) accepted the authenticity of paranormal claims while others remained skeptical (narratives 1, 2, 5, and 6). Investigators encountered fraud and unusual behaviors associated with fraud. Participants variously confessed to fraud, denied fraud, seemed unaware that fraud had occurred, and regarded fraud as part of a natural process (narratives 9, 10, 11, 14, and 15). Effects were related to altered states of consciousness (narratives 8 and 10). The phenomena seemed shaped by personalities within the group, yet also had universal features (narratives 9 and 10). The phenomena had a contagious quality; witnessing events increased one's potential for observing similar effects (narrative 14). Scientists claiming to have verified anomalous effects were labeled as deviant (narratives 1, 2, 10, and 11). Investigators attributed a capricious, hiding quality to the phenomena (narratives 9, 10, and 11).

This evidence supports the argument that scientific investigations of psychic phenomena reveal recurrent patterns. I predict that future researchers will encounter similar patterns.[18]

Sociological Theories Pertaining to Recruitment and Retention

SORRAT participants' motivations seemed unrelated to spiritual, psychological, or social deprivations. SORRAT members shared a group ideology but did not achieve consensus (narratives 3, 7, and 14). The original SORRAT members attracted by John Neihardt were fascinated with unexplained phenomena rather than attracted by an ideology (narratives 7 and 14). After Neihardt's death, the group did not become bureaucratized but remained covert. The wondrous quality of the phenomena continued to attract members (narratives 13 and 14). Social interaction was important for inspiring long-term participation since it coincided with rapport and anomalous experience. Table tippers, who experienced more robust phenomena, were more committed to the group than letter writers, who perceived fewer anomalous events (narratives 4, 7, 8, 9, 12, 13, and 14). Batcheldor's (1966, 1979, 1984) and Owen and Sparrow's (1976) groups seemed similarly motivated by scientific curiosity and anomalous perceptions (narrative 15). These observations support both the social networks theory and the recruitment-through-experience hypothesis.

Members of SORRAT, Batcheldor's group, and the "Philip" group may be atypical in that they attempted to influence scientific, rather than religious, audiences. I suspect that many occult assemblies use ideological factors and social networks to a greater degree than do these experimental groups.

A Theory Regarding Wondrous Events in Small Groups

I hypothesize that social-psychological needs, networks, and group processes can work contiguously to increase the probability of group wondrous experiences. I do not seek to "explain away" anomalous claims, but rather to describe processes contributing to their incidence. Groups with sufficient cohesion (rapport), aesthetically suitable narratives, psychic performers (who need not be aware of their roles), and the willingness to overcome their initial resistance to wondrous perceptions can experience spiraling levels of wondrous experience and belief.

Elements in Batcheldor's theory can be translated into social-psychological terms. Batcheldor argued that witness inhibition and ownership resistance prevent the incidence of psychokinesis; such obstacles are overcome by artifact effects which induce temporary states of absolute belief leading to authentic PK events. This theory can be rephrased in a manner that does not presume the existence of PK. Skepticism in groups thwarts interpretations of events as paranormal (witness inhibition) while belief encourages wonderment. Believers tend to deny that wondrous experiences are mental or social products (ownership resistance). They generally attribute wondrous events to supernatural agencies (overcoming ownership resistance). Groups with members who stimulate wondrous events (either consciously or unconsciously) can develop absolute beliefs conducive to further wondrous perceptions (overcoming witness inhibition and skepticism). Artifact effects contribute to this process. Experience leads to belief, allowing further, and more astonishing, anomalous experiences and greater belief. This model describes extremely anomalous wondrous perceptions in small groups as a product of progressively greater levels of experience and belief. Some groups appear able to generate effects that overcome moderate levels of individual skepticism.

Many shamanic groups demonstrate processes that are consistent with this social-psychological model. Psychic practitioners often create artifact effects (secondary wondrous events) in order to kindle belief. This seemingly stimulates further anomalous experiences (tertiary wondrous events). Such incidents then provide a foundation for future performances.

Subconscious effects are particularly suitable for triggering the cycle of experience and belief. For example, in a typical shamanic performance, Taiwanese Taoists hold the legs of a small chair. They believe that the deity inhabiting the chair activates it to perform religious functions. Sometimes the chair moves so violently that the members have difficulty holding it. (It can vibrate in the same manner as a SORRAT table.) The chair can also form Chinese characters with one leg, providing messages for onlookers. Although the chair may be affected by subconscious muscular movements, its performances are thought to be magical since holders are often illiterate (Jordan, 1972). When an observer states the correct reading of the characters, the chair provides a confirmatory rap on the table. (As with the SORRAT system, the chair gives two raps for a wrong interpretation.)

According to the sect members' beliefs, gods, using the divination chair, can descend to earth to act as guests, overseers, guides, or decision makers. Figure 18 shows a ritual performance during which the chair, and its invisible godly presence, send healing energy to a baby. A similar practice involves a divination stick—held by a person in trance—that writes messages (Jordan and Overmyer, 1986). Such devices, like the Ouija board, harness unconscious muscular energy to provide communication with spiritual forces. Variations of these procedures are common throughout the world.

Such group practices can lead to highly anomalous perceptions.

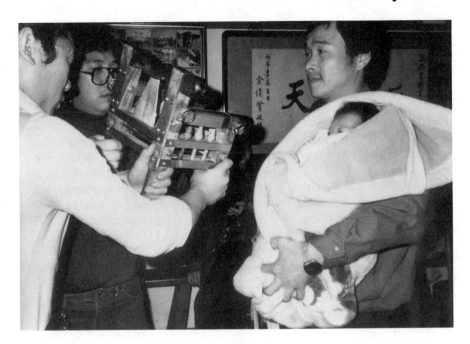

Figure 18. Taoists hold chair believed occupied by a deity (photo by J. McClenon).

Taiwanese Taoist sect members claim they gain information, later verified as true, which was unknown to any of those holding the chair. Messages also foretell future events. This leads to greater certainty regarding supernatural phenomena. The pattern is universal: secondary wondrous events produce belief and stimulate tertiary wondrous effects, generating even greater faith.

Aesthetic and archetypical qualities within folk narratives appear to influence the subconscious mind/body processes related to wondrous experience. *Aesthetics*, as noted in Chapter 3, can be defined as that quality which resonates with an audience's needs, producing a sense of truth, completeness, balance, drama, or beauty. Groups that use potent stories seem better able to recruit new members, achieve unity, and generate wondrous effects. Throughout the centuries, certain patterns have been found to work effectively to accomplish this end. Groups focus on narratives with archetypical heroes, heroines, magicians, wise people, healers, villains, victims, and tricksters. Taiwanese divination sects summon a pantheon of archetypical deities, each with a special personality. SORRAT spirits include a wise poet (Neihardt), Native American healers (Black Elk and Good Thunder), and a seventeenth-century buccaneer/trickster (John King). The Philip group sought to demonstrate that narrative "truth" is not a necessary factor for producing anomalous experience. They communicated with a fictitious victim, Philip, the central character in an aesthetically powerful haunting narrative.

Many of the narratives that established archetypical spirits were based on actual events. The individual who is central to the narrative dies, is perceived to create wondrous effects, and then becomes the focus for narratives used within wondrous performances. The Chinese general Kuan Yu, for example, distinguished himself during the Han dynasty, but was executed in 220 B.C. After his death, he made apparitional visits and was thought to produce miraculous events. He was worshiped for his integrity and loyalty, and Asian shamans still believe he delivers messages through them. Today he is known as the Chinese God of War (Chamberlain, 1983).

Christian history mirrors this process: a hero-victim became the focus of collective worship due to a series of wondrous experiences. Jesus' wondrous performances aided his disciples in overcoming their witness inhibitions. He made apparitional visits following his death. After his final departure, his followers lived communally. We would assume they developed rapport, since love was central to Jesus' teachings. The Resurrection story became a suitable narrative for inducing further wondrous experiences. According to the New Testament (Acts: 2), Jesus' followers heard the sound of a mighty windstorm, saw flames and tongues of fire, spoke in unknown languages, and felt filled with the Holy Spirit (the SORRAT group reports equivalent incidents: anomalous lights, sounds, earthquake effects, powerful feelings of rapport). Early Christian groups out-performed their competitors in producing magical events, aided by their superior, unifying narratives.

Various anthropologists have observed processes that coincide with this social-psychological model. Paul Stoller (1989) described increasingly frightening sorcery effects after he submerged himself in Songhay culture. Edith Turner (1992) participated wholeheartedly in Ndembu ceremonies and witnessed a spiritform. These anthropologists did not begin their studies as believers, but they exposed themselves to ambiguous circumstances. Puzzling events seemingly prepared them for more anomalous perceptions.

In the course of my SORRAT investigation, I also subjected myself to a series of unusual situations, establishing a basis for increasingly anomalous experiences. I cannot be certain that my perceptions were valid; my PK experiences could be like apparitions, seeming to be real but lacking a physical basis. Yet my wondrous stories are equivalent to Stoller's (1989) sorcery accounts and Turner's (1992) vision of a spirit.

Our perceptions took place within mythologically rich environments, in which small groups produced ambiguous effects. Social scientists who partake fully in group magical ceremonies increase their probability of experiencing such events.

I speculate that witnessing a wondrous event can change a participant's mind/body processes, creating a foundation for accepting the possibility of even more anomalous perceptions. Observers' autonomic nervous systems are affected, at times, by wondrous perceptions, and tertiary experiences may then result. This process occurs most effectively in small groups since members can effectively exclude the participation of skeptics and directly reinforce one another's perceptions. I suspect that members' outward expressions of belief are less important than their capacity for autonomic changes, an aptitude probably related to hypnotic suggestion.

These formulations are testable within social scientific paradigms. Small groups from many cultures have claimed similar anomalous perceptions; participant observation of groups claiming wondrous experiences provide modern data. Group anomalous reports have had important ramifications for religious history, contributing to belief in spirits, souls, life after death, and wondrous capacities. These universal features suggest predictions regarding the future of religion, an issue I explore in the next chapter.

Chapter 12
Wondrous Events and the Future of Religion

Wondrous perceptions have contributed to similarities within folk traditions throughout the ages. Shamanism arose from the capacity for altered states of consciousness (ASC) coupled with experiences that lead to belief in spirits, souls, life after death, and anomalous abilities. With increased complexity of political organization, priestly roles evolved which were less associated with ASC (Winkelman, 1992). Modern religious assemblies reflect this disjunction: Large denominations place less emphasis on ASC, whereas some small groups continue to seek individual-based wondrous experiences. The latter groups have the potential for innovative impacts on religious belief and mass culture (Stark and Bainbridge, 1985; Tiryakian, 1974). The universal features found within such experiences provide a basis for predictions regarding the future of religion.

My study indicates the following patterns related to wondrous events:

1. Apparitions, ESP, PK, out-of-body and near-death experiences, and sleep paralysis contain universal features supporting belief in spirits, souls, life after death, and extraordinary abilities.
2. Some people are more prone to these experiences than others. Those with greater belief in anomalous faculties and capacity for dissociative experience, hypnotic states, and artistic achievement report more wondrous episodes. Folklore suggests the involvement of other factors such as genetics, particular religious activities, power of thought, ascetic practices, and exposure to a special person or location.
3. Some groups report more wondrous experiences than others. For example, Icelanders, Chinese, and Americans have a greater propensity for such experiences than do elite American scientists or

Japanese students. This suggests that socialization influences the incidence of these experiences.

4. Those reporting frequent wondrous events become psychic practitioners far more frequently than do those reporting few experiences. Wondrous perceptions contribute to the development of occult practices.

5. Wondrous performers often generate audience experiences using trance, sleight-of-hand, and unusual physiological effects. Experiencing a wondrous event, even an artifact effect, increases the probability that one will perceive other such incidents.

6. Wondrous events are related to collective behavior. They can involve group processes, as in hauntings, and have stimulated the formation of social and religious movements.

7. Wondrous events have contributed to equivalencies in religious doctrines by supporting belief in heavens, hells, prayer, rituals, and the value of specific individuals as intermediaries.

8. Wondrous events are a factor in the recruitment and retention within some small, alternative religious groups. Group experiences may include contacts with the dead, percussive rapping sounds, spiritual healing, and other alleged psychokinetic events. Small group processes, coupled with aesthetically powerful narratives, can contribute to collective wondrous experiences.

9. Wondrous events often involve fraud, misperception, embellished accounts, fantasy-proneness, altered mental states, and unusual behaviors possibly related to dissociation. These features encourage skepticism. Anomalous incidents frequently stimulate fear, psychological resistance, and derision among audiences learning of them. Many investigators believe that psi is thwarted by disbelief and has a hiding or obscured quality.

Because various features appear cross-culturally and are temporally consistent, it is logical to assume that wondrous events also affected early human societies. Winkelman (1992: 1) provides data pertaining to this assertion. His examination of a stratified subsample ($N = 47$) of a standard sample of the world's societies indicates that magico-religious practices have three bases:

(1) psychobiologically based altered states of consciousness and their functions in healing, divination and human development (Shamanistic Healers and "magic"); (2) sociopolitical organizations uniting secular and sacred power in complex societies (Priests and "religion"); and (3) individuals persecuted in the conflict between magico-religious power bases and traditions (Sorcerer/Witch and "black magic" or "witchcraft").

Winkelman (1992) used social complexity data from Murdock and Provost (1973) to investigate the relationship between social conditions and the incidence of different types of occult practitioners. Shamans are generally found in hunting and gathering societies. Priests and shaman/healers emerge in agricultural subsistence societies. Societies with greater social complexity (political integration beyond the local level) have priests, sorcerer/witches, mediums, and healers. Although shamanic healers using altered states of consciousness are universal, priests and sorcerer/witches occur only in more complex societies. Winkelman (1992: 127) notes:

The original basis of magico-religious practice is in the potential provided by ASC. This original basis manifested in shamanism provides the basis for a subsequent differentiation of magical-religious practice. The original ASC basis persists in all societies, and provides one of the bases for the Priest. As this sociopolitical basis develops, it ultimately comes into conflict with the local level ASC based practitioners, represented by Shaman and Shaman/Healers. This ultimately manifests itself as the Sorcerer/Witch practitioner, the conflict of magic and religion, and the manifestation of black magic.

Contemporary proponents of Durkheim's thesis portray magic as derived from religion (O'Keefe, 1982). Winkelman's (1992) data refute this hypothesis. ASC activities—or individualized cults, as Durkheim labels them—cannot be totally derived from collective religious practices; ASC activities are universal, while specific religious traditions are not. "The collective religious activities cannot be the source of a universal phenomena when it is not universal itself" (Winkelman, 1992: 126). This conclusion coincides with my observations regarding primary wondrous events. Wondrous perceptions cannot entirely be products of cultural traditions since elements within wondrous experiences are universal. Rather than being purely products of belief, wondrous events have the capacity to produce belief (the experiential source theory).

Various studies have indicated a physiological basis for ASC, a theory that would explain their universal features (Cooperstein, 1992; Noll, 1983; Winkelman, 1992). Winkelman (1992: 93) hypothesizes that a variety of procedures used to induce ASC cause similar brain functions "characterized by a state of parasympathetic dominance in which the frontal cortex is dominated by slow wave patterns originating in the limbic system and related projections into the frontal parts of the brain." Shamanism and other ASC traditions were and are, in Winkelman's view, natural manifestations of the human mind. Independent inventions of ASC practices, such as soul flight, vision quests, spirit dialogue, and spirit possession, were likely (p. 109).

Although I cannot specify the mechanisms, various wondrous events probably do have physiological bases, which helps to account for the universal features within many anomalous narratives. In many folk traditions, the faculty for wondrous experience is believed to be partly inherited (D1737, "Magic power inherited"; G224.9, "Witch's power inherited"). Tests of identical twins indicate that hypnotic suggestibility, a trait correlated with frequency of wondrous reports, has a genetic component (Morgan, 1973). The "genetic basis" hypothesis could be tested by comparisons of anomalous report rates among identical and fraternal twins. Nash and Buzby (1965) found a statistically significant correspondence in clairvoyance test scores among identical twins, suggesting that clairvoyant faculties are inherited.

The possible physiological basis for wondrous experience may have primitive origins. Animals reportedly have acted in ways that foretold unanticipated events, have demonstrated anomalous navigational abilities, and have behaved unusually in haunted houses and mediumistic sittings (Bayless, 1970; Fodor, 1974: 3; Morris, 1977). Firsthand reports and folk narratives cite many incidents in which animals seemed more capable of perceiving ghosts than humans were (E421.1.2–E421.1.6, "Ghost visible to animal alone").[1]

Brain mechanisms allowing ASC and wondrous perceptions may have been shaped by evolutionary processes. Even if subjective wondrous events have no basis in physical reality, their role in primitive health care systems suggests that ASC and the capacity for wondrous perception have a genetic basis. Shamanic performances affect emotional states, thereby enhancing health. This process could in turn select for genotypes that favor ASC and wondrous perceptions. This hypothesis, however, requires further grounding and development in the psychobiology of consciousness.

The sporadic incidence of wondrous events may have created "superstitious" behaviors among early societies. Like Skinner's (1948) pigeons, who came to believe that their unusual dancing and cooing brought the random pellets they received, early humans may have sought to induce wondrous events through ASC, since the two are often linked.[2] Advantageous reinforcement can reinforce superstition.

This behaviorist paradigm can also explain the longevity of magical traditions. Magic may be defined as occult practices intended to influence nature in a causal way for practical purposes. Magical traditions may have evolved from attempts to derive practical applications from wondrous experiences (Winkelman, 1982). Erratic paranormal perceptions sporadically "reward" those engaging in magical performances, making "superstitious" behaviors difficult to extinguish, even by disconfirmation. The frequencies of spontaneous OBE and ESP correlate with the capacity for hypnotic suggestion and dissociation.

Some occult practices have practical value. Groups experiencing hauntings or other unplanned, recurring anomalous episodes might seek to control the phenomena. Collective ceremonies, a source of magical traditions, might successfully reduce the incidence of negative experiences. Such occult performances can also provide psychosomatic treatments. Since these performances also have social functions, magical practices would persist, even though they often might fail from a practical standpoint.

The functional use of ASC varies with cultural development. Priestly practitioners' involvement with ASC declines in societies with greater levels of organizational complexity (Winkelman, 1992: 106). Priests in societies with hierarchical political structures stigmatize locally based competitors as sorcerers or witches, giving rise to the conflict between religion and magic. This process moves the use of ASC into the folk domain.

The struggle between large organizations and small ASC groups continues to the present, particularly in the West. Large churches reduce their emphasis on magic, while many small, alternative religious groups seek benefits from wondrous experiences. Groups claiming wondrous perceptions are labeled deviant. The term "cult" has a stigmatizing quality.

Yet some observers point to a huge body of parapsychological literature that they regard as strong evidence for wondrous capacities. Michael Murphy (1992), a cofounder of the Esalen Institute, provides heavily documented arguments for the authenticity of various anomalous claims. He contends that people's extraordinary abilities can be improved through training. He argues that most psychic practitioners advocate development of specific wondrous capacities through a single method. He suggests that extraordinary capacities can be cultivated through balanced practice of a variety of procedures (yoga, meditation, martial arts, etc.) and that such development will be the next stage in human cultural evolution.

Projections from my data lead to alternate conclusions, at least in the short term. Factors within modern hierarchical societies serve to restrict the development of psychic capacities. Wondrous phenomena have qualities that make them less valuable to large organizations than to small groups. Established religions, whose membership's include the majority of religious people, do not support the sort of movement Murphy (1992) envisions.

One source of conflict between folk and established religions originates from differences in ideological complexity. Large organizations develop doctrines derived from a variety of perspectives. Their established formulations tend to be more theoretical and less "experience-near" than those conceived by small groups. The large groups' creeds must be useful in a variety of circumstances. In contrast, folk beliefs tend to be less abstract. They are more "experience-near," placing greater emphasis on individual observations. The conflict between established religion and alternative groups is illustrated by their attitudes toward wondrous events.

Wondrous perceptions sometimes clash with doctrines that serve the status quo. For example, people who report religious visions may emphasize the ideas of equality and unity rather than hierarchy. They tend to claim that their miraculous sensations supersede the authority of church canons. As a defense against these unacceptable reports, religious authorities generally evaluate atypical perceptions as being less important than established doctrines; they rarely encourage psychic experiences.

Although ASC are not intrinsically linked with social change, examples abound of their use within religious movements. ASC performances provide ways for subjugated people to ignore established customs and hierarchies. Trance utterances are more likely to reflect current concerns than are established, written doctrines. For example, the Native American Ghost Dance movement, originating in 1889, involved ASC performances. It was perceived as threatening by U.S. authorities, resulting in the 1890 massacre of nearly three hundred Sioux at Wounded Knee Creek (Miller, 1985: 283–286; Mooney, 1896). The Spiritualist movement shocked traditionalists by allowing American women their first opportunities to address large audiences; Spiritualists became major figures in the early women's rights movement (Braude, 1989). Modern Western witches, and equivalent ASC groups, continue to advocate sexual equality. Various trance speakers within the New Age movement focus on ecological issues, ignoring traditional Christian concerns.

Established religious elites are unlikely to encourage development of abilities that threaten their authority. They, like most in their congregations, are less motivated by the desire for magic than by the other benefits of religious participation.

Wondrous events have characteristics that seem to limit their incidence among large organizations. Skilled wondrous performance requires charisma, while leadership positions in most large religious denominations have a legal/rational basis. Priest-leaders generally have less training in ASC since wondrous perceptions are unrelated to their bureaucratic tasks. Most shun these practices, which are often associated with fraud. Psi is thought to have a hiding, elusive quality that avoids the skeptical scrutiny associated with large audiences; it reportedly acts more robustly in small, secretive groups.

The central elements of wondrous experiences make it unlikely that future complex organizations will emphasize their performance. Murphy's (1992) projections of the widespread development of psychic abilities, although possible, appear based more on wishful thinking than on social analysis.

Although wondrous events may not have all the qualities desired by some believers, they will continue to provide foundations for folk beliefs. People in the future will experience apparitions, ESP, OBEs, PK, and sleep paralysis. No matter how highly secularized future societies may become, folk traditions regarding spirits, souls, life after death, and the existence of psychic abilities will continue to survive (Hufford, 1987b).

Wondrous events have had particular impact when experienced within small groups. Stark and Bainbridge (1985) link small group behavior to religious change. As mentioned in Chapter 1, they argue that large denominations are affected by secularization, a process that creates fertile fields for small groups to step in and reinvigorate the religious marketplace. Religious history can be viewed as a process of secularization, revival, cult and sect formation, growth of cult movements, and the eventual development of new churches from cult movements. Although wondrous events influence religious traditions at many levels, they are particularly important within "client cults." My findings help delineate features that grant some small, alternative religious groups the potential to survive and grow.

Although my appraisal of magic differs from Stark and Bainbridge's (1985), their orientation provides a valuable framework for prediction. They contend that religion deals with general compensators while magic involves specific compensators. They argue that, since "magic competes with science in attempting to produce tangible results" it is "very vulnerable to empirical disconfirmation" (p. 432). They note that magical claims are more susceptible to refutation than religious doctrines (p. 433). This leads them to speculate that "faiths suited to the future will contain no magic, only religion. . . . Faiths containing only religion will be immune to scientific attack and thus will avoid the accelerated secularization in effect during recent centuries" (p. 456).

My disagreements with Stark and Bainbridge's (1985) discussion are related to their definition of magic. They describe magical practices as "compensators that are offered as correct explanations without regard for empirical evaluations and that, when evaluated, are found wanting" (p. 32). (Because this definition is not central to their argument, their theory, after modification, retains its explanatory value.) I argue that it is incorrect to state that magical practitioners are unconcerned with empirical evaluations. Many of my respondents tested their perceptions to the best of their abilities. They often based their beliefs on the positive feedback they received from clients. Psychic practitioners and associated alternative groups operate in a spiritual marketplace. If clients find that a particular strategy does not work, they tend to seek solutions elsewhere. Magic is sometimes effective and sometimes not.

It is likewise incorrect to define magical practices as a collection of endeavors that, "when evaluated, are found wanting." Many magical practices involve areas of scientific uncertainty which have not yet been adequately tested. Scientists, for example, have not reached consensus regarding ESP. Most parapsychologists believe that ESP occurs, and they have presented experimental results supporting their arguments. The majority of American science professors feel there is a "likely possibility" that ESP exists. On the other hand, most elite American scientists feel this possibility is either very remote or nonexistent (Mc-Clenon, 1984). We do not know what future scientists will conclude regarding this matter.

Problems with the definition of magic are, however, peripheral to Stark and Bainbridge's and my overall formulations. Our differences arise from divergent evaluations of the social effects of magical claims. Such disagreements are subject to resolution through empirical research. I hypothesize that the incidence of wondrous experience and magical practice will wax and wane over time, rather than decline steadily. While wondrous events are unlikely to play a significant role within official institutions, they will not die out. I propose that primary wondrous experiences have a genetic basis that is moderated by cultural factors.

In my view, the human propensity to experience wondrous events provides support for magical traditions. People with a proclivity for wondrous experience will continue to feel compelled to engage in psychic performances and in spiritual healing. They will attract audiences and many patrons will feel they have benefited.

Although magic is more susceptible to empirical disconfirmation than is religion, the motivations supporting religion create similar demands for magic. Some church members who want general compensators also seek specific ones. People will continue to experience emotional, spiritual, and psychosomatic problems that magical performances can sometimes resolve.

Even though specific claims are subject to refutation, magical traditions show great potential for longevity. Magic generally does not compete with science but is undertaken in areas where there is scientific uncertainty or inadequacy, such as in the realm of psychosomatic healing. Magical traditions resonate with human needs. Occult believers use unconscious processes for decision making. They dissociate in service of the ego, thereby gaining confidence in their deductions. The benefits they receive reinforce their efforts. People unable to tap intuitive abilities are at a disadvantage in this context. The value of ASC practices insures the survival of magical traditions. Future psychic performers will continue to fulfill the demand for magical services.

The impact of future psychic practitioners will depend, in part, on the resonant aesthetic and dramatic qualities within the accounts of their performances. Narratives containing archetypical elements will be most suitable for stimulating further wondrous experiences. Skilled charismatic performers who have organized cohesive groups could have a great impact on future religious thought. Such groups will experience spiraling levels of perception and belief, thereby generating new narratives and attracting new followers.

The contagious qualities of wondrous events are magnified by modern media. As a result, future occult movements could grow more rapidly than any in the past. Secularized societies, in particular, provide environments ripe for religious innovation. If wondrous abilities are inherited, random genetic mutations could eventually give rise to an *extremely* adept performer, one whose abilities exceed those of all previous psychic practitioners. The resulting movement could rapidly attract many converts and create a large following.

Yet, as I have shown, wondrous events also have an elusive quality. They cannot withstand close scrutiny and often involve fraud, illusion, delusion, and misperception. In modern societies, they stimulate both belief *and* skepticism. Future wondrous exhibitions will not sway all observers, and demands for "proofs" will not be completely satisfied. Psychic performers will continue to be attacked by established churches and scientific organizations. They and their followers will be accused of fraud and demonism.

Some occult movements, however, will thrive and become established churches. As specified in Stark and Bainbridge's (1985) model, maturing organizations tend to attract more mainstream members. Such members generally have less desire for wondrous performances than do earlier converts. With time, charismatic performers are replaced by legal/rational leaders with greater administrative skills. Hierarchical denominations cannot create the same frequency of anomalous perceptions as can small groups.

Because established churches tend to reduce their dependence on magic, they risk losing those clients who seek specific compensators. Although sects within some large organizations attempt to fulfill magical needs, this endeavor often leads to conflicts.

The recurring features within wondrous experience insure that some people will continue to offer and to seek magical benefits. Small, alternative religious groups, and the new churches evolving from them, will provide the magic that these people pursue. This will allow more skillful movements to prosper. The features that comprise wondrous experience contribute to the cyclic nature of religious development as hypothesized by Stark and Bainbridge.

My model has three basic elements. Each provides a starting point for future verification, refutation, or modification:

1. Wondrous experiences have features related to ASC and human physiology which contribute to similar beliefs in many cultures and eras. These elements allow us to predict that future wondrous accounts will support faith in spirits, souls, life after death, and wondrous abilities. This argument coincides with Hufford's (1987b) formulations. This argument does not preclude the existence of anomalous or spiritual forces; I merely hypothesize that humans have physiological features that cause them to have experiences which lead them to believe in anomalous or spiritual forces.

2. Those reporting frequent wondrous experiences have a tendency to provide wondrous performances, particularly psychosomatic treatments. Their proclivity for spiritual healing can lead to the formation of small, alternative religious groups. Cohesive groups with skilled performers, using aesthetically powerful narratives, will experience extremely anomalous events. Movements originating with such groups have the potential to become established churches.

3. Wondrous events have a restricted quality and, in complex societies, a tendency to stimulate both belief *and* skepticism. Groups that evolve into large organizations tend to place less reliance on wondrous experiences due to their destabilizing aspects, their association with fraud, and their obscured qualities. Rejection of individual wondrous perceptions makes large assemblies vulnerable to competition from smaller groups that do support wondrous experiences and magical performances.

This model does not seek to "explain" wondrous events. Anomalous experiences retain a mysterious quality. The theory I have described provides a framework for interpreting the social uses of these unusual, yet universal, perceptions. These hypotheses are subject to empirical testing, refutation, and revision.

Bias is a particular problem within studies of wondrous events. Psychic phenomena evoke deep-seated emotions, generating religious awe in some and skeptical hostility in others. The irrationality associated with these strong passions has restricted social scientific understanding of such episodes.

Some believers assume that miracles support their faith and invalidate opposing doctrines. They are unsettled by the implications of cross-cultural analyses of the wondrous. Yet people from all cultures report equivalent wondrous perceptions. My findings are therefore best interpreted within a relativistic framework.

Scholars who reject wondrous claims tend to ignore the prevalence and influence of these episodes. They sometimes cannot understand the difference between social scientific and parapsychological orientations. They fail to perceive that the academic "culture of disbelief" restricts discourse regarding psychic phenomena. They label folk beliefs as trivial, overlooking the role that anomalous events have played in cultural evolution.

My model explains the impact of wondrous perceptions on human societies. Anomalous experiences support the universal features within folk beliefs. They are central to shamanic health care systems. They have had an important, but restricted, role in the development of modern religious doctrines. Recognizing the patterns within wondrous events allows us to make certain predictions regarding the future of religion.

This is an empirically grounded approach. Social surveys, participant observation of groups making anomalous claims, and analysis of parapsychological, folkloric, and historical data have been used to help delineate the universal features within anomalous perceptions. By studying wondrous events, we can gain insights into the foundations of religious belief.

Appendix:
Unusual Experience Questionnaire

Versions of this questionnaire were administered to randomly selected Caucasian-American, African-American, Japanese, and Chinese students (see Chapter 2).

Please mark one response for each question.

Sex: Male _____   Age: _____

      Female _____   Major: _____

How often have you had any of the following experiences?

1. Have you thought you were somewhere you had been before but knew that it was impossible?

| | Once or | Several | |
| Never _____ | Twice _____ | Times _____ | Often _____ |

2. Have you woken in the night and found that you could not move?

| | Once or | Several | |
| Never _____ | Twice _____ | Times _____ | Often _____ |

3. Have you thought you were in touch with someone when you knew that it was impossible (ESP or sixth sense)?

| | Once or | Several | |
| Never _____ | Twice _____ | Times _____ | Often _____ |

4. Have you thought you were really in touch with someone who had died?

| | Once or | Several | |
| Never _____ | Twice _____ | Times _____ | Often _____ |

5. Have you thought you were out of your body?

	Once or		Several			
Never _____	Twice _____		Times _____		Often _____

6. Do you think that it is possible that people have extrasensory perception?
a) It is a fact. _____
b) It is a likely possibility. _____
c) It is a remote possibility. _____
d) It is impossible. _____
e) It is merely an unknown. _____

7. How religious do you consider yourself?

Extremely	Somewhat	Slightly	Not at all
Religious _____	Religious _____	Religious _____	Religious _____

8. What is your religion? _____

9. What is your academic class?   Freshman _____
                                   Sophomore _____
                                   Junior _____
                                   Senior _____
                                   Grad. Student _____

10. What is your race?   African-American _____
    [for USA]   Caucasian _____
                             Chicano _____
                             Native American _____
                             Other _____

11. If you have had a very unusual experience, would you describe it briefly? [American and Japanese respondents were asked if they would allow an interviewer to contact them and, if so, to give their names and telephone numbers]

Notes

Chapter 1. Wondrous Events and Social Science

1. Keel's (1975) UFO investigations and Rogo's (1982a) discussion of miracles provide insights into the obscure nature of collective wondrous experience.

Chapter 4. Haunting and Poltergeist Cases

1. One reader noted that this incident was "not all that unusual, especially since they're smokers without ashtrays." Bruce, who experienced this event, felt he could provide no explanation. He suspended judgment since he could not evaluate the probability of the smoke detector's malfunctioning. The reader's comment illustrates the kind of "unpacking" that observers, particularly skeptics, often make regarding anomalous reports. The assumption is that experiencers fail to consider alternative possibilities besides the paranormal explanation.

2. At this point, I am playing an outsider's role. Since I was not present to interview witnesses, I assumed that those accepting the paranormal explanation for the fire had not adequately considered "normal" alternatives.

3. Although it is unusual for cases to end by allegedly paranormal fires, it is not unprecedented. Of the 116 cases discussed by Roll (1977), two ended in this manner. In the context of the Alexandria case, haunting episodes regarding smoke, fire alarms, and the events immediately preceding the fire might be interpreted by believers as paranormal warnings of impending disaster rather than as indications that spiritual forces caused the accident.

Chapter 5. Psychic Practitioners and Wondrous Events

1. Stevenson (1977) notes that reports, like C.'s, of children remembering past lives occur in a wide variety of societies, even those that lack reincarnation beliefs. Although cultural factors influence the nature and frequency of these reports, they apparently are not always "produced" by belief—otherwise they would not occur in localities where they were not accepted.

2. This technique coincides with the motif of occult practitioners "reversing"

mainstream customs and etiquette. In Thailand, the foot is the least sacred part of a person's body because it is farthest from the head. Touching someone with the foot, or pointing it at them, is taboo.

3. Although Terte's account may be fabricated, his story coincides with other shamanic biographies. I did not interview Terte (he is deceased); I rely on Licauco's (1982) biography.

Chapter 6. Performing Wondrous Events

1. If the patient does not attain a hypnotic state, we might assume that psychosomatic benefits are due to placebos. The situation is complicated by the fact that people can fall into hypnotic states without formal induction. Some researchers even suggest that all humans are perpetually in hypnotic states, to a degree, an argument that blurs the distinction between hypnotic and placebo effects.

2. Sufi dervishes demonstrate their confidence that the spiritual powers of their master, part of a "chain of masters" leading back to the Prophet Muhammad, surpass and transcend natural laws, and that the master who saves their bodies can also save their spirits. People perceive that the masters of Tariqa Casnazaniyyah paranormally intervene to resolve people's problems (saving them from fatal accidents or curing them of serious diseases, for example). Tariqa Casnazaniyyah has spread mainly in Iraq, Iran, Jordan, and Turkey.

3. Rousseau ignored New Testament verses indicating that Jesus, and the Gospel writers, felt that miracles *were* grounds for belief (see, for example, John 20:31). Jesus clearly directed his followers to do exorcisms and healings (Matthew 10:1; Mark 6:7) and stated that they would be able to perform wonders even greater then his (John 14:12).

4. This is a paradigm established by the American firewalking seminar leader Tolly Burkan and adopted by many other Western workshop organizers.

Chapter 7. Wondrous Events and Audience Attraction

1. Controversy surrounds this assertion. It is often difficult to specify exactly which deprivations or "dispositional susceptibilities" are associated with cult recruitment and social movements (Jorgensen, 1982, 1992).

2. Like many educated residents on Sequijor Island, L. regards psychic practitioners skeptically. "For a long time, I believed," he told me, "but now I cannot be certain."

3. Jaime Licauco tells of an Australian factory worker, Jim Bernard. Although Australian doctors could not remove slivers of aluminum from his eye without blinding him, a psychic surgeon barehandedly performed the operation and restored his sight.

4. Ikegami (1992) argues that N.'s appeal is derived from the similarities between charismatic Christianity and Okinawan shamanism. I would suggest that these parallel qualities also reflect features that are universal in wondrous experiences.

5. A born-again Christian in North Carolina described a parallel story to me. Christian faithful entered a broad river to be baptized during a thunderstorm,

even though lightning threatened their lives. A rainbow appeared during the ceremony.

6. Okinawan shamans typically find that ancestral spirits are the cause of people's problems and that certain young women suffering from severe spiritual distress can be healed by becoming shamans. Some Okinawan psychotherapists believe that schizophrenic patients have been cured through this process.

Chapter 8. Wondrous Events and Religious History in Medieval Asia and Europe

1. Within traditional Chinese medicine, practitioners take note of different "pulses," or characteristics of the pulse such as frequency, rhythm, intensity, etc., using varying pressures at different points. They arrive at a diagnosis by evaluating the relationships between these readings.

2. Fittingly, the book itself contains references to late-sixteenth-century historical episodes which indicate it could not have been compiled in its entirety by T'ang Yin as suggested.

Chapter 10. The Scientific Investigation of Wondrous Events

1. Wiseman (1992) suggests that the effects could have been created by an accomplice, an argument that has stimulated controversy and rebuttals in the *Journal of the Society for Psychical Research*.

2. For example, PK cases from all eras include percussive raps. Fodor (1974: 321–324) sites European cases which involve rapping sounds from the years 858, 1520, 1521, 1610, 1661, and 1716. Equivalent communicative percussive effects occurred around Frau Frederica Hauffe, the Seeress of Prevorst (early nineteenth century), the Fox sisters (loud raps occurred around Margaretta even as she was immobilized on her deathbed), Henry Slade (even after he sank into senile dementia), D. D. Home, Stainton Moses, Madame Blavatsky (1831–1891), Eusapia Palladino, and Mina Crandon. People have perceived raps originating within their bodies, on living trees, on a sheet of glass, on a stretched iron wire, on the roof of a cab, and on the floor of a railway station. A case described in Chapter 11 includes equivalent rapping phenomena.

3. Kasahara's (1993) *The Elusiveness Problem of Psi*, a collection of articles translated into Japanese, has an extensive bibliography in English regarding psi's "hiding" quality. Beloff (1977, 1993, 1994) provides historical overviews of the field of psychical research which also suggest a hiding quality.

4. As with many psychic performers, Kiyota has been involved in a number of ambiguous situations. He seemed to confess to fraud on Japanese television. I talked with him soon afterward. His "confession" has been misinterpreted to imply more guilt than he wished to assume, a common "quirky" pattern among psychic performers.

5. One skeptic points out that my observations cannot be trusted. He has observed that people often perceive that metal is bending when this is not the case. This kind of performance was one of three occasions when I witnessed metal bending without anyone touching it. I described one incident in Chapter

3 and noted the videotape of Professor Soji Otani, of the Japanese Defense Academy (McClenon, 1989). Chinese and European researchers have video-taped similar events. None has produced irrefutable proof of a paranormal event, however, since videotape images can be simulated.

Chapter 11. Wondrous Events in a Small Group

1. Dr. Richards writes, "I am *not* a medium any more than everyone is in the sense that even a turnip may be *somewhat* psychic." W. Edward Cox refers to him as a medium probably because much allegedly paranormal phenomena seem to occur around him.

2. W. Edward Cox writes, "The filming was far from 'clumsy.' Only the camera was cheap, but this *per se* can hardly detract at all from its sharply filmed product's evidentiality." Cox (1984) presented a paper regarding SORRAT at a later Parapsychological Association meeting in 1983, amid much controversy. Hansen (1985) critiques his report.

3. A SORRAT member writes, "If there is evidence of trickery, it ought to be exposed. If not, it should not be implied." Skeptics requested that I insert words such as "alleged" or "ostensible" before phrases hinting at anomalous events, such as "paranormal experience." They desired complete descriptions of the normal means by which paranormal effects might be simulated. Believers, however, found such insertions to be offensive. These comments reveal that both skeptics and believers wish I would frame my observations in light of their preconceptions.

4. Reactions to this hypothesis regarding Three-times-three's nature illustrate the wide varieties of SORRAT belief. One member writes, "There is no more evidence that the phenomenon Three-times-three is tied to Ed Cox's subconsciousness than that it is some independent force which manifests in connection with Cox." Another points out that Three-times-three could be a demonic entity. He cites arguments based on the tarot. Cox suspends judgment but tends to believe that psychokinetic phenomena originate within the human subconscious.

5. Many people, including myself, have carefully inspected the floorboards at the Richardses' and found nothing unusual. Dr. William Braud, then with the Mind Science Foundation, stated that during his visit to the Richardses an associate was in the basement inspecting the beams while raps occurred. She saw no devices that would account for the raps. I have discussed methods for creating raps with a number of magicians but have yet to devise a normal explanation for my experiences. The skeptical parapsychologist George Hansen, who is knowledgeable regarding magical performances, faces a similar dilemma; he has visited the Richardses, remains skeptical, but has not been able to explain the rapping sounds.

6. The raps here reveal a quirky sense of humor, which exemplifies trance logic. They literally followed the suggestion to rap out "on the wall over there." SORRAT phenomena are like poltergeists, in that events often reveal intelligence, humor, and wisdom, but still fail to provide evidence convincing to skeptical observers.

7. Ed Cox and Elaine Richards's argument illustrates a typical pattern of discourse between believers and scientists. The majority of parapsychologists feel that the evidence they gather does not constitute proof of life after death

but merely reveals a scientific anomaly. My sociological observations mirror their findings: many people have unusual experiences, but these episodes do not scientifically verify their faith.

8. Later, I also had these experiences: hearing and feeling the raps' vibrations come from concrete floors and also from the ground. Many SORRAT members have had similar experiences.

9. Table tipping was a favorite method for common people to communicate with spirits during the Spiritualist era (1848 through the early 1900s.) In 1852, the English scientist Michael Faraday (1791–1867) devised and conducted an experiment which indicated that table-tipping effects could be explained by conscious or unconscious pressure of the sitters' fingers on the table's edge. However, this explanation cannot explain levitations that occur without any sitters' touching the table. Only through misobservation or conjuring could reports of "hands-off" levitations be interpreted as normal events.

10. A skeptic validly observed that Calvin is not an outside observer, implying that this reduces the evidential quality of his comments. I present this narrative to portray Calvin's reasons for personal belief, not to inspire belief in others. Calvin's *experiences* made him into an "insider." It was not his attraction to SORRAT ideology or social networks that drew him to this case.

11. The British researcher Tony Cornell created a film using stopframe photography which appears similar to the SORRAT version. His "mini-lab" was missing one glass side.

12. Richards's book, *SORRAT: A History of the Neihardt Psychokinesis Experiments, 1961–1981*, was published in 1982. His fictional work, *The Year of the Sorrats*, Vol. 1, published in 1992, and Vol. 2, published in 1994, describes the early recruitment processes. Although social networks were important to SORRAT recruitment, anomalous experiences were central to maintaining group identity and solidarity.

13. Many SORRAT members who had participated over a number of years stated that they had grown bored with the limited nature of the entities' doctrines. SORRAT members do not regard the spirit messages as infallible.

14. Patience Worth's postcard message coincided with her 1920s writings in that it imitated, but failed to reflect exactly, an Elizabethan style. Later spirit writers claimed to be members of the "Imperator Group" (most frequently, Rector and Imperator), using the sixteenth-century buccaneer John King as their scribe. These entities have been associated with many mediums during the Spiritualist era. The Reverend Stainton Moses (1839–1892) wrote the book *Spirit Teachings* under the guidance of the Imperator Group. John King was the first spirit to speak through a medium's trumpet during the Spiritualist era.

15. Author's note: One respondent to my mail survey of SORRAT members reported seeing a similar incident. She states, "I believe that most of J. T. Richards's experiments with raps and table levitations are authentic. However, I believe I have seen him tap his foot to imitate raps on a few occasions (Tom's 'raps' may be unconscious). I have never confronted him on this, as we are friends. I do watch him most carefully during experiments because of this and am convinced that most phenomena are genuine."

16. George Hansen also wishes to state that "The evidence for fraudulent manipulation is considerably more than discussed in [*Wondrous Events*]."

17. One of Neihardt's signatures appeared in a book published after his death at a home geographically distant from the Richardses. I received two letters allegedly written and signed by Neihardt more than a decade after his

death. An analysis of these signatures by a court-qualified handwriting expert revealed one to be fraudulent and two to be of such quality that the expert could not pass judgment.

18. Haraldsson's (1987) report on Sai Baba also contains many of these recurring features. Sai Baba's miracles seem authentic to many observers, but he has not allowed testing under controlled conditions. Anthropologists have also told me about their anomalous field research experiences in Asia, which included percussive raps. One informant told me of wondrous events during a Native American ceremony. Lay people, too, have described anomalous incidents during modern table-tipping sessions, religious meetings, and occult ceremonies. The SORRAT claims, therefore, are not unique but rather portray elements within the pool of recurring psychic phenomena.

Chapter 12. Wondrous Events and the Future of Religion

1. Skeptics might argue that psychic capacities, if they exist, should substantially contribute to an organism's survival, perhaps through warnings of danger, but this assertion ignores other factors: First, many faculties exist in an undeveloped state. Second, collections of wondrous accounts indicate that most incidents do not contribute to survival or procreative success. A dog's howling at the time of its owner's death, for example, does not affect the distribution of future canine genotypes. Wondrous experiences typically reflect emotional bonding rather than survival needs.

2. Folk literature motifs reflect the relationship between wondrous experience and ASC (D1817.0.1.6, "Wizard detects thief by trance"; E721.2, "Body in trance while soul is absent"; F11.1, "Journey to heaven in trance").

References

Achterberg, Jeanne. 1985. *Imagery and Healing: Shamanism and Modern Medicine*. Boulder, CO: Shambhala.

Ahern, Emily M. 1973. *The Cult of the Dead in a Chinese Village*. Stanford, CA: Stanford University Press.

Anderson, Susanne Andrea. 1969. "Legends of Holy Men of Early Japan." Unpublished MA thesis, UCLA.

Asin y Palacios, Miguel. 1926. *Islam and the Divine Comedy*. Translated by Harold Sunderland. London: J. Murray.

Atkinson, Rita L., R. C. Atkinson, E. E. Smithy, and D. J. Bem. 1990. *Introduction to Psychology*. San Diego, CA: Harcourt Brace Jovanovich.

Bainbridge, William Sims. 1978. *Satan's Power*. Berkeley, CA: University of California Press.

Bainbridge, William Sims, and Rodney Stark. 1980a. "Superstitions: Old and New." *Skeptical Inquirer* 4: 18–31.

———. 1980b. "Client and Audience Cults in America." *Sociological Analysis* 41: 199–214.

Balch, Robert W., and David Taylor. 1977. "Seekers and Saucers: The Role of the Cultic Milieu in Joining a UFO Cult." *American Behavioral Scientist* 20: 839–859.

Barnouw, Victor. 1942. "Siberian Shamanism and Western Spiritualism." *Journal of the American Society for Psychical Research* 36: 140–168.

———. 1975. *An Introduction to Anthropology*, Vol. 2: Ethnology. rev. ed. Homewood, IL: Dorsey.

Batcheldor, Kenneth J. 1966. "Report on the Case of Table Levitation and Associated Phenomena." *Journal of the Society for Psychical Research* 43: 339–356.

———. 1979. "PK in Sitter Groups." *Psychoenergetic Systems* 3: 77–93.

———. 1984. "Contributions to the Theory of PK Induction from Sitter-Group Work." *Journal of the American Society for Psychical Research* 78: 105–132.

Bayless, Raymond. 1970. *Animal Ghosts*. New York: University Books.

Becker, Carl B. 1981. "The Centrality of Near-Death Experience in Chinese Pure Land Buddhism." *Anabiosis* 1: 154–171.

———. 1984. "The Pure Land Revisited: Sino-Japanese Meditations and Near-Death Experiences of the Next World." *Anabiosis* 4: 51–68.

Beloff, John. 1977. "Historical Overview." In *Handbook of Parapsychology*, edited by Benjamin B. Wolman, 3–24. New York: Van Nostrand Reinhold Company.

———. 1985. "What Is Your Counter-Explanation? A Plea to Skeptics to Think Again." In *A Skeptic's Handbook of Parapsychology*, edited by Paul Kurtz, 359–377. Buffalo, NY: Prometheus Books.

———. 1993. *Parapsychology: A Concise History*. London: Athlone.

———. 1994. "Lessons of History." *Journal of the American Society for Psychical Research* 88: 7–22.

Bennett, Gillian. 1987. *Traditions of Belief, Women, Folklore and the Supernatural Today*. New York: Penguin Books.

Benor, Daniel J. 1990. "Survey of Spiritual Healing Research." *Complementary Medical Research* 4: 9–33.

Bierman, Dick J. 1979. "A Methodological Hint for Research in RSPK Cases." *European Journal of Parapsychology* 2: 137–162.

Birnbaum, Raoul. 1979. *The Healing Buddha*. Boulder, CO: Shambhala.

Blacker, Carmen. 1975. *The Catalpa Box*. London: George Allen and Unwin.

Blackmore, Susan J. 1988. "Do We Need a New Psychical Research?" *Journal of the Society for Psychical Research* 55: 49–59.

Blake, Julianne. 1985. "Attribution of Power and the Transformation of Fear: An Empirical Study of Firewalking." *Psi Research* 4: 64–90.

Bourguignon, Erika. 1973. *Religion, Altered States of Consciousness, and Social Change*. Columbus: Ohio State University Press.

Braud, William G. 1974. "Relaxation as a Psi Conducive State." *Bulletin of the Psychonomic Society* 3: 115–118.

———. 1975. "Psi Conducive States." *Journal of Communication* 25: 142–152.

———. 1985. "The Two Faces of Psi: Psi Revealed and Psi Obscured." In *The Repeatability Problem in Parapsychology*, edited by B. Shapin and L. Coly, 150–182. New York: Parapsychology Foundation.

———. 1990. "Distant Mental Influence of Rate of Hemolysis of Human Red Blood Cells." *Journal of the American Society for Psychical Research* 84: 1–24.

Braud, William G., G. Davis, and R. Wood. 1979. "Experiments with Matthew Manning." *Journal of the Society for Psychical Research* 50: 199–223.

Braude, Ann. 1989. *Radical Spirits: Spiritualism and Women's Rights in Nineteenth-Century America*. Boston: Beacon Press.

Braude, Steven E. 1986. *The Limits of Influence: Psychokinesis and the Philosophy of Science*. New York: Routledge and Kegan Paul.

Braxell, Karen, trans. 1973. *The Confessions of Lady Nijo*. Stanford, CA: Stanford University Press.

Brookes-Smith, Colin. 1973. "Data-tape Recorded Experimental PK Phenomena." *Journal of the Society for Psychical Research* 47: 69–89.

———. 1975. "Paranormal Electrical Conductance Phenomena." *Journal of the Society for Psychical Research* 48: 73–86.

Brookes-Smith, Colin, and D. W. Hunt. 1970. "Some Experiments in Psychokinesis." *Journal of the Society for Psychical Research* 45: 265–81.

Broughton, Richard S. 1988. "If You Want To Know How It Works, First Find Out What It's For." In *Research in Parapsychology 1987*, edited by D. H. Weiner and R. L. Morris, 187–202. Metuchen, NJ: Scarecrow Press.

———. 1991. *Parapsychology: The Controversial Science*. New York: Ballantine Books.

Brunvand, Jan. 1981. *The Vanishing Hitchhiker*. New York: W.W. Norton.

Byrd, Eldon. 1976. "Uri Geller's Influence on the Metal Alloy Nitinol." In *The Geller Papers*, edited by Charles Panati, 67–73. Boston: Houghton Mifflin Co.

Campbell, Bernard G. 1988. *Humankind Emerging*. Glenview, IL: Scott, Foresman.

Cerullo, John J. 1982. *The Secularization of the Soul*. Philadelphia, PA: Institute for the Study of Human Issues.

Chamberlain, Jonathan, 1983. *Chinese Gods*. Hong Kong: Long Island Publishers.

Chapman, L., H. Goodell, and H. Wolff. 1959. "Increased Inflammatory Reaction Induced by Central Nervous System Activity." *Transactions of the Association of American Physicians* 72: 84–110.

Ch'en, Kenneth. 1964. *Buddhism in China: A Historical Survey*. Princeton, NJ: Princeton University Press.

Chou Yi-liang. 1944–45. "Tantrism in China." *Harvard Journal of Asiatic Studies* 8: 241–245.

Christian, William A. 1981. *Apparitions in Later Medieval and Renaissance Spain*. Princeton, NJ: Princeton University Press.

Christopher, Milbourne. 1970. *ESP, Seers & Psychics*. New York: Thomas Y. Crowell.

Clarke, George W. 1893–94. "The Yu-li or Precious Records." *Journal of the China Branch of the Royal Asiatic Society* 28: 233–400.

Coates, Harper Havelock, and Ryugaku Ishizuka, eds. and trans. 1930. *Honen the Buddhist Saint: His Life and Teaching*. 2nd ed. Tokyo: Kodokaku.

Coe, Mayne Reid, Jr. 1958. "Firewalking and Related Behaviors." *Journal of the American Society for Psychical Research* 52: 85–97. Reprint of *The Psychological Record* (1957) 7: 101–110.

———. 1978. "Safely Across the Fiery Pit." *Fate* (June): 84–86.

Cohn, Norman. 1957. *The Pursuit of the Millennium*. Fairlawn, NJ: Essential Books.

Colgrave, Bertram, and R. A. B. Mynors, eds. and trans. 1969. *Bede's Ecclesiastical History of the English People*. Oxford: Oxford University Press.

Collins, Harry M., and Trevor J. Pinch. 1982. *Frames of Meaning: The Social Construction of Extraordinary Science*. London: Routledge and Kegan Paul.

Cooke, Pete. 1982. "Ghost Kills a Young Couple." *Weekly World News* (August 10): 1, 15.

Cooperstein, M. Allan. 1992. "The Myths of Healing: A Summary of Research into Transpersonal Healing Experiences." *Journal of the American Society for Psychical Research* 86: 99–133.

Covell, Alan Carter. 1983. *Ecstasy: Shamanism in Korea*. Elizabeth, NJ: Hollym International.

Cox, William Edward. 1984. "Selected Static-PK Phenomena Under Exceptional Conditions of Security." In *Research in Parapsychology 1983*, edited by R. A. White and R. S. Broughton, 107–110. Metuchen, NJ: Scarecrow Press.

Crossan, John Dominic. 1991. *The Historical Jesus: The Life of a Mediterranean Jewish Peasant*. San Francisco: HarperCollins.

Danforth, Loring M. 1989. *Firewalking and Religious Healing: The Anastenaria of Greece and the American Firewalking Movement*. Princeton, NJ: Princeton University Press.

Davis, G. A., J. M. Peterson, and F. H. Farley. 1974. "Attitudes, Motivation, Sensation Seeking, and Belief in ESP as Predictors of Real Creative Behavior." *Journal of Creative Behavior* 8: 31–39.

Davis, J. A., and T. W. Smith. 1990. *General Social Surveys, 1972–1990*. Storrs,

CT: The Roper Center for Public Opinion Research, University of Connecticut. Data file.

De Groot, J. M. M. [1892] 1967. *The Religious System of China.* Vol. 4. Reprint. New York: Paragon Book Gallery.

de Vesme, C. 1931. *A History of Experimental Supernaturalism:* Vol. 1, *Primitive Man,* translated by S. de Barth. London: Rider.

de Visser, M. W. 1935. *Ancient Buddhism in Japan.* Leiden, Holland: E.J. Brill.

De Woskin, Kenneth J. 1977. "The Six Dynasties Chih-kuai and the Birth of Fiction." In *Chinese Narrative: Critical and Theoretical Essays,* edited by Andrew H. Plaks, 21–52. Princeton, NJ: Princeton University Press.

———. trans. 1983. *Doctors, Diviners, and Magicians of Ancient China: Biographies of Fang-shih.* New York: Columbia University Press.

Dean, Douglas, and E. Brame. 1975. "Physical Changes in Water by the Laying-on of Hands. *Proceedings of the Second International Congress of Psychotronic Research.* Paris: Institute Metaphysique International.

Demieville, Paul. 1985. *Buddhism and Healing: Demieville's Article "Byo" from Hobogirin,* translated by Mark Tatz. Lanham, MD: University Press of America.

Doherty, Jim. 1982. "Hot Feat—Firewalkers of the World." *Science Digest* (August): 66.

Donovan, Rose Marie. 1981. "Local Places Where Things Go Bump in the Night." *Alexandria Journal* (October 30): 1.

Donovan, Rose Marie, and Elizabeth George, 1982. "Death in the Haunted House." *Alexandria Journal* (July 6): 1.

Douglas, Alfred. 1977. *Extra-Sensory Powers: A Century of Psychical Research.* Woodstock, NY: Overlook Press.

Doyle, Arthur Conan. 1926. *History of Spiritualism,* Vol. 2. London: Cassell and Company.

Duanne, B. J., and J. Bisaha. 1979. "Precognitive Remote Viewing in the Chicago Area: A Replication of the Stanford Experiment." *Journal of Parapsychology* 43: 17–30.

Duke, Gail, and George Hansen. 1991. "Bibliography on the SORRAT Phenomena and Experiments." *Artifex* 9: 45–49.

Durant, Will, and Ariel Durant. 1965. *The Age of Voltaire.* New York: Simon and Schuster.

Durkheim, Emile. [1895] 1938. *The Rule of Sociological Method.* Reprint. Chicago: University of Chicago Press.

———. [1912] 1965. *The Elementary Forms of Religious Life.* Reprint. New York: Free Press.

Duyuendak, J. J. 1952. "A Chinese 'Divina Commedia.'" *T'oung Pao* 41: 255–316.

Edge, Hoyt L., Robert L. Morris, Joseph H. Rush, and John Palmer, 1986. *Foundations of Parapsychology: Exploring the Boundaries of Human Capability.* Boston: Routledge and Kegan Paul.

Edwards, Emily, and James McClenon. 1993. "Wondrous Events: Foundations for Folk Belief." 57 min. video presentation.

Eisenberg, David. 1985. *Encounters with Qi.* New York: W.W. Norton.

Eisenbud, Jule. 1963. "Psi and the Nature of Things." *International Journal of Parapsychology* 5: 245–273.

———. 1967. *The World of Ted Serios.* New York: William Morrow.

———. 1972. "Some Notes on the Psychology of the Paranormal." *Journal of the American Society for Psychical Research* 66: 27–41.

———. 1977. "Paranormal Photography." In *Handbook of Parapsychology*, edited by Benjamin B. Wolman, 414–432. New York: Van Nostrand Reinhold.

———. 1983. *Parapsychology and the Unconscious.* Berkeley, CA: North Atlantic Books.

Eliade, Mircea. 1969. *Patanjali and Yoga*, translated by Charles Lam Markmann. New York: Funk and Wagnalls.

———. 1974. *Shamanism: Archaic Techniques of Ecstasy*, translated by Willard R. Trask. Princeton, NJ: Princeton University Press.

Ellwood, Robert S. 1977. *Alternative Altars: Unconventional and Eastern Spirituality in America.* Chicago: University of Chicago Press.

Emmons, Charles F. 1982. *Chinese Ghosts and ESP: A Study of Paranormal Beliefs and Experiences.* Metuchen, NJ: Scarecrow Press.

Emmons, Charles F., and J. Sobal. 1981a. "Paranormal Beliefs: Testing the Marginality Hypothesis." *Sociological Focus* 14: 49–56.

———. 1981b. "Paranormal Beliefs: Functional Alternative to Mainstream Religion?" *Review of Religious Research* 22: 301–312.

Erikson, Kai T. 1966. *Wayward Puritans.* New York: Wiley.

Escandor-Sisson, Josephina T. 1987. *God Does the Work and I Am Only His Instrument: Autobiography of a Spiritual Healer.* Manila, Philippines: Josephina T. Escandor-Sisson.

Evans, Hilary. 1984. *Visions * Apparitions * Alien Visitors: A Comparative Study of the Entity Enigma.* Wellingborough, Northamptonshire, England: Aquarian Press.

———. 1987. *Gods * Spirits * Cosmic Guardians: A Comparative Study of the Encounter Experience.* Wellingborough, Northamptonshire, England: Aquarian Press.

———. 1989. *Alternate States of Consciousness: Unself, Otherself, and Superself.* Wellingborough, Northamptonshire, England: Aquarian Press.

Feilding, Everand. 1963. *Sittings with Eusapia Palladino and Other Studies.* New Hyde Park, NY: University Books.

Feilding, Everand, W. W. Baggally, and Hereward Carrington. 1909. "Report on a Series of Sittings with Eusapia Palladino." *Proceedings of the Society for Psychical Research* 23: 306–569.

Feinberg, Leonard. 1964. "Fire Walking in Ceylon." *Atlantic Magazine* (October) 214: 73–76.

Finucane, Ronald C. 1984. *Appearances of the Dead: A Cultural History of Ghosts.* Buffalo, NY: Prometheus Books.

Fodor, Nador. 1974. *Encyclopaedia of Psychic Science.* New York: University Books.

Fox, John W. 1992. "The Structure, Stability, and Social Antecedents of Reported Paranormal Experiences." *Sociological Analysis* 53: 417–431.

Frank, Jerome. 1973. *Persuasion and Healing.* Baltimore: Johns Hopkins University Press.

Frazier, Kendrick. 1985. "Firewalker Challenged, Gets Cold Feet." *Skeptical Inquirer* 10, no. 1: 9–10.

Fuller, Robert C. 1982. *Mesmerism and the American Cure of Souls.* Philadelphia, PA: University of Pennsylvania Press.

———. 1989. *Alternative Medicine and American Religious Life.* Oxford: Oxford University Press.

Gaddis, Vincent M. 1967. *Mysterious Fires and Lights.* New York: David McKay.

Galilei, G. [The Assayer]. [1623] 1960. Reprinted in *The Controversy over the*

Comets of 1618, edited and translated by S. Drake and C. D. O'Malley. Philadelphia: University of Pennsylvania Press.

Gallup, George, Jr. 1979. *The Gallup Poll: Public Opinion, 1978.* Wilmington, DE: Scholarly Research. (Survey dated June 15, 1978.)

Gallup, George, Jr., with W. Proctor. 1982. *Adventures in Immortality: A Look Beyond the Threshold of Death.* New York: McGraw-Hill.

Gallup, George, Jr., and F. Newport. 1991. "Belief in Paranormal Phenomena Among Adult Americans." *Skeptical Inquirer* 15: 137–147.

Gardner, Martin. 1966. "Dermo-Optical Perception: A Peek Down the Nose." *Science* 151: 654–657.

———. 1977. "Geller, Gulls, and Nitinol." *The Humanist* 37, 3: 25–32.

Gauld, Alan. 1968. *The Founders of Psychical Research.* New York: Schocken.

———. 1977. "Discarnate Survival." In *Handbook of Parapsychology,* edited by Benjamin B. Wolman, 577–630. New York: Van Nostrand Reinhold.

———. 1982. *Mediumship and Survival, A Century of Investigations.* London: Heinemann.

Gauld, Alan, and A. D. Cornell. 1979. *Poltergeists.* London: Routledge and Kegan Paul.

Gernet, Jacques. 1956. *Les Aspects Économiques du Bouddhisme dans la Société Chinoise du Ve an Xe Siècle.* Paris: Ecole Francaise D'extreme-Orient. Paper presented by Stephen F. Teiser at the 1989 National Endowment for the Humanities Summer Seminar, "Buddhism and Culture: China and Japan," UCLA.

Gibbons, Don, and James de Jarnette. 1972. "Hypnotic Susceptibility and Religious Experience." *Journal for the Scientific Study of Religion* 11: 152–156.

Giesler, Patric V. 1984. "Parapsychological Anthropology: I. Multi-method Approaches to the Study of Psi in the Field Setting." *Journal of the American Society for Psychical Research* 78: 289–330.

———. 1985a. "Parapsychological Anthropology: II. A Multi-Method Study of Psi and Psi-related Processes in the Umbanda Ritual Trance Consultation." *Journal of the American Society for Psychical Research* 79: 113–166.

———. 1985b. "Differential Micro-PK Effects Among Afro-Brazilian Cultists: Three Studies Using Trance-Significant Symbols as Targets." *Journal of Parapsychology* 49: 329–366.

———. 1986. "GESP Testing of Shamanic Cultists." *Journal of Parapsychology,* 50: 123–153.

Gissurarson, Loftur Reimar. 1992. "Studies of Methods of Enhancing and Potentially Training Psychokinesis: A Review." *Journal of the American Society for Psychical Research* 86: 303–346.

Glik, Deborah C. 1986. "Psychosocial Wellness among Participants in Spiritual Healing Groups: A Comparison Groups Survey." *Social Science and Medicine* 22: 579–586.

Glock, Charles Y., and Rodney Stark. 1965. *Religion and Society in Tension.* Chicago: Rand McNally.

Gooch, Stan. 1984. *Creatures from Inner Space.* London: Rider.

Goodman, Felicitas D. 1988. *How about Demons? Possession and Exorcism in the Modern World.* Bloomington, IN: Indiana University Press.

Grad, Bernard. 1965. "Some Biological Effects of the 'Laying on of Hands': A Review of Experiments with Animals and Plants." *Journal of the American Society for Psychical Research* 59: 95–127.

Grad, Bernard, Remi J. Cadoret, and G. I. Paul. 1961. "The Influence of an

Unorthodox Method of Treatment of Wound Healing in Mice." *International Journal of Parapsychology* 3: 5–24.

Greeley, Andrew M. 1975. *Sociology of the Paranormal: A Reconnaissance.* Beverly Hills, CA: Sage Publications.

———. 1987. "Mysticism Goes Mainstream." *American Health* 6, no. 1: 47–49.

Gregory, Anita. 1974. "Ethics and Psychical Research." *Journal of the Society for Psychical Research* 47: 283–305.

———. 1985. *The Strange Case of Rudi Schneider.* Metuchen, NJ: Scarecrow Press.

Greyson, Bruce, and C. P. Flynn, eds. 1985. *The Near-Death Experience: Problems, Prospects, Perspectives.* Springfield, IL: Charles C. Thomas.

Gurney, Edmund, F. W. H. Myers, and Frank Podmore. [1886] 1918. *Phantasms of the Living*, edited by Mrs. Henry Sidgwick. London: Tubner; reprint, New York: E. P. Dutton.

Hallowell, A. Irving. 1934. "Some Empirical Aspects of Northern Saulteaux Indians." *American Anthropologist* 36: 389–404.

———. 1942. *The Role of Conjuring in Saulteaux Society.* Philadelphia, PA: University of Pennsylvania Press.

Hansen, George P. 1982. "Review of *SORRAT: A History of the Neihardt Psychokinesis Experiments, 1961–1981*, by John Thomas Richards." *Journal of Parapsychology* 46: 373–376.

———. 1985. "Critique of Mr. Cox's Mini-lab Experiments." *Archaeus* 3: 17–27.

———. 1990. "Deception by Subjects in Psi Research." *Journal of the American Society for Psychical Research* 84: 25–80.

———. 1992. "Magicians on the Paranormal: An Essay with a Review of Three Books." *Journal of the American Society for Psychical Research* 86: 151–185.

Hansen, George P., and Richard S. Broughton. 1983. "An Investigation of Macro-PK: The SORRAT." In *Research in Parapsychology 1982*, edited by William G. Roll, John Beloff, and Rhea A. White, 115–116. Metuchen, NJ: Scarecrow Press.

———. 1991. "Card-Sorting Tests with SORRAT." *Artifex* 9: 19–26.

Hansen, George P., Marilyn J. Schlitz, Charles T. Tart. 1984. "Bibliography—Remote-Viewing Research 1973–1982." In *The Mind Race: Understanding and Using Psychic Abilities*, by Russell Targ and Keith Harary, 265–269. New York: Villard Books.

Haraldsson, Erlendur. 1981. "Some Determinants of Belief in Psychical Phenomena." *Journal of the American Society for Psychical Research* 75: 297–309.

———. 1985. "Representative National Surveys of Psychic Phenomena: Iceland, Great Britain, Sweden, USA, and Gallup's Multinational Survey." *Journal of the Society for Psychical Research* 53: 145–158.

———. 1987. *Modern Miracles: An Investigative Report on Psychic Phenomena Associated with Sathya Sai Baba.* New York: Fawcett Columbine.

———. 1988–89. "Survey of Claimed Encounters with the Dead." *Omega* 19: 103–113.

Haraldsson, Erlendur, and J. M. Houtkooper. 1991. "Psychic Experience in the Multinational Human Values Study: Who Reports Them." *Journal of the American Society for Psychical Research* 85: 145–165.

Harris, Marvin. 1988. *Culture, People, Nature: An Introduction to General Anthropology.* New York: HarperCollins.

Hay, David, and Ann Morisy. 1978. "Reports of Ecstatic, Paranormal or Religious Experience in Great Britain and the United States—A Comparison of Trends." *Journal for the Scientific Study of Religion* 17: 255–268.

Haynes, Renee. 1970. *Philosopher King—The Humanist Pope Benedict XIV.* London: Weidenfeld and Nicolson.

Heber, A. S., W. P. Fleisher, C. A. Ross, and R. S. Stanwick. 1989. "Dissociation in Alternative Healers and Traditional Therapists." *American Journal of Psychotherapy* 43: 562–574.

Heinze, Ruth-Inge. 1984. *Trance and Healing in Southeast Asia Today.* Berkeley, CA: Ruth-Inge Heinze.

———. 1990. *Shamans of the 20th Century.* New York: Irvington.

Hilgard, Ernest R. 1965. *Hypnotic Susceptibility.* New York: Harcourt, Brace, and World.

Hillgarth, J. N., ed. 1986. *Christianity and Paganism, 350–750, The Conversion of Western Europe.* Philadelphia, PA: University of Pennsylvania Press.

Hobsbawn, Eric J. 1959. *Primitive Rebels: Studies in Archaic Forms of Social Movement into the 19th and 20th Centuries.* Manchester, UK: Manchester University Press.

Hodgson, Richard. 1892. "Mr. Davey's Imitations by Conjuring of Phenomena Sometimes Attributed to Spirit Agency." *Proceedings of the Society for Psychical Research* 8: 253–310.

Honorton, Charles. 1977. "Psi and Internal Attention States." In *Handbook of Parapsychology,* edited by Benjamin B. Wolman, 435–472. New York: Van Nostrand Reinhold.

———. 1985. "Meta-analysis of Psi Ganzfeld Research: A Response to Hyman." *Journal of Parapsychology* 49: 51–92.

Honorton, Charles, R. Berger, M. Varvoglis, M. Quant, P. Derr, E. Schechter, and D. Ferrari. 1990. "Psi Communication in the Ganzfeld: Experiments with an Automated Testing System and a Comparison with a Meta-Analysis of Earlier Studies." *Journal of Parapsychology* 54: 99–139.

Honorton, Charles, and Diane C. Ferrari. 1989. "'Future Telling': A Meta-Analysis of Forced-Choice Precognition Experiments, 1935–1987." *Journal of Parapsychology* 53: 281–308.

Honorton, Charles, M. Ramsey, and C. Cabibbo. 1975. "Experimenter Effects in Extrasensory Perception." *Journal of the American Society for Psychical Research* 69, 135–49.

Honorton, Charles, and Ephraim Schechter. 1987. "Ganzfeld Target Retrieval with an Automated Testing System: A Model for Initial Ganzfeld Success." In *Research in Parapsychology 1986,* edited by Debra H. Weiner and Roger D. Nelson, 36–39. Metuchen, NJ: Scarecrow Press.

Hoy, David. 1981. "Psychic Surgery: Hoax or Hope?" *Zetetic Scholar* 8: 37–46.

Hufford, David J. 1982a. *The Terror That Comes in the Night: An Experience-Centered Study of Supernatural Assault Traditions.* Philadelphia, PA: University of Pennsylvania Press.

———. 1982b. "Traditions of Disbelief." *New York Folklore Quarterly* 8: 47–56 (Reprinted in *Talking Folklore* 1, no. 3, (1987a): 19–31.

———. 1983a. "The Supernatural and the Sociology of Knowledge: Explaining Academic Belief." *New York Folklore Quarterly* 9: 47–56.

———. 1983b. "Folk Healers." In *Handbook of American Folklore,* edited by Richard M. Dorson, 306–319. Bloomington, IN: Indiana University Press.

———. 1985a. "Reason, Rhetoric and Religion: Academic Ideology Versus Folk Belief." *New York Folklore* 11: 177–207.

———. 1985b. "Commentary: Mystical Experience in the Modern World." In

The World Was Flooded with Light: A Mystical Experience Remembered, by Genevieve Foster. 87–183. Pittsburgh, PA: University of Pittsburgh Press.

———. 1987b. "Afterword to 'Traditions of Disbelief.'" *Talking Folklore* 1, no. 3: 29–31.

———. 1988. "Contemporary Folk Medicine. In *Unorthodox Medicine in America,* edited by Norman Gevitz, 228–264. Baltimore, MD: Johns Hopkins University Press.

———. 1990. "Rational Skepticism and the Possibility of Unbiased Folk Belief Scholarship." *Talking Folklore* 1, no. 9: 19–31.

———. 1992. "Commentary: Paranormal Experiences in the General Population." *The Journal of Nervous and Mental Disease* 180: 362–368.

———. 1993. "Epistemologies of Religious Healing." *The Journal of Philosophy and Medicine* 18: 173–192.

Hultkrantz, Åke. 1992. *Shamanic Healing and Ritual Drama, Health and Medicine in Native North American Religious Traditions.* New York: Crossroad Publishing.

Hume, David. [1748] 1967. *An Inquiry Concerning Human Understanding.* Reprint, edited by L. A. Selby-Bigge II. New York: Oxford University Press.

Huxley, Aldous. 1945. *The Perennial Philosophy.* New York: Harper and Row.

Hyman, Ray. 1977. "Cold Reading." *Zetetic* 1: 18–37.

———. 1985. "The Psi Ganzfeld Experiment: A Critical Appraisal." *Journal of Parapsychology* 49: 3–49.

Hyman, Ray, and C. Honorton. 1986. "A Joint Communiqué: The Psi Ganzfeld Controversy." *Journal of Parapsychology* 50: 351–364.

Ikegami, Yoshimasa. 1992. "Okinawan Shamanism and Charismatic Christianity." Paper presented at the meetings of the Society for the Scientific Study of Religion, Washington, DC, November.

Im Bang and Yi Ryuk. [1913] 1962. *Korean Folk Tales: Imps, Ghosts and Fairies,* translated by James S. Gale. Rutland, VT: Charles E. Tuttle Company. Reprint, New York: E. P. Dutton.

Inglis, Brian. 1986. "The Fire-Walk." *Speculations in Science and Technology* 9: 163–167.

Irwin, H. J. 1985a. *Flight of Mind: A Psychological Study of the Out-of-Body Experience.* Metuchen, NJ: Scarecrow Press.

———. 1985b. "Parapsychological Phenomena and the Absorption Domain." *Journal of the American Society for Psychical Research* 79: 1–11.

———. 1992. "Origins and Functions of Paranormal Belief: The Role of Childhood Trauma and Interpersonal Control." *Journal of the American Society for Psychical Research* 86: 199–208.

Jahoda, G. 1968. "Scientific Training and the Persistence of Traditional Beliefs among West African University Students." *Nature* 220: 1,356.

James, William. [1909] 1960. *William James on Psychical Research,* edited by Gardner Murphy and R. D. Ballou, 309–325. Reprint. New York: Viking. Originally published as "The Final Impressions of a Psychical Researcher." *The American Magazine* (October).

Johnson, Donald M. 1945. "The Phantom Anesthetist of Mattoon: A Field Study of Mass Hysteria." *Journal of Abnormal and Social Psychology* 40: 175–186.

Jordan, David K. 1972. *Gods, Ghosts, and Ancestors: Folk Religion in a Taiwanese Village.* Berkeley, CA: University of California Press.

Jordan, David K., and Daniel L. Overmyer. 1986. *The Flying Phoenix, Aspects of Chinese Sectarianism in Taiwan.* Princeton, NJ: Princeton University Press, 1986.

Jorgensen, Danny L. 1982. "The Esoteric Community, An Ethnographic Investigation of the Cultic Milieu." *Urban Life* 10: 383–407.

———. 1992. *The Esoteric Scene, Cultic Milieu, and Occult Tarot.* New York: Garland.

Kaagan, L. 1984. "Black Cats, Cracked Mirrors and the Dow Jones." *Psychology Today* 18: 8.

Kakar, Sudhir. 1982. *Shamans, Mystics, and Doctors.* Boston: Beacon Press.

Kane, Stephen M. 1982. "Holiness Ritual Fire Handling: Ethnographic and Psychological Considerations." *Ethos* 10: 369–384.

Kao, Karl S. Y., ed. 1985. *Classical Chinese Tales of the Supernatural and the Fantastic: Selections from the Third to the Tenth Century.* Bloomington, IN: Indiana University Press.

Kasahara, Tosio, ed. and trans. 1993. *The Elusiveness Problem of Psi* (in Japanese). Tokyo: Shunju-Sha Publishers.

Keel, John A. 1975. *The Mothman Prophecies.* New York: Dutton.

Kelsey, Morton. 1987. "Miracles: Modern Perspectives." In *The Encyclopedia of Religion,* Vol. 9, edited by Mircea Eliade, 548–552, New York: Macmillan and Free Press.

Kennedy, J. E., and J. L. Taddonio. 1976. "Experimenter Effects in Parapsychological Research." *Journal of Parapsychology* 40: 1–33.

Kiev, Ari. 1964. *Magic, Faith, and Healing, Studies in Primitive Psychiatry Today.* New York: Free Press.

Kleinman, Arthur. 1980. *Patients and Healers in the Context of Culture.* Berkeley, CA: University of California Press.

———. 1986. *Social Origins of Distress and Disease: Depression, Neurasthenia, and Pain in Modern China.* New Haven, CT, and London: Yale University Press.

Kmetz, J. M. 1981. "Cell Culture Experiments with Dean Kraft." In *Portrait of a Psychic Healer,* by Dean Kraft, 181–187 (appendix). New York: Putnam's.

Kraft, Dean. 1981. *Portrait of a Psychic Healer.* New York: Putnam's.

Krippner, Stanley. 1989. "A Call to Heal: Entry Patterns in Brazilian Mediumship." In *Altered States of Consciousness and Mental Health,* edited by Colleen A. Ward, 186–206. Newberry Park, CA: Sage.

Krippner, Stanley, and Alberto Villoldo. 1976. *The Realms of Healing.* Millbrae, CA: Celestial Arts Press.

Krippner, Stanley, and Patrick Welch. 1992. *Spiritual Dimensions of Healing.* New York: Irvington Publishers.

Kurtz, Paul, ed. 1985. *A Skeptic's Handbook of Parapsychology.* Buffalo, NY: Prometheus Books.

Kurtz, Paul, James Alcock, Kendrick Frazier, Barry Karr, Philip J. Klass, and James Randi. 1988. "Testing Psi Claims in China: Visit by a CSICOP Delegation." *Skeptical Inquirer* 12, no. 4: 364–375.

Landes, Ruth. 1968. *Ojibwa Religion and the Midewiwin.* Madison, WI: University of Wisconsin Press.

Lang, Andrew [1898] 1968. *The Making of Religion.* Reprint. New York: AMS Press. New York: Longmans, Green, and Co.

Lava, Jesus B., and Antonio S. Araneta. 1982. *Faith Healing and Psychic Surgery in the Philippines.* Manila: Philippine Society for Psychical Research Foundation.

Lawrence, Tony R. 1993. "Gathering in the Sheep and Goats . . . A Meta-

Analysis of Forced-Choice Sheep-Goat ESP Studies, 1947–1993." *Parapsychological Association, 36th Annual Convention, Proceedings of Presented Papers,* 75–86, Toronto.

Le Bon, Gustave. [1895] 1969. *The Crowd.* Reprint. New York: Viking. Originally published as *Psychologie des Foules.* Paris: F. Alcan.

Lebra, William P. 1966. *Okinawan Religion: Belief, Ritual, and Social Structure.* Honolulu: University Press of Hawaii.

Leikind, Bernard J., and William J. McCarthy. 1985. "An Investigation of Firewalking." *Skeptical Inquirer* 10, no. 1: 23–34.

Licauco, Jaime T. 1978. *Born to Heal: The Amazing Story of Spiritual Healer Rev. Alex Orbito.* Manila: Jaime T. Licauco.

———. 1981. *The Magicians of God.* Manila: National Book Store.

———. 1982. *The Truth Behind Faith Healing in the Philippines.* Manila: Navotas Press.

Linton, Ralph. 1943. "Nativistic Movements." *American Anthropologist* 45: 230–40.

Long, Joseph K. ed., 1977. *Extrasensory Ecology: Parapsychology and Anthropology.* Metuchen, NJ: Scarecrow Press.

Lowie, Robert Harry. 1924. *Primitive Religion.* New York: Boni and Liveright, Inc.

Lundahl, Craig R. 1982. *A Collection of Near-Death Research Readings.* Chicago: Nelson-Hall.

Lynch, Frederick R. 1977. "Toward a Theory of Conversion and Commitment to the Occult." *American Behavioral Scientist* 20: 887–907.

Lyons, Arthur, and Marcello Truzzi. 1991. *The Blue Sense: Psychic Detectives and Crime.* New York: Mysterious Press.

MacDonald, William L. 1992. "Idionecrophanies: The Social Construction of Perceived Contact with the Dead." *Journal for the Scientific Study of Religion* 31: 215–223.

Mack, Mary Peter, ed. 1969. *A Bentham Reader.* New York: Pegasus.

MacKenzie, Brian, and S. Lynne MacKenzie. 1980. "Whence the Enchanted Boundary? Sources and Significance of the Parapsychological Tradition." *Journal of Parapsychology* 44: 125–166.

Manning, Matthew. 1974. *The Link: Matthew Manning's Own Story of His Extraordinary Psychic Gifts.* New York: Holt Rinehart and Winston.

Marks, David, and Richard Kammann. 1980. *The Psychology of the Psychic.* Buffalo, NY: Prometheus Books.

Markwick, Betty. 1978. "The Soal-Goldney Experiments with Basil Shackleton: New Evidence of Data Manipulation. *Proceedings of the Society for Psychical Research* 56: 250–277.

———. 1985. "The Establishment of Data Manipulation in the Soal-Shackleton Experiments." In *The Skeptic's Handbook of Parapsychology,* edited by Paul Kurtz, 287–311. Buffalo, NY: Prometheus.

Matsubayashi, Herbert Hideto. 1970. "A Study of the Sambo-e-Kotoba." Unpublished MA Thesis, UCLA.

McCarthy, William J., and Bernard J. Leikind. 1986. "Walking on Fire: Feat of Mind?" *Psychology Today* 20 (February): 10, 12–13.

McClenon, James. 1981. "A Summary of an Investigation of a Haunting in Baltimore." *Theta* 9 (4): 12–14.

———. 1982. "A Survey of Elite Scientists: Their Attitudes Toward ESP and Parapsychology." *Journal of Parapsychology* 46: 127–152.

———. 1984. *Deviant Science: The Case of Parapsychology.* Philadelphia, PA: University of Pennsylvania Press.

———. 1985. "Firewalking and Psychic Surgery: Defining the Paranormal by Investigating Its Boundaries." *Journal of Indian Psychology* 4: 85–97.

———. 1988a. "A Survey of Chinese Anomalous Experiences and Comparison with Western Representative National Samples." *Journal for the Scientific Study of Religion* 27: 421–426.

———. 1988b. "Firewalking in Japan, Sri Lanka, and the USA: The Social Uses of an Unusual Phenomenon," *International Journal of Comparative Sociology* 29, nos. 3–4: 202–213.

———. 1989. "Parapsychology in Japan." *Parapsychology Review* 20, no. 4: 13–15.

———. 1990. "Chinese and American Anomalous Experiences: The Role of Religiosity." *Sociological Analysis* 51: 53–67.

———. 1991. "Near-Death Folklore in Medieval China and Japan: A Comparative Analysis." *Asian Folklore Studies* 50: 319–342.

———. 1993. "The Experiential Foundations of Shamanic Healing." *Journal of Medicine and Philosophy* 18: 107–127.

McClenon, James, and Ray Hyman. 1987. "A Remote Viewing Experiment Conducted by a Skeptic and a Believer." *Zetetic Scholar* 12–13: 21–33.

———. 1989. "A Remote Viewing Experiment Conducted by a Skeptic and a Believer." In *The Elusive Quarry: A Scientific Appraisal of Psychical Research,* edited by Ray Hyman, 347–361. Buffalo, NY: Prometheus Books.

McCready, William C. and Andrew M. Greeley. 1976. *The Ultimate Values of the American Population.* Beverly Hills, CA: Sage Publications.

Medalia, N. Z., and O. N. Larsen. 1958. "Diffusion and Belief in a Collective Delusion: The Seattle Windshield Pitting Epidemic." *American Sociological Review* 23: 221–232.

Medhurst, R. G., K. M. Goldney, and M. R. Barrington. 1972. *Crookes and the Spirit World.* New York: Taplinger.

Meek, George W., ed. 1977. *Healers and the Healing Process.* Wheaton, IL: Theosophical Publishing House.

Mill, John Stuart. [1884] 1973. *A System of Logic Ratiocinative and Inductive, Being a Connected View of the Principles of Evidence and the Methods of Scientific Investigation,* edited by J. M. Robson. Reprint, Toronto: University of Toronto Press. 8th edition, London: Longmans, Green, and Co.

Miller, David L. 1985. *Introduction to Collective Behavior.* Belmont, CA: Wadsworth.

Mills, D. E. 1970. *A Collection of Tales from Uji: A Study and Translation of Uji Shui Monogatari.* Cambridge, England: Cambridge University Press.

Mischo, J. 1971. "Personality Structure of Psychokinetic Mediums." In *Proceedings of the Parapsychological Association,* Vol. 5, 1968, edited by W. G. Roll. Durham, NC: Parapsychological Association.

Mitchell, Janet L. 1981. *Out-of-Body Experiences: A Handbook.* Jefferson, NC: McFarland.

Mitchell, Stephen. 1991. *The Gospel According to Jesus: A New Translation and Guide to His Essential Teaching for Believers and Unbelievers.* New York: HarperCollins.

Moody, Raymond A., Jr. 1975. *Life after Life.* Atlanta, GA: Mockingbird Books.

———. 1989. *Elvis after Life.* New York: Bantam.

Moon, M. L. 1975. "Artists Contrasted with Non-artists Concerning Belief in ESP: A Poll." *Journal of the American Society for Psychical Research* 69: 161–166.

Mooney, James. 1896. *The Ghost-Dance Religion and the Sioux Outbreak of 1890*. Fourteenth Annual Report of the Bureau of Ethnography to the Secretary of the Smithsonian Institution, 1892–1893, J. W. Powell, Director. Washington, DC: Government Printing Office.

Morgan, A. H. 1973. "The Heritability of Hypnotic Susceptibility in Twins." *Journal of Abnormal Psychology* 82: 55–61.

Morris, Robert L. 1977. "Parapsychology, Biology, and Anpsi." In *Handbook of Parapsychology*, edited by Benjamin B. Wolman, 687–715. New York: Van Nostrand Reinhold.

Mumford, Emily. 1983. *Medical Sociology: Patients, Providers, and Policies*. New York: Random House.

Murdock, G. P., and C. Provost. 1973. "Measurement of Cultural Complexity." *Ethnology* 12: 379–92.

Murphy, Gardner. 1963. "Creativity and Its Relation to Extrasensory Perception." *Journal of the American Society for Psychical Research* 57: 203–214.

———. 1966. "Research in Creativeness: What Can It Tell Us about Extrasensory Perception." *Journal of the American Society for Psychical Research* 60: 8–22.

Murphy, K., and D. Lester. 1976. "A Search for Correlates of Belief in ESP." *Psychological Reports* 38: 82.

Murphy, Michael. 1992. *The Future of the Body: Explorations into the Future Evolution of Human Nature*. Los Angeles, CA: Jeremy P. Tarcher.

Nadon, R., and J. F. Kihlstrom. 1987. "Hypnosis, Psi, and the Psychology of Anomalous Experience." *Behavioral and Brain Sciences* 10: 597–599.

Nakamura, Kyoko Motomochi, trans. 1973. *Miraculous Stories from the Japanese Buddhist Tradition: The Nihon Ryoiki of the Monk Kyokai*. Cambridge, MA: Harvard University Press.

Narayan, Kirin. 1989. *Storytellers, Saints, and Scoundrels: Folk Narrative in Hindu Religious Teaching*. Philadelphia, PA: University of Pennsylvania Press.

Nash, Carroll B., and Dallas E. Buzby. 1965. "Extrasensory Perception of Identical and Fraternal Twins: Comparison of Clairvoyance Test Scores." *Journal of Heredity* 56: 52–54.

———. 1978. *Science of Psi: ESP and PK*. Springfield, IL: Charles C. Thomas.

Neppe, Vernon M. 1983. *The Psychology of Déjà Vu*. Johannesburg: Witwatersrand University Press.

———. 1985/86. "Déjà Vu in the Survival Context." *Theta* 13/14, no. 2: 26–29.

Neuman, W. Lawrence. 1991. *Social Research Methods*. Needham Heights, MA: Allyn and Bacon.

Nolen, William A. 1974. *Healing: A Doctor in Search of a Miracle*. New York: Random House.

Noll, Richard. 1983. "Shamanism and Schizophrenia: A State-Specific Approach to the 'Schizophrenia' Metaphor of Shamanic States." *American Anthropologist* 10: 443–459.

Okazaki, Toji. 1977. *Pure Land Buddhist Painting*. Translated by Elizabeth ten Grotenhuis. Tokyo: Kodansha International and Shibundo.

O'Keefe, Daniel L. 1982. *Stolen Lightning: The Social Theory of Magic*. Oxford: Continuum.

Orne, Martin T. 1959. "The Nature of Hypnosis: Artifact and Essence." *Journal of Abnormal and Social Psychology* 58: 277–299.

Osis, Karlis. 1981. "Assassin's Shadow Disrupts Experiment." *ASPR Newsletter* 8, no. 3: 16.

Osis, Karlis, and E. Haraldsson. 1977. *At the Hour of Death.* New York: Avon.

Osis, Karlis, and Donna McCormick. 1980. "Kinetic Effects at the Ostensible Location of an Out-of-Body Projection During Perceptual Testing." *Journal of the American Society for Psychical Research* 74: 319–329.

Otis, L. P., and J. E. Alcock. 1982. "Factors Affecting Extraordinary Belief." *Journal of Social Psychology* 118: 77–85.

Otto, Rudolf. 1953. *The Idea of the Holy.* Translated by John W. Harvey. London: Oxford University Press.

Owen, Iris M., and Margaret Sparrow. 1976. *Conjuring Up Philip: An Adventure in Psychokinesis.* New York: Harper and Row.

PA News and Annual Report. 1993. "Membership." (March): 3.

Padgett, V. R., V. A. Benassi, and B. F. Singer. 1981. "Belief in ESP Among Psychologists." In *Paranormal Borderlands of Science,* edited by Kendrick Frazier, 66–67. Buffalo, NY: Prometheus Books.

Palmer, John. 1974. "A Case of RSPK Involving a Ten-year-old Boy: The Powhattan Poltergeist." *Journal of the American Society for Psychical Research* 68: 1–33.

———. 1978. "Extrasensory Perception: Research Findings." In *Advances in Parapsychological Research,* Vol. 2, edited by Stanley Krippner, 59–243. New York: Plenum Press.

———. 1979. "A Community Mail Survey of Psychic Experiences." *Journal of the American Society for Psychical Research* 73: 221–251.

———. 1992. "President's Message." *PA News and Annual Report,* 1.

Palmer, John, and I. Van der Velden. 1983. "ESP and 'Hypnotic Imagination,' A Group Free-Response Study." *European Journal of Parapsychology* 4: 413–434.

Park, Robert Ezra, and Ernest W. Burgess. 1921. *Introduction to the Science of Sociology.* Chicago, IL: University of Chicago Press.

Pekala, Ronald J., V. K. Kumar, and James Cummings. 1992. "Types of High Hypnotically-Susceptible Individuals and Reported Attitudes and Experiences of the Paranormal and Anomalous." *Journal of the American Society for Psychical Research* 86: 135–150.

Perry, Joseph B., and Meredith David Pugh. 1978. *Collective Behavior: Response to Social Stress.* St. Paul, MN: West Publishing.

Podmore, Frank. [1902] 1963. *Mediums of the Nineteenth Century.* 2 vols. New Hyde Park, NY: University Books. Originally published as *Modern Spiritualism.*

———. [1909] 1964. From Mesmer to Christian Science. New Hyde Park, NY: University Books.

Prabhavananda, Swami, and Christopher Isherwood. 1953. *How to Know God: The Yoga Aphorisms of Patanjali.* New York: New American Library.

Price, Harry. 1936. *Bulletin II: A Report on Two Successful Firewalks.* London: London Council for Psychical Investigation.

———. 1937. "Firewalking." *Nature* 139 (May 29): 928–929.

Price, Walter Franklin. 1927. *The Case of Patience Worth.* Boston: Boston Society for Psychic Research.

Radin, D. I., and R. D. Nelson. 1989. "Evidence for Consciousness-Related Anomalies in Random Physical Systems." *Foundations of Physics* 19: 1,499–1,514.

Randall, J. L. 1978. "Correspondence." *Journal of the Society for Psychical Research* 49: 968–969.

Randall, J. L., and C. P. Davis. 1982. "Paranormal Deformation of Nitinol Wire: A Confirmatory Experiment." *Journal of the Society for Psychical Research* 51: 368–373.

Randi, James. 1980. *Flim-Flam! Psychics, ESP, Unicorns, and Other Delusions.* Buffalo, NY: Prometheus Books.

———. 1987. *The Faith-Healers.* Buffalo, NY: Prometheus Books.

Rauscher, E. A., and B. A. Rubik. 1980. "Effects on Motility Behavior and Growth of Salmonella Typhimurium in the Presence of a Psychic Subject." In *Research in Parapsychology 1979,* edited by W. G. Roll, 140–142. Metuchen, NJ: Scarecrow Press.

———. 1983. "Human Volitional Effects on a Model Bacterial System." *Psi Research* 2: 38–48.

Reischauer, August Karl. 1917. *Studies in Japanese Buddhism.* New York: Macmillan.

———. 1930. "Genshin's Ojo Yoshu: Collected Essays on Birth into Paradise." *The Transactions of the Asiatic Society of Japan* 7: 16–97.

Rhine, Joseph Banks. 1934. *Extra-sensory Perception.* Boston: Boston Society for Psychic Research. Reprint. Brookline Village, MA: Branden Press, 1964.

———. 1974. "Comments: A New Case of Experimenter Unreliability." *Journal of Parapsychology* 38: 215–25.

Rhine, Louisa. 1977. "Research Methods with Spontaneous Cases." In *Handbook of Parapsychology,* edited by Benjamin B. Wolman, 59–80. New York: Van Nostrand Reinhold.

———. 1981. *The Invisible Picture: A Study of Psychic Experiences.* Jefferson, NC: McFarland.

Richards, Douglas G. 1990a. "Hypnotic Susceptibility and Subjective Psychic Experiences." *Journal of Parapsychology* 54: 35–51.

———. 1990b. "Dissociation and Transformation." *Journal of Humanistic Psychology* 30: 54–83.

———. 1991. "A Study of the Correlations Between Subjective Psychic Experiences and Dissociative Experience." *Dissociation* 4: 83–91.

Richards, John Thomas. 1982. *SORRAT: A History of the Neihardt Psychokinesis Experiments, 1961–1981.* Metuchen, NJ: Scarecrow Press.

———. 1984. "The Question of Artifact Introduction in Psychical Research." *Archaeus Project Newsletter* 3 (Summer/Fall): 10.

———. 1992. *The Year of the Sorrats.* Vol. 1. Ashland, OH: BookMasters.

———. 1994. *The Year of the Sorrats.* Vol. 2. Ashland, OH: BookMasters.

Richardson, James T., and Mary Stewart. 1977. "Conversion Process Models and the Jesus Movement." *American Behavioral Scientist* 20: 819–838.

Ring, Kenneth. 1980. *Life at Death: A Scientific Investigation of the Near-Death Experience.* New York: Coward, McCann and Geoghegan.

———. 1984. *Heading toward Omega: In Search of the Meaning of the Near-Death Experience.* New York: William Morrow.

Rogo, D. Scott. 1976. *In Search of the Unknown.* New York: Taplinger.

———. 1982a. *Miracles: A Parascientific Inquiry into Wondrous Phenomena.* New York: Dial Press.

———. 1982b. "The Poltergeist and Family Dynamics: A Report on a Recent Investigation." *Journal of the Society for Psychical Research* 51: 233–237.

———. 1985. "J. B. Rhine and the Levy Scandal. In *The Skeptic's Handbook of Parapsychology*, edited by Paul Kurtz, 313–326. Buffalo, NY: Prometheus.

Rojcewicz, P. M. 1987. "The 'Men in Black' Experience and Tradition: Analogues with the Traditional Devil Hypothesis." *Journal of American Folklore* 100: 148–160.

Roll, William G. 1972. *The Poltergeist*. Garden City, NY: Doubleday. Reprint, Metuchen, NJ: Scarecrow Press, 1976.

———. 1977. "Poltergeists." In *Handbook of Parapsychology*, edited by Benjamin B. Wolman, 382–413. New York: Van Nostrand Reinhold.

Rose, Dan. 1989. *Patterns of American Culture: Ethnography and Estrangement*. Philadelphia, PA: University of Pennsylvania Press.

Ross, C. A., and S. Joshi. 1992. "Paranormal Experiences in the General Population." *Journal of Nervous and Mental Disease* 180: 357–361.

Rousseau, Jean-Jacques. 1972. *The Miscellaneous Works of Mr. J. J. Rousseau*. Vol. 4. New York: Burt Franklin.

Sabom, Michael. 1982. *Recollections of Death: A Medical Investigation*. New York: Simon and Schuster.

Saltmarsh, H. F. [1938] 1975. *Evidence of Personal Survival from Cross-Correspondences*. Reprint, New York: Arno Press. London: Bell.

Schechner, Richard. 1985. *Between Theater and Anthropology*. Philadelphia, PA: University of Pennsylvania Press.

Schechter, Ephraim. 1984. "Hypnotic Induction vs. Control Conditions: Illustrating an Approach to the Evaluation of Replicability in Parapsychological Data." *Journal of the American Society for Psychical Research* 78: 1–27.

Schepps, Solomon J. [1820] 1979. "Foreword." In *Lost Books of the Bible: Being All the Gospels, Epistles, and other pieces now extant attributed in the first four centuries to Jesus Christ, His Apostles and their companions, not included by its compilers, in the Authorized New Testament. . . .* Translated by Jeremiah Jones. Collected by William Hone. Reprint, New York: Bell Publishing Company. Originally published as *The Apocryphal New Testament*.

Schetky, L. McDonald. 1979. "Shape-Memory Alloys." *Scientific American* 241: 68–76.

Schlitz, Marilyn. 1991. "Video Review—'Psychic Surgery': A Case History of Shamanic Sleight-of-Hand," produced by Philip Singer; edited by Thomas Peterson. *Journal of the American Society for Psychical Research* 85: 213–216.

Schlitz, Marilyn, and Elmer Gruber. 1980. "Transcontinental Remote Viewing." *Journal of Parapsychology* 44: 305–318.

Schlitz, Marilyn, and Charles Honorton. 1992. "Ganzfeld Psi Performance within an Artistically Gifted Population." *Journal of the American Society for Psychical Research* 86: 83–98.

Schmidt, Helmut. 1970. "PK Experiments with Animals as Subjects." *Journal of Parapsychology* 34: 255–261.

Schumaker, John F. 1990. *Wings of Illusion: The Origin, Nature, and Future of Paranormal Belief*. Buffalo, NY: Prometheus Books.

Seligman, Martin E. P. 1991. *Learned Optimism*. New York: Alfred A. Knopf.

Sheils, Dean. 1978. "A Cross-Cultural Study of Beliefs in Out-of-the-Body Experiences, Waking and Sleeping." *Journal of the Society for Psychical Research* 49: 697–741.

Sheils, Dean, and P. Berg. 1977. "A Research Note on Sociological Variables Related to Belief in Psychic Phenomena." *Wisconsin Sociologist* 14: 24–31.

Sherman, Harold. 1967. *Wonder Healers of the Philippines*. London: Psychic Press.

Shibutani, Tamotsu. 1966. *Improvised News: A Sociological Study of Rumor.* Indianapolis, IN: Bobbs-Merrill.

Sidgwick, Henry, and Committee. 1894. "Report on the Census of Hallucinations." *Proceedings of the Society for Psychical Research* 10: 25–422.

Singer, Barry, and V. A. Benassi. 1981. "Occult Beliefs." *American Scientist* 69: 49–55.

Skinner, B. F. 1948. "Superstition in the Pigeon." *Journal of Experimental Psychology* 38: 168–712.

———. 1953. *Science and Human Behavior.* New York: Macmillan.

Smelser, Neil. 1962. *Theory of Collective Behavior.* New York: Free Press.

Smith, Morton. 1978. *Jesus the Magician.* San Francisco, CA: Harper and Row.

Smith, Susy. 1964. *The Mediumship of Mrs. Leonard.* New Hyde Park, NY: University Books.

Snow, D. A., and L. A. Zurcher, Jr., and S. Ekland-Olson. 1980. "Social Networks and Social Movements: A Microstructural Approach to Differential Recruitment." *American Sociological Review* 45: 787–801.

Snow, D. A., and R. Machalek. 1982. "On the Presumed Fragility of Unconventional Beliefs." *Journal for the Scientific Study of Religion* 21: 15–26.

Stark, Rodney, and William Sims Bainbridge. 1980. "Networks of Faith: Interpersonal Bonds and Recruitment to Cults and Sects." *American Journal of Sociology* 85: 1,376–1,395.

———. 1985. *The Future of Religion: Secularization, Revival, and Cult Formation.* Berkeley, CA: University of California Press.

Stelter, Alfred. 1976. *Psi Healing.* New York: Bantam Books.

Stevenson, Ian. 1970. "Characteristics of Cases of the Reincarnation Type in Turkey and Their Comparison with Cases in Two Other Cultures." *International Journal of Comparative Sociology* 11: 1–17.

———. 1977. "Reincarnation: Field Studies and Theoretical Issues." In *Handbook of Parapsychology,* edited by Benjamin B. Wolman, 631–663. New York: Van Nostrand Reinhold.

———. 1987. *Children Who Remember Previous Lives: A Question of Reincarnation.* Charlottesville, VA: University Press of Virginia.

Stillings, Dennis. 1991. "The Society for Research on Rapport and Telekinesis: Experiences and Experiments." *Artifex* 9: 4–18.

Stoller, Paul. 1989. *The Taste of Ethnographic Things: The Senses in Anthropology.* Philadelphia, PA: University of Pennsylvania Press.

Stoller, Paul, and Cheryl Olkes. 1987. *In Sorcery's Shadow, A Memoir of Apprenticeship Among the Songhay of Niger.* Chicago: University of Chicago Press.

Straus, R. 1976. "Changing Oneself: Seekers and the Creative Transformation of Life Experiences." In *Doing Social Life,* edited by J. Lofland, 252–272. New York: John Wiley.

Takakusu, Junjiro. 1947. *Essentials of Buddhist Philosophy.* Honolulu, HI: University Press of Hawaii.

Tanous, Alex (with Harvey Ardman). 1976. *Beyond Coincidence: One Man's Experiences with Psychic Phenomena.* New York: Doubleday and Company.

Targ, Russell, and Harold Puthoff. 1977. *Mind Reach.* New York: Dell Publishing.

Tart, Charles. 1984. "Acknowledging and Dealing with the Fear of Psi." *Journal of the American Society for Psychical Research* 78: 133–143.

———. 1986. "Psychics' Fears of Psychic Powers." *Journal of the American Society for Psychical Research* 80: 279–292.

Tart, Charles, and C. M. Labore. 1986. "Attitudes toward Strongly Functioning Psi: A Preliminary Survey." *Journal of the American Society for Psychical Research* 80: 163–173.

Teiser, Stephen F. 1988a. *The Ghost Festival in Medieval China.* Princeton, NJ: Princeton University Press.

———. 1988b. "Having Once Died and Returned to Life: Representations of Hell in Medieval China." *Harvard Journal of Asiatic Studies* 48: 433–464.

Thalbourne, Michael A. 1981. "Extroversion and the Sheep-Goat Variable: A Conceptual Replication." *Journal of the American Society for Psychical Research* 75: 105–119.

———. 1984. "Some Correlates of Belief in Psychical Phenomena: A Partial Replication of the Haraldsson Findings." *Parapsychology Review* 15: 13–15.

Thomas, William I. (with Dorothy S. Thomas). 1928. *The Child in America.* New York: Alfred A. Knopf.

Thompson, Stith. 1966. *Motif-Index of Folk-Literature.* 6 vols. Bloomington, IN: Indiana University Press.

Thurston, Herbert, and Donald Attwater, eds. 1956. *Butler's Lives of the Saints.* Rev. ed., 4 vols. New York: P. J. Kenedy.

Tietze, Thomas R. 1973. *Margery.* New York: Harper and Row.

Tiger, Lionel. 1979. *Optimism: The Biology of Hope.* New York: Simon and Schuster.

Tiryakian, Edward A. 1974. *On the Margin of the Visible.* New York: John Wiley and Sons.

Tobacyk, J., and G. Milford. 1983. "Belief in Paranormal Phenomena: Assessment Instrument Development and Implications for Personality Functioning." *Journal of Personality and Social Psychology* 44: 1,029–1,037.

Truzzi, Marcello. 1972. "The Occult Revival as Popular Culture: Some Random Observations on the Old and Nouveau Witch." *Journal of Popular Culture* 8: 906–911.

———. 1977. "Editorial: On Pseudo-sciences and Proto-sciences." *Zetetic Scholar* 1, no. 2: 3–8.

———. 1978. "On the Extraordinary: An Attempt at Clarification." *Zetetic Scholar* 1: 11–19.

———. 1983. "A Bibliography on Fire-Walking." *Zetetic Scholar* 11: 105–108.

Turner, Edith. 1992. *Experiencing Ritual: A New Interpretation of African Healing.* Philadelphia, PA: University of Pennsylvania Press.

Turner, Ralph H., and Lewis M. Killian. [1957] 1972. *Collective Behavior.* Second edition. Englewood Cliffs, NJ: Prentice-Hall.

Tylor, Edward B. 1920. *Primitive Culture.* 2 vols. New York: Putnam's.

Ullman, M. 1947. "Herpes Simplex and Second Degree Burn Induced under Hypnosis." *American Journal of Psychiatry* 103: 823–830.

Ury, Marian Bloom. 1970. "Genko Shakusho, Japan's First Comprehensive History of Buddhism: A Partial Translation with Introduction and Notes." Unpublished Ph.D. Dissertation, UCLA.

———. 1979. *Tales of Times Now Past: Sixty-Two Stories from a Medieval Japanese Collection.* Berkeley, CA: University of California Press.

Valentine, Tom. 1975. *Psychic Surgery.* New York: Pocket Books.

Valla, Jean-Pierre, and Raymond H. Prince. 1989. "Religious Experiences as Self-Healing Mechanisms." In *Altered States of Consciousness and Mental Health: A Cross-Cultural Perspective,* edited by Colleen A. Ward, 149–166. Newbury Park, CA: Sage.

Vermes, Geza. 1986. *Jesus the Jew: A Historian's Reading of the Gospels.* Philadelphia, PA: Fortress Press.

Vilenskaya, Larissa, and Joan Steffy, 1991. *Fire Walking: A New Look at an Old Enigma.* Falls Village, CT: Bramble Company.

Virtanen, Leea. 1990. *"That Must Have Been ESP!",* translated by John Atkinson and Thomas Dubois. Bloomington, IN: Indiana University Press.

Wagner, M. W., and Mary Monnet. 1979. "Attitudes of College Professors Toward Extra-Sensory Perception." *Zetetic Scholar* 5: 7–16.

Wagner, M. W., and F. H. Ratzeburg. 1987. "Hypnotic Suggestibility and Paranormal Belief." *Psychological Reports* 60: 1,069–1,070.

Walker, Jearl. 1977. "The Amateur Scientist." *Scientific American* 237, no. 2 (August): 126–131.

Wallis, Roy. 1976. *The Road to Total Freedom.* New York: Columbia University Press.

Ward, Benedicta. 1982. *Miracles and the Medieval Mind: Theory, Record, and Event, 1000–1215.* Philadelphia, PA: University of Pennsylvania Press.

Watkins, Graham K., and Anita M. Watkins. 1971. "Possible PK Influence on the Resuscitation of Anesthetized Mice." *Journal of Parapsychology* 35: 257–272.

Weatherhead, Leslie Dixon. 1953. *Psychology, Religion, and Healing.* London: Abingdon-Cokesbury.

Weiner, Debra H., and Dean I. Radin. eds. 1986. *Research in Parapsychology, 1985.* Metuchen, NJ: Scarecrow.

West, D. J. 1948. "A Mass-Observation Questionnaire on Hallucinations." *Journal of the Society for Psychical Research* 34: 187–196.

Westrum, Ron. 1977. "Science and Social Intelligence about Anomalies: The Case of UFOs." *Social Studies of Science* 7: 271–302.

White, Rhea A. 1976. "The Limits of Experimenter Influence on Psi Test Results: Can Any Be Set?" *Journal of the American Society for Psychical Research* 70: 333–369.

———. 1982. "An Analysis of ESP Phenomena in the Saints." *Parapsychology Review* 13, no. 4: 15–18.

Wickramasekera, Ian E. 1988. *Clinical Behavioral Medicine: Some Concepts and Procedures.* New York: Plenum Press.

———. 1989. "Risk Factors for Parapsychological Verbal Reports, Hypnotizability and Somatic Complaints." In *Parapsychology and Human Nature,* edited by Betty Shapin and Lisette Coly, 19–35. New York: Parapsychology Foundation.

Wiebe, Phillip. 1991. "Apparitions of Christ: Contemporary Accounts and Philosophical Appraisal." Paper presented to the Society for the Scientific Study of Religion, Pittsburgh, PA, November.

Wilson, Bryan. 1959. "An Analysis of Sect Development." *American Sociological Review* 24: 3–15.

Wilson, Sheryl C., and Theodore X. Barber. 1983. "The Fantasy-Prone Personality: Implications for Understanding Imagery, Hypnosis, and Parapsychological Phenomena." In *Imagery: Current Theory, Research, and Application,* edited by Anees A. Sheikh, 340–386. New York: John Wiley and Sons.

Winkelman, Michael. 1981. "The Effect of Formal Education on Extrasensory Ability: The Ozolco Study." *Journal of Parapsychology* 45: 321–336.

———. 1982. "Magic: A Theoretical Reassessment." *Current Anthropology* 23: 37–44, 59–66.

———. 1992. *Shamans, Priests and Witches: A Cross-Cultural Study of Magico-Religious Practitioners.* Tempe, AZ: Arizona State University Anthropological Research Papers #44.

Wiseman, Richard. 1992. "The Feilding Report: A Reconsideration." *Journal of the Society for Psychical Research* 58: 129–152.

Wolf, Arthur P., ed. 1974. *Religion and Ritual in Chinese Society.* Taiwan: Rainbow Bridge.

Wolkomir, Richard. 1992. "If Those Cobras Don't Get You, the Alligators Will." *Smithsonian* (November): 167–176.

Wolman, Benjamin B., ed. 1977. *Handbook of Parapsychology.* New York: Van Nostrand Reinhold.

Worrall, Ambrose A. (with Olga N. Worrall). 1970. *The Gift of Healing: A Personal Story of Spiritual Therapy.* New York: Harper and Row.

Wright, A. 1948. "Fo-t'u-teng." *Harvard Journal of Asiatic Studies* 11: 322–370.

Wuthnow, Robert. 1978. *Experimentation in American Religion: The New Mysticisms and Their Implications for the Churches.* Berkeley, CA: University of California Press.

Yang, Richard F. S. and Howard S. Levy, eds. and trans. 1971. *Monks and Nuns in a Sea of Sins.* Washington, DC: Warm-Soft Village Press.

Youngsook, Kim Harvey. 1978. *Six Korean Women: The Socialization of Shamans.* St. Paul, MN: West Publishing.

Yu, Anthony C. 1987. " 'Rest, Rest, Perturbed Spirit!' Ghosts in Traditional Chinese Prose Fiction." *Harvard Journal of Asiatic Studies* 47: 397–434.

Zaleski, Carol. 1987. *Otherworld Journeys: Accounts of Near-Death Experience in Medieval and Modern Times.* New York: Oxford University Press.

Zha, Leping, and Tron McConnell. 1991. "Parapsychology in the People's Republic of China: 1979–1989." *Journal of the American Society for Psychical Research* 85: 119–143.

Zurcher, Eric. 1959. *The Buddhist Conquest of China.* Leiden: E. J. Brill.

Zusne, Leonard, and Warren H. Jones. 1982. *Anomalistic Psychology.* Hillsdale, NJ: Lawrence Erlbaum Associates.

Index

This book was set in Baskerville and Eras typefaces. Baskerville was designed by John Baskerville at his private press in Birmingham, England, in the eighteenth century. The first typeface to depart from oldstyle typeface design, Baskerville has more variation between thick and thin strokes. In an effort to insure that the thick and thin strokes of his typeface reproduced well on paper, John Baskerville developed the first wove paper, the surface of which was much smoother than the laid paper of the time. The development of wove paper was partly responsible for the introduction of typefaces classified as modern, which have even more contrast between thick and thin strokes.

Eras was designed in 1969 by Studio Hollenstein in Paris for the Wagner Typefoundry. A contemporary script-like version of a sans-serif typeface, the letters of Eras have a monotone stroke and are slightly inclined.

Printed on acid-free paper.